OUTSOURCING AMERICA

What's Behind Our National Crisis and
How We Can Reclaim American Jobs

RON HIRA
AND
ANIL HIRA

American Management Association

New York • Atlanta • Brussels • Chicago • Mexico City • San Francisco
Shanghai • Tokyo • Toronto • Washington, D. C.

Special discounts on bulk quantities of AMACOM books are available to corporations, professional associations, and other organizations. For details, contact Special Sales Department, AMACOM, a division of American Management Association, 1601 Broadway, New York, NY 10019.
Tel.: 212-903-8316. Fax: 212-903-8083.
Web site: www. amacombooks.org

This publication is designed to provide accurate and authoritative information in regard to the subject matter covered. It is sold with the understanding that the publisher is not engaged in rendering legal, accounting, or other professional service. If legal advice or other expert assistance is required, the services of a competent professional person should be sought.

Library of Congress Cataloging-in-Publication Data

Hira, Ron.
Outsourcing America : what's behind our national crisis and how we can reclaim American jobs / Ron Hira and Anil Hira.— 1st ed.
     p. cm.
     Includes index.
     ISBN 0-8144-0868-0
1. Manpower policy—United States. 2. Labor market—United States.
3. United States—Commercial policy. I. Hira, Anil. II. Title.

HD5724.H54 2005
331.12—dc22

2004026948

Printing number

10 9 8 7 6 5 4 3 2 1

TO OUR LATE FATHER, INDU

Contents

Foreword

Americans at the beginning of this new millennium are concerned not only about our security from terrorism but also about our economic future. This insecurity hits right at the heart of the American Dream, the idea that people who work hard will improve their lots and the lots of their children. This concept, which makes America unique, is being shattered by the outsourcing of American jobs to cheap foreign labor markets, which is nothing less than a direct assault on hardworking middle-class men and women in this country.

Remarkably, many "American" corporations, in their pursuit of their own interests, are leading the fight to destroy American jobs. They all but dismiss any responsibility to their broader stakeholders—American workers, communities, and country. It is rational for corporations to pursue their own interests, but it is folly for policymakers to turn a blind eye to the effects on American workers and our national interest. Unfortunately, corporate lobbyists have so much influence over our political process that they have rendered policymakers impotent in the face of outsourcing and the destruction of high-quality American jobs.

The exporting jobs story has become a regular feature in newspapers and magazines across the country. We have reported on the issue vigorously on my television show on CNN and in my recent book, *Exporting America*. The principal author of *Outsourcing America*, Ron Hira, has appeared several times on the show. We have received an overwhelmingly positive response from middle-class Americans who have lost their jobs to outsourcing or are afraid that they soon will. To our astonishment, we heard

of literally thousands of cases of our fellow Americans being forced to train their foreign replacements before being laid off.

The American people are extremely bright, and none of us should ever underestimate the power of their insight into complex issues. They understand at an intuitive level that it is absurd to argue that destroying American jobs, without any plans for assuring replacement, is good for America. They also understand that the executives of large multinational corporations put the company's interests above all else, including America's national interest. This schism between corporate and national interest is obvious to all but the policymakers in Washington.

The misalignment of corporate and national interests is most obviously manifested in our trade policies. Every other nation pursues a trade policy that serves their national interest, but we in the United States have abdicated our trade policy to multinational corporations, who pursue their own corporate interests. The result? We have a record and unsustainable annual trade deficit of more than one-half trillion dollars and an accumulated deficit of almost four trillion dollars. No economist has explained how we get out from under this enormous and potentially crippling burden without a major upheaval for the American economy and American people. There is nothing 'free' about our so-called free trade agreements. We are trading away our wealth while enriching other countries. No other country pursues such a shortsighted trade policy that actually works against its citizens and their future.

As viewers of my show know, I have long been an advocate of a market-based system and a strong private sector. In regard to trade, I neither espouse nor promote protectionism or isolationism. I believe in balanced trade and fair trade. I believe that we should reject the absolutism of both the strict protectionists *and* the free trade evangelists. The former want to turn back the clock, and the latter put their blind faith in the primacy of markets to solve all ills. We need a pragmatic approach to trade policy that promotes our national interest, not a dogmatic blind faith that all will be OK in the long run. *Outsourcing America* is an important step in this direction.

Many of our business leaders have lost all sense of responsibility for their country, communities, employees, and the public trust. These leaders have promoted the false notion that American workers are not capable or are overpaid. The truth is that American workers are the most productive

in the world. They shouldn't be forced to compete for their jobs with Indian or Chinese workers who can afford to earn a fraction of U.S. wages. Corporate America cannot expect to charge American prices for their products, but pay third-world wages for their labor. Corporations are on a dangerous race to the bottom that can only result in a lower standard of living for Americans.

I have called for a moratorium on outsourcing until we can understand how to address it with reasoned solutions and sound policy. We need a national debate on outsourcing. The American way of life depends upon it.

Outsourcing America will provide you a balanced and comprehensive description of outsourcing, how much is happening, why it is occurring, the challenges it poses all of us, and what we can do about it. Ron Hira, a leading expert on outsourcing who has influenced the national debate, brings you a unique perspective on the subject. The authors describe the good and bad that comes with outsourcing for both America and developing economies, and put it in the broader context of globalization. We are consistently told that on balance, globalization will provide not only benefits to consumers but also new jobs to replace the ones lost in inefficient industry. But for the unemployed steel worker, or the now-unemployed computer programmer, where are the new jobs? The Hiras ground their analysis in what matters—how globalization affects middle-class America, the backbone of our great nation. They also describe, in only the way an insider can, why the policy debate has been miscast and misleading. They suggest a new and pragmatic way to think about having a national strategy for jobs from trade. With this book, you will be well equipped to join the national dialogue on the issue of outsourcing American jobs.

Lou Dobbs

Preface

For the United States and for Americans, this is a time of great unease
and increasing insecurity. The uneasiness comes not just from the violation
of our territory by terrorists and not just from an insecurity in terms of our
personal safety. We also suffer now from profound economic unease and
insecurity. In fact, this unease reflects major shifts in our world—shifts that
may be long-term but are certainly changing in perceptible ways our way of
life and possibly the quality of our lives.

After World War II, America had great hopes that were matched by
an unprecedented period of prosperity and improvement in our living standards up to and including the 1960s. Although that period was polarized by
social issues and the Vietnam War, it was also marked by a strong optimism
about America's role in the world and our ability to solve problems and
continue to make a better life for ourselves and future generations.
Americans remained positive that our prosperity could be shared by the
rest of the world, as Japan and Europe rose out of the ashes of war to
become thriving democracies.

During the early 1970s, the OPEC oil crisis signaled that we were
not in complete control of our own destiny. Long lines at the gas pumps,
the shamed withdrawal from Vietnam, and the ensuing economic "stagflation" (inflation and lack of economic growth) all brought a sense of self-
questioning to our country, a questioning that was heightened by the res-
ignation of President Richard Nixon and was capped by the taking of
American hostages in Iran amid a second oil crisis by the end of the
decade.

With Ronald Reagan's election in 1980, the country seemed able to reaffirm its old trajectory of progress and international leadership. Reagan spoke openly about our values in calling for the destruction of the Berlin Wall, in referring to the Soviet Union as an "evil empire," and with his promises of prosperity through hard work and entrepreneurship. But Ronald Reagan could only delay our recognition of the shifts taking place in the world's economy and their implications for our way of life.

Reagan's administration made an important contribution in finally controlling inflation, though this came at the price of a major recession and an international debt crisis, and was aided by lower oil prices. Despite the promise of a balanced budget and simultaneous growth, we were able seemingly to get our economy going only by massive increases in government and private consumption, funded by borrowing from abroad, by deregulating our markets at home, and by ramping up our own consumer debt.

Reagan made most Americans feel proud because he stood for American values, including supporting democracy and free markets abroad. Reagan's successors, George H.W. Bush, Bill Clinton, and George W. Bush, have more or less followed the same recipe. This path led to American leadership in the North American Free Trade Agreement (NAFTA), which, its Republican and Democratic proponents argued, would lead to mutual benefits and gains: We would expand our markets and help to raise the Mexican standard of living at the same time. In supporting democracy, whether it was in Panama or in Iraq, we could create regimes that share our values, thus improving our security and helping local populations to have legitimate governments at the same time.

This is a formula that seems hard to argue against, as the goals are so noble. What we do argue in this book is that this view of American foreign policy and of the world we live in is both naïve and dangerous. We deal with the economic realm, but the same arguments could be made of foreign policy as well. We suggest what too many American workers already know: that the key decision makers in Washington are missing some basic facts about the international economy. That the formula of free, deregulated markets and faith in American superiority ignores how the international economy has slowly and gradually shifted in the last few decades. And that unless we

carefully reconsider our own domestic and international economic policies, our—and more importantly, our children's—way of life is in doubt.

We focus in this book on a particular development within the international economy to illustrate our point: the growing practice of outsourcing overseas our advanced and high-tech jobs. We demonstrate through this example that the superficial views of the economy held by American leaders in the last two decades have been more "muddling through" than a serious acknowledgment or a plan for the future. We document the growing number of job losses and suggest the underlying reasons for them. We predict and attempt to document the short-term impact of such losses. And we close the book with some suggestions for a plan of action that could best deal with this loss of jobs, and offer ideas for how to preserve the American way of life in these new international conditions.

We write this book unapologetically for the layperson rather than the academic or expert. We think all Americans should understand the issues at hand so that they can have a chance to participate in making the decisions that affect their livelihood.

Acknowledgments

We would like to thank Lou Dobbs of CNN who was kind enough to write the foreword for the book, and more importantly has asked the right sets of questions about the implications of outsourcing on America and American workers. We would like to thank Congressman Donald Manzullo for demonstrating his leadership by holding the first hearings on outsourcing, and persistently pushing for solutions to the problems caused by it. Karl Froschauer, Chris Brantley, and Jamie Winebrake all provided helpful comments on the manuscript. We would like to thank our wives for their patience while the book was being written. Charles McMillion, Bob Morgan, Vin O'Neill, and Chris Hill provided valuable input and encouragement as our ideas on outsourcing were being formed. We would also like to thank Robert Mackwood, our agent, Adrienne Hickey, our editor, and Barry Richardson, who helped significantly with the development and editing of the book, and Mithu Dey for being a source of ideas and critiques. We would like to thank Patricia Hira for her help in editing this book. This book is largely the work of Ron Hira, reflecting his three years of research on the topic. Anil Hira helped with the writing and organization, and took the lead on the Preface, Chapter 2, Chapter 8, and some sections of the other chapters.

CHAPTER 1

What Outsourcing Means for America

The cover of the February 3, 2003, issue of *BusinessWeek* showed a man in a business suit hanging on for dear life to cargo that was going to be shipped overseas. "Is Your Job Next?" the headline blared, followed by this disturbing preview of the article inside:

> A new round of GLOBALIZATION is sending upscale jobs offshore. They include chip design, engineering, basic research—even financial analysis. Can America lose these jobs and still prosper?

This story started the debate over whether transferring good jobs to cheap overseas locations—outsourcing, or more specifically, offshore outsourcing—is good for America.

The debate raged in relatively small circles until nearly a year later, when President Bush's chief economic adviser, Dr. Gregory Mankiw, flippantly answered a reporter's question as to whether outsourcing was good or bad, "Yes, it is probably good for America in the long run." That's when the story hit the front pages of nearly every major newspaper in the country. The reaction was swift and divided. The elites in corporations, policy circles, and newspaper editorial boards unequivocally and resoundingly supported Mankiw's assertion that exporting high-paying U.S. jobs is a

good thing, while most "average" Americans reacted in just the opposite way, with grave concern about the consequences of outsourcing for themselves and their children's futures.

Who is right, and why is there such difference in opinion about whether this is good for America? Unfortunately, the public debate has been drenched with innuendo presented by both sides as unassailable natural laws and sensationalism. This has made it nearly impossible to explore the positive and negative consequences of outsourcing and what we should do about it.

The problem isn't so much that outsourcing is happening as *how* it is happening. In this book, we investigate outsourcing by presenting the full set of facts—what we know and, more important, what we don't know about how it is affecting America's economy, jobs, national security, and future.

Outsourcing Cannot Be Ignored

As the twenty-first century moves through its first decade, Americans have begun to notice a growing trend in their economy: the accelerating loss of jobs to overseas workers. Whether it's called "outsourcing," "offshore outsourcing," "offshoring," or some other term,[1] it's a phenomenon that cannot be ignored. The media have started to highlight the devastating impacts on individuals and communities, and some politicians have begun to pay attention. But the trends indicated by the facts and figures are truly alarming.

• *What does the future hold?* We are at just the beginning of the outsourcing phenomenon, or as some experts like to put it, "the outsourcing tidal wave." It will only grow in scale, scope, and speed by dragging out to sea many good-paying U.S. jobs with it. Experts at the University of California have estimated that a staggering 14 million white-collar jobs— *nearly one in nine of all U.S. jobs*—are vulnerable to being outsourced. These are high-paying jobs, with more than half of them paying above the average salary of $31,720. A 2004 report predicted that approximately 3.5 million white-collar jobs and $151 billion in wages would move overseas by 2015, with 830,000 jobs leaving by the end of 2005.

• *What types of jobs are involved?* A wide array of jobs have already been shipped overseas, including call-center operators, information tech-

nology, accounting, architecture, newspaper reporting, medical and legal services, and high-level engineering design. One report estimates that 2.3 million U.S. jobs in banking and securities may move overseas. Another study predicts that 700,000 customer service and corporate back-office jobs will move from the United States to India by 2008. According to one outsourcing CEO, any work that can be sent over a wire can be sent offshore. As a result, highly sensitive information on personal finances and medical records is being handled offshore.

● *Who's driving the outsourcing phenomenon?* U.S. companies are enthusiastically embracing offshoring. Company managers and executives are being told that offshoring is an "imperative," and if they want to keep their jobs, they must outsource. Many companies have employed programs to accelerate the process that they euphemistically call "knowledge transfer," whereby they force their U.S. workers to train foreign replacements. The U.S. worker is then laid off after his or her knowledge has been extracted. Venture-capital firms are forcing their start-up firms to outsource as much work as possible. Venture-capital-funded start-up firms are recognized as the lifeblood of future innovation and a major reason for Silicon Valley's success. If these jobs are outsourced, what are the implications for future innovation?

● *Can the United States compete with low-cost labor abroad?* Wages in developing countries such as India and China are 10 to 20 percent of comparable U.S. workers, and there is a nearly endless supply of educated underemployed workers in those countries. And it is much cheaper to live in a developing country. For example, the cost of living in India or China is one-fifth that of the United States. Wages in those countries will not reach parity with those in the United States for many years, maybe decades. Many other developing countries, such as those in Eastern Europe and Latin America, are trying to emulate India's success, adding even more competition for U.S. workers.

● *Will the United States be out front in the next technological revolution?* Not necessarily. Many of our best and brightest students are not majoring in technology disciplines because of the fear of offshoring. For example, computer science enrollment dropped by 20 percent in the 2003–04 academic year. This threatens America's future ability to innovate. The

next generation of innovative jobs easily could move overseas as India, China, and other low-cost countries attract high-level research and development work. So, the expectation that the United States will generate the next wave of innovation in biotechnology or nanotechnology is just blind faith. No one knows when those jobs will appear and, more important, how many of them will be captured by other countries. China is the number two producer of scientific papers on nanotechnology, a field that is considered on the cutting edge.

• *Can displaced U.S. workers find other jobs?* The track record for the reemployment of displaced U.S. workers is abysmal. The Department of Labor reports that more than *one in three workers who are displaced remains unemployed,* and many of those who are lucky enough to find jobs take major pay cuts. Many former manufacturing workers who were displaced a decade ago because of manufacturing that went offshore took training courses and found jobs in the information technology sector. They are now facing the unenviable situation of having their second career disappear overseas. And no one can point to the logical replacement occupation of the future, the way that information technology once served for manufacturing.

• *Can't the government help?* The U.S. government is actively pursuing policies that accelerate outsourcing by undermining U.S. workers' primary competitive advantage over foreign workers: their physical presence in the United States. The government has a guest-worker policy that enables companies to bring cheap foreign white-collar professionals to America to work on-site, replacing U.S. workers. The process also accelerates outsourcing as the United States transfers knowledge to foreign workers. Many then go back to their countries and compete with U.S. workers from there. Even more ominously, the U.S. Trade Representative, the chief U.S. representative for negotiating trade agreements, wants to make this process even easier through the World Trade Organization and trade agreements.

And here's another thought to ponder: While private companies are spearheading the outsourcing movement, they are not alone. Federal, state, and local governments are outsourcing government services, raising the question of whether it is right to use tax dollars to create jobs offshore while there are so many unemployed people in America.

What Actually Happens with Outsourcing

Contrary to popular belief, understanding the impact of offshore outsourcing doesn't require any formal economics training. Most economists assume the following *ideal* scenario when thinking about outsourcing.

Before Outsourcing	*After Outsourcing*
U.S. workers do tasks A, B, C.	U.S. workers do tasks B, C, D.
Offshore workers are idle.	Offshore workers do tasks A and some of B.

In this scenario, U.S. workers were doing tasks A, B, and C and offshore workers were idle before the outsourcing occurred. After the outsourcing, U.S. workers no longer do task A, but have moved on to a new task, D. And instead of being idle, offshore workers are now doing tasks A and some of B. So, in the ideal scenario, U.S. workers remain fully employed but the mix of tasks they do has changed because of outsourcing. Offshore workers are now fully employed with tasks A and B. This is what one hopes will happen.

There are two important problems with this scenario. First, the presumption is that the U.S. workers who were previously doing task A will easily be reabsorbed into the workforce by doing tasks such as B, C, and D. This is what economists refer to as the "adjustment" process. Unfortunately, the practical problems with adjustment are substantial. For example, let's assume that task A is computer programming, which is increasingly moving offshore, and task C is nursing, which is in high demand in the United States. Is it realistic to expect computer programmers to easily become nurses? The track record for adjustment is terrible, and there are no resources to facilitate the adjustment process.

The second problem is whether the new mix of tasks B, C, and D is better than tasks A, B, and C. Does the United States have a better set of jobs after outsourcing? No one really knows. It is important to note that many of the jobs being outsourced are very high paying jobs, and they are not being replenished with better jobs. In other words, task D has yet to appear. Plus, developing countries are targeting high-wage jobs for their own citizens. So, even in the ideal scenario there are major disruptions and uncertainties caused by outsourcing as U.S. jobs are destroyed, and there is

only hope that those workers find better jobs. Reality, of course, rarely follows the ideal scenario.

The Outsourcing Debate Is Misleading

For the most part, companies and politicians have been in a state of denial about the impact of outsourcing on America. Companies believe that outsourcing is good for them because it helps them cut their expenses, and as a result, they conceal the extent of the outsourcing they are doing and dismiss any criticism as outdated thinking. In order to influence public opinion and politicians, they go even further by sponsoring one-sided "studies" that find that outsourcing is good for the United States. These studies downplay the negatives of outsourcing and in some cases completely ignore them.

Not surprisingly, politicians with strong ties to the business community believe that outsourcing is good for the United States, and they often quote the studies sponsored by industry as proof. Their thinking goes along the lines of the old saying, "What's good for General Motors is good for America." A few politicians have raised concerns about outsourcing, but they are overwhelmed by the politicians, pundits, and experts who favor outsourcing. And there seems to be no real action on outsourcing in good part because there has been little serious study of it.

Not only has outsourcing been largely dismissed by the experts, but they look at it as a one-time, relatively minor issue that will largely disappear on its own or even be to our benefit. Gregory Mankiw, a Bush Administration advisor, summed up the accepted wisdom of the experts by cavalierly stating that outsourcing "is just another form of trade, and it is probably good for us in the long run."

Outsourcing is not a limited, one-time phenomenon. It is part of a larger trend of changes in our economy that will have profound implications for how we run our economy and determine our standard of living. Outsourcing is not really trade, though. Instead, it is U.S. companies forcing U.S. workers to compete head-to-head with foreign workers. This is not fair competition, though, since the foreign workers can afford to be paid less because their cost of living is so much lower. Plus, U.S. companies are taking away U.S. workers' other advantages by providing those overseas

workers with the latest tools and technologies. Lastly, outsourcing will impact our national security in ways that cannot be modeled by economists, so the security implications have been largely ignored.

Many Americans have asked the following practical questions because of outsourcing: "What field should my son or daughter study in college?" And, "I am an information technology worker and have been laid off twice in the last three years because of outsourcing. Should I stay in the information technology field or transition to another field?" The answer from the experts who support outsourcing, such as Federal Reserve Chairman Alan Greenspan, is vague and unsatisfactory. They say that the jobs are coming, but they don't know in which field. They are sure that the new jobs that will be created will require higher levels of skill and will be better.

But these are hopeful answers that are effectively useless. The media and politicians have allowed the experts to duck any responsibility for answering them. As a result, there is a paralysis in policymaking. Even in policy areas where there is a large consensus that something should be done, such as expanding adjustment assistance, there has been no action.

Is Outsourcing Inevitable?

Offshore outsourcing is not a natural result of market forces; it has been helped by U.S. immigration and tax laws; foreign governments explicitly targeting U.S. jobs; and U.S. companies and management consultants who have actively promoted outsourcing. The federal government and some state governments have even begun to outsource public-sector jobs, including welfare and food-stamp service jobs!

Outsourcing is not some isolated phenomenon. It reflects longer-term changes in our global economy. Yet these changes, going back three decades, have largely been ignored by the U.S. government and successive presidential administrations. Instead, our policies toward outsourcing, as toward trade and economic policy in general, have been characterized by knee-jerk, Band-aid reactions rather than long-term planning. Meanwhile, our new competitors, such as India and China, have long-term designs to outcompete us in every major industry and service. And their plans do not rely just on pitiful wage levels but also on an accelerating technological capability and deliberate government policies to increase competitiveness

and attract outsourced jobs from America. If the U.S. doesn't wake up to this reality, we will find our economy full of craters where there were once vibrant communities and industries—while the experts assure us that this is all just good free-market forces at work.

The Potential Impacts Are Far-Reaching

The stakes are enormous, not just for our economic future but also for all other aspects of our quality of life. Without good, high-paying jobs there are no tax revenues to fund our education, health, infrastructure, and social security systems. Economists want to claim dogmatically that workers will simply retrain for other jobs, but where are those jobs going to come from? Retraining has never proven itself reliable. More important, can an outsourced IT worker or engineer, who has been forced to train her overseas replacement, find comparable work with comparable salary to support her family and pay for her kids' education? The answer is clearly not, as the growing multitude of devastated, overqualified workers has been crying out.

Outsourcing is not just about jobs. Its potential impact is not only on our quality of life but also on our national competitiveness and national security. Our competitive edge—the reason, until now, America has been the beacon for immigrants to come and achieve the American Dream—has been our ability to create new high-wage jobs. And a good part of that job creation has been in technology, with government and private support for developing the most highly skilled workforce and the most innovative products. The IT, the aerospace, and the biotechnology industries, to name a few, depend on a careful partnership among publicly funded research, our leading-edge universities, the private sector, and the most productive workers in the world.

Outsourcing is taking away the workforce that has been a key part of our winning formula. Once we lose the high-tech jobs, then why would our most capable minds study engineering, computer science, biotechnology, or any of the other promising fields that will create national competitiveness in the future? Already we are seeing record unemployment rates in these occupations and a major drop in enrollments in these fields, in good part owing to outsourcing.

Moreover, our national security is based in large part on this techno-

logical edge. Our soldiers depend upon a solid core of engineers, computer technicians, and research and development scientists to provide the equipment and logistical support that protect our country. Now that terrorist forces are using technology, including the Internet and high-tech communications equipment, we need to maintain the national capability to stay ahead of their technological knowledge. If we allow outsourcing to wipe out our base of technical workers, we will leave the nation vulnerable to foreign powers, much as unhappy consumers have found their personal, medical, and tax information in the hands of overseas computer technicians.

Why Outsourcing Is Fool's Gold for Companies

Companies believe that offshore outsourcing is good for their bottom line. Like economists and politicians, they seem to forget that the greatness of this country was built on the backs of its workers. When they lose their base of skilled workers, companies will find that they have lost not only their best employees—what economists call human capital—but also the consumers who buy their products! Obviously, unemployed workers can neither pay taxes nor buy products. Unemployed workers cannot provide retirement savings to banks and pension funds to invest in new companies. In their short-term mentality, companies that outsource jobs are cutting the lifeline that keeps the American economy robust.

America's companies are not irrational, just shortsighted. Their economic gamble is like the proverbial game of chicken, where two cars race toward each other, waiting for the other to swerve. Because they do not think of the wider national interests, these companies refuse to acknowledge that the few thousand jobs they ship overseas are just part of a much larger trend, a trend they are encouraging as other companies follow their lead. The fear of being underpriced is leading the stampede to outsourcing, without adequate consideration of whether the job shift is necessary or what its longer-term impacts will be.

Many companies claim that the job losses are limited to low-level jobs. Yet this is hardly the case; company management positions and others of the highest paid jobs are being outsourced as well. This brings us to the saddest part of all. U.S. companies have claimed that they need to set up shop overseas in order to gain a foothold in the emerging markets of China and

India. Yet there is no evidence that they will be able to outcompete local Chinese and Indian companies, who are very rapidly assimilating the technology and know-how from the local U.S. plants. In fact, studies show that Indian IT companies have been consistently outcompeting their U.S. counterparts, even in U.S. markets. Thus, it is time for CEOs to start thinking about whether they are fine with their own jobs being outsourced as well.

What the U.S. Can Do About Outsourcing

Equipped with a fuller picture of what outsourcing is, what its impacts have been, and how it fits into larger historical trends in the world economy, the United States can move forward with a plan based on confidence rather than denial or fear. Our concerns are not so much that outsourcing is happening, but how it is happening. The United States must shape the ways in which outsourcing unfolds in order to harness its positive effects and mitigate its negative effects. Here are the nine ways in which this can be done.

1. Acknowledge that outsourcing causes major problems. Surprisingly enough, many policymakers and pundits continue to deny the negative outcomes of outsourcing.

2. There must be full disclosure. Make consumers aware of where products are made and when those products are the result of jobs that have been outsourced. Force companies to disclose such activities.

3. The government, experts, and private sector must make a serious effort to document and study outsourcing. This book tackles some basic questions—such as the magnitude of outsourcing; the impacts in communities; what happens to workers who are outsourced; and what happens to other social institutions, such as tax bases and the education system—that need systematic data in order to be really answered. But it is nearly impossible to address these questions in the current atmosphere.

4. Companies, as well as the federal and state governments, must stop promoting outsourcing. The visa, immigration, and tax laws that promote outsourcing should be rewritten. American workers must have a level playing field upon which to compete. Communities should be well equipped to

maintain good jobs, and not be used as pawns by companies seeking tax subsidies that lead only to short-term jobs.

5. Those who have lost their livelihoods to outsourcing must be helped. It is in America's best interest to get these people back to work as soon as possible. They need a greater safety net, including affordable healthcare coverage, job training, and jobs search. This will require more resources, not less, and since the U.S. track record on reemployment is so poor, new and innovative ways of supporting the process will have to be devised.

6. America needs to recognize that its priorities of national competitiveness and security include maintaining a technological edge and encouraging the engineers, scientists, and programmers to keep the United States a step ahead of its potential enemies.

7. America is the economic engine that drives the world: Every country's economy and much of international trade are based on gaining access to the U.S. economy. Instead of dividing up the spoils for a few particular interests, America needs to rethink its trade policy. There should be a long-term plan for economic growth and competitiveness based on a pragmatic understanding of historical trends in the world economy, on our national assets, and on where the nation wants to be, not dogmatic adherence to some abstract economic theory that dismisses any possible challenges.

8. For decades, American workers have not been the lowest-cost competitors in the labor marketplace. The higher wages of American workers have derived from a combination of hard work, better technology, higher skills, and greater productivity. Instead of burying their heads in the sand, Americans should see the international competition as a national challenge to make investments in our own workers and create policies that help our workers thrive. After all, American workers have run the world economy's engine.

9. The "powers that be" have basically ignored and weakened any institutional voice that workers once had. That is why the United States is now in a jobless recovery, in which the economic output is rosy but thousands of workers are in trouble. U.S. top management, as well as the government, has largely dismissed the importance of middle-class workers, who are the people who buy the world's goods and ultimately pay the

salaries of those CEOs. Outsourcing is a wake-up call for the United States to create and maintain high-quality, long-term employment that will guarantee the desirable quality of life in America.

Conclusion

How much outsourcing is happening? This is a very difficult question to answer because companies have been going out of their way to keep their outsourcing activities quiet. It should not be surprising, given the media coverage of widespread job losses and communities torn asunder by the impact of jobs lost to overseas. Moreover, unlike in previous years when the job losses were limited to blue-collar workers and, more recently, to lower-paying service jobs like telemarketers and customer service operations, outsourcing has gained attention precisely because it threatens the livelihoods of some of the best-paid workers in America.

Companies have not been revealing their job movements because they know that outsourcing devastates the workers laid off and kills the morale of those who remain. However, some investigative work can piece together a basic picture of what is happening. Let's review some of the basic facts on outsourcing:

- While the actual figures are hard to determine for the reasons described above, economists and consultants have estimated that millions of jobs will move overseas in the next decade.
- Outsourcing cuts across all occupations. Blue-collar, white-collar, manufacturing, and service jobs have all begun to fly overseas. Lawyers, medical technicians, accountants and financial services, architects, engineers, and, of course, computer programmers are all seeing their jobs outsourced.
- Newspaper reports have already documented huge sudden losses of jobs, such as EDS moving 20,000 jobs and Siemens moving 15,000 jobs overseas. So outsourcing is not some minor, isolated phenomenon, but a real and accelerating trend.
- We need to seriously study the outsourcing phenomenon—to understand how much is happening, why it is increasing, the over-

all ramifications on a global, national, local, and individual level, and what can be done to deal with outsourcing in the future.

The next chapter will review the discussion that has occurred around outsourcing so far, and explore why the loss of thousands of jobs has been dismissed by experts and many politicians as a limited, relatively unimportant blip on the economic radar screen.

Note

1. Throughout the book, we use the term "outsourcing" to refer to offshore outsourcing and offshoring. The definitions of each different type of outsourcing are included in Appendix A.

CHAPTER 2

Outsourcing in a Larger Context

Offshore outsourcing is part of the globalization of the economy that has been accelerating in the last three decades. Economic globalization has sped up through the development of currency exchange markets, free trade areas, and new technologies, namely the Internet, that enable low-cost and quick communication around the planet.

Global markets for investments and goods and services now exist. Thus, a significant and growing portion of our economy is susceptible to changes in the relative value of our currency and to actions against our products by foreign governments and companies. So, in this sense, globalization naturally brings a sense of insecurity and vulnerability. It is this sense of vulnerability that may be at the heart of the debate about globalization. In his 1992 presidential campaign, Ross Perot talked about the "giant sucking sound" of jobs that would be lost if we signed the NAFTA agreement with Mexico. Today, antiglobalization protestors cite the lack of national sovereignty and of labor and environmental rights as examples of a loss of control that has accompanied globalization.

These debates about globalization miss the mark, but the question of whether free trade is good or bad for the economy and for American workers is a fine place to start. Time after time, politicians from both parties have told us that free trade "lifts all boats," that prosperity comes with open

15

markets. In short, economists almost always claim that open trade is a win-win situation. For example, with access to an expanded market, U.S. producers can sell more goods in Mexico and U.S. consumers enjoy lower prices here as a result of the increased competition that imported Mexican goods will bring.

On the other hand, the antiglobalization camp would have us believe that free trade is eroding American jobs and the American way of life. Moreover, free trade is "exploitative," taking advantage of workers in developing countries and putting us at the mercy of multinational corporations over which we have no control. Given the disheartening information on job outsourcing and its rapid acceleration, it would be all too easy to follow this path and present a dire picture of the future for the American worker. But a nuanced view of free trade and globalization yields more hope.

What economists discuss, but don't reveal in their public pronouncements about free trade, is that there are some important facets to free trade that go well beyond the win-win theory discussed above. A few examples will give you the idea of how complicated the practice of free trade really is.

Free Trade Is Not Really "Free"

The first thing to notice is that there really is no such thing as "free" trade. Every free-trade agreement is, in fact, a negotiated document. That is, a free-trade agreement involves all kinds of bargaining by each nation's negotiators. So, for example, the NAFTA agreement contains a section on agriculture with important clauses about the gradual lowering of tariffs; treats various fruits, vegetables, and meat differently by product; and preserves room for governments to erect "emergency" barriers in the event they need to protect their domestic producers. When you consider the different ways countries run their economies and how those procedures affect trade, such as varying tax schedules and social spending goals, as well as the dynamism of the whole process, it's clear that no human being (or economic model) could possibly predict the exact outcome of a trade agreement over time.

The Effects Can Vary Greatly

More important, the effects of a trade agreement may vary considerably from one region of the country to another. Whereas U.S. corn producers

seem to have benefited from the NAFTA agreement, for example, U.S. textile workers have not. One would be tempted to believe, then, that Mexicans should have experienced mirror effects. In fact, Mexican farmers have been devastated by U.S. corn imports, but textile workers have not gained, either. Instead, increases in textile production have occurred mostly in China. So Mexicans have a right to wonder where the vaunted benefits of NAFTA and free trade are.

Some economists do acknowledge that free trade and globalization can have negative impacts on our economy. In fact, recent studies of NAFTA have called into question the assumed benefits, citing both the high level of job losses, particularly in sectors such as U.S. textiles and Mexican agriculture, and the growing inequalities.[1]

While many mainstream economists will argue that the overall benefits to U.S. consumers outweigh the net losses of jobs in particular sectors, this does not help the now-unemployed textile worker, who has no means of earning a living, let alone buying these cheap foreign goods. The same economists would argue that these workers can best be employed elsewhere, "in a growing area of the economy." What the economists fail to explore, or even acknowledge, is that gains from trade vary by industry and that some industries provide more employment and higher-wage jobs. In this sense, a country could have net consumer gains through lower prices but at the same time experience net job losses. For example, losing a local steel mill will affect more people than gaining a travel agency. Thus, there is a net labor component for each industry, so as trade affects each economic sector, it also affects the number and quality of jobs in a particular region.

Of course, free trade can provide benefits in terms of competition, a greater variety of products, and lower prices, but that depends on what kind of free-trade arrangement is negotiated. Not every high-wage job necessarily must be kept, but the cost in terms of jobs must be weighed against the net consumer benefit. And keep in mind that not all of the cost savings from outsourcing are passed on to consumers. Company executives and stockholders take their share of the savings. Looking at the forecasted net reductions in prices (and projections are tough even here) tells only part of the story. Not only are the number and types of jobs important, but also the volatility of those jobs and the wages behind them are key considerations for the United States to move toward a rational, long-term policy on trade.

Understanding Historical Developments

A sensible trade policy entails a revision of economists' depiction of what happens to our jobs under globalization. NAFTA is the key to understanding these historical developments. With NAFTA, the United States began to embrace a developing country for the first time as a significant partner in a regionally exclusive, rather than an international, trade agreement. What led to this change in strategy? In the 1970s there were several major shifts in the world economy that set up this change.

The first shift was the flood of Japanese imports in the 1970s. With the 1973 OPEC rise in oil prices, American consumers began to buy the more efficient Japanese automobile models. Detroit was set back on its heels, and the Japanese were transformed from an oversight in American diplomacy to a front-page threat, not only in autos but also in electronics and a wide variety of other products whose field America had dominated.

The same forces pushed the Western European countries toward creation of an integrated, protected market, called the European Community. The Europeans concluded that they needed to create a larger market to compete internationally. The surprising successes of Europe and Japan, then, led American manufacturers and the U.S. government to develop NAFTA.

The underlying idea of NAFTA was to reduce American labor costs by using cheaper Mexican labor. By integrating Mexican labor into a unified market, U.S. auto and other manufacturers could lower the costs of their products and thereby outcompete the Japanese. The supposedly free-market Reagan Administration resorted to voluntary export and other restraints on trade as well. The upshot is that, despite the economists' trade theories, NAFTA was designed for U.S. manufacturers, not for disorganized and largely powerless consumers-at-large

The Reagan Administration further strengthened the hand of the business owners by dismantling much of the social welfare state and taking deliberate actions to reduce labor power. Rarely is business now encumbered by major strikes and shutdowns. The migration of businesses to the southeastern United States with lax labor laws, including the allowance of nonunionized foreign auto plants—such as Toyota in that region—as well as a look the other way on most illegal immigration, are

further examples of a deliberate policy to reduce the power of labor in the United States.

Some adjustments by the United States were needed to equip the country for globalization—just not the adjustments chosen by our leaders. By the late 1970s, other nations began to outcompete the U.S.'s tired industries. They were faster and leaner, and worked harder. American companies began sending management teams to Japan to learn the secrets of lean and just-in-time production, and to set up separate units, such as General Motors's Saturn company, that would help to reproduce the magic formulas of higher productivity and employer-worker comanagement. This situation was ironic, since the Japanese concepts of lean manufacturing were actually designed by American management gurus Deming and Juran.

Could the United States simply have cut off the Japanese from our market and preserved the existing labor-business situation? It seems unlikely in hindsight that such a policy could have been followed indefinitely, considering the U.S.'s role in the world as a security force and a political leader. Indeed, with the fall of the Soviet Union, and the supposed triumph of the capitalist way of life, the ties between markets and politics seemed more intertwined than ever before. Moreover, would Americans really be satisfied to live a subpar way of life based on protectionism, when the American dream has always been that of doing things best and of continually improving one's standard of living?

Trading Jobs for Competitive Advantage

The hidden gamble in the American trade strategy from the late 1980s thereafter was, first, to trade away American manufacturing jobs in certain sectors in the hope that the gains from greater competitiveness (the buzzword of the 1980s) would lead to jobs elsewhere in the economy, particularly in services and technology goods. Second, we would deregulate our markets and allow all kinds of mergers and acquisitions—basically watering down antitrust regulations—in the hope of creating larger companies that could dominate world markets by their sheer size.

This paradigm shift was all about politics, of course. At first it was about Republican Party union-bashing in order to help business owners reduce their taxes and labor costs through mergers and moves overseas.

Mergers and acquisitions created all kinds of phony wealth and golden parachutes for their financial engineers, rather than revamped investment and productive capacity as their proponents had argued.

By the early 1990s, Bill Clinton and his supporters signaled a sea change in the formerly union-focused Democratic Party by embracing the new trade agreements. Clinton cultivated major contributors to the Party who were business owners, many from emerging sectors such as IT. But Clinton did not address the anxiety of American workers alarmed at the shifts in international trade. He abandoned the traditional concerns of the Democratic Party base and adopted a Republican Party stance on trade, a balanced budget, and welfare reform.

The underlying promise made by Clinton was that eased trade arrangements would allow the United States to remain at the top of the international economic pyramid. America would retrain manufacturing and agricultural workers not only to be smarter and more productive but also to use high technology to outcompete lower-wage workers overseas. American companies would be allowed to merge, and thereby have the increased financial capital and market presence to dominate most world markets. And, as the IT sector began to take off in the mid-1990s, it began to be seen as a source not only of productivity growth but also of jobs. This helped to mask the pain felt by the loss of manufacturing jobs and the continued decline in union power, which went hand in hand with labor's decreasing representation in the Democratic Party.

So, America would eventually be where the best and the brightest came to make the leading-edge products, including not only IT but also high-end services like finance, consulting, and investment. By the end of the 1990s, this was the American trade strategy and the focus of negotiations at the international bargaining table. Unfortunately, things have not played out as anticipated. While American negotiators may have been content to trade some manufacturing jobs for the competitive advantages of free trade, they will have to rethink this strategy if the high-paying service jobs that they want for their children continue to disappear as well.

How Other Nations Handled Trade Competition

Did the United States have any choice but to push for competition via free trade? Comparing U.S. trade policy with other nations' strategies is instruc-

tive. Note that the fastest-growing economies in the world during the last three decades—namely, those in East Asia—quite consciously follow "strategic" trade policies. Japan, seeking to recover from the devastation of World War II, intentionally promoted certain industries through its Ministry of International Trade and Investment (MITI). Japan went from being a country of toy and gadget manufacturers to one that leads the world in technology and manufacturing, including most recently the first commercially successful hybrid automobiles.

There are many reasons Japan was successful, but free trade is never one of them. For years, Japan has protected its domestic markets, especially agriculture, while competing in world markets through strong promotion of its exports. The JETRO agency is an arm of the Japanese government whose main job is to help Japanese manufacturers market their products abroad. The Japanese tradition of "lifetime employment" and strong bond between company and employees was legendary, even if the relationship has dissipated in the wake of Japan's recession.

The governments of South Korea, Singapore, and Taiwan also promoted policies that boosted certain industries. Free trade did not determine that South Korea would enter the domestic and world automobile market; a partnership of government, large national champions, and heavy investment in the country's workers did. The government of Singapore similarly has made strong efforts to educate its population and create a base of information technology firms, thereby taking that country from a dilapidated colony in 1960 to one that offers a world-class standard of living today. Taiwan also began to compete in producing personal computers when its government decided that this was a policy to pursue.

The latest example of a country's pro-competitiveness policy is that of China, where the government keeps a tight lid on the level and types of foreign investment and controls key sectors of its economy. China has policies to compete on all levels of manufacturing and the latest technologies. In sum, its trade policy coordinates various tools to increase national competitiveness, from promoting applied research links among institutes, students abroad, and national companies, to supporting an artificially low exchange rate for its currency. Most projections show that the largest and fastest-growing U.S. trade deficit is with China, and that imbalance of trade will not change after China enters the World Trade Organization. It is not free

trade or the free market that has led to China's highest growth rates in the world. It is China's government policy to find ways to enter new markets.

In short, several countries in the developing world now compete head-on with the United States in key industries ranging from steel to automobiles. These countries have proactive economic policies to attract new industries and technologies, train workers, steal technology, and lure outsourced jobs from the United States.

By contrast, every man or woman in the United States is supposed to be uniquely responsible for his or her own fate; if a company downsizes, the employees somehow must find a way to survive. Yet, globalization and free trade agreements affect everyone in this economy but are outside most individuals' control. How can each person be totally responsible for his or her fate when shortsighted government policies constrain their options?

Conclusion

World economic competition is a national, not an individual, endeavor. The end result of government's efforts should be a focus on maintaining and improving Americans' quality of life, including stable income, asset growth, and full employment, rather than the short-term corporate bottom line. Studies have shown that, since World War II, even social welfare states such as Norway, or moderate welfare countries such as Germany, have economic growth rates within 1 to 3 percentage points of United States—and at times have even exceeded U.S. growth rates.[2] Therefore, the myth that totally "free" markets are always the ultimate good and that any government intervention is ultimately "bad" is nothing but a fairy tale.

Having a market economy does *not* mean that you have to abandon workers to the whims of the marketplace; that the higher tax income from increased growth can provide all the basic social services to insulate society from the roller-coaster effects of market fluctuations; that monies invested in retraining people weaken a country's international competitiveness; or that integration with less developed markets means you have to lower your labor and environmental standards to their level.

In the United States, the ideologues of free trade have caused unnecessary suffering by transforming the American dream into a means of satisfying special interests instead of considering the welfare of the majority. It is no surprise that CEOs in the United States are paid many more times

the rate of their Japanese and European counterparts. The United States's economic strategy is an homage to "the market" that goes beyond the results of that strategy, that has not benefited the nation as a whole. U.S. politicians tout their actions to reduce taxes while they run up record deficits for spending that has little long-term economic return. Instead of making a larger pie for mutual benefit, a few Americans are gorging themselves.

It is hoped that by highlighting the outsourcing of jobs as part of this deteriorating economic situation, we will precipitate a long-overdue rethinking of American economic strategy. Let us now turn to why outsourcing itself has fallen victim—like our trade policies—to deception and short-sightedness by special political interests.

Notes

1. See John Audley, Sandra Polaski, Demetrious Papademetriou, and Scott Vaughan, *Nafta's Promise and Reality: Lessons from Mexico for the Hemisphere* (Washington, D.C.: Carnegie Endowment for International Peace, 2003) for a highly critical assessment of the outcomes of NAFTA. Even the strongly pro-free-trade World Bank released the report "Lessons from NAFTA for Latin America and the Caribbean Countries: A Summary of Research Findings," by Daniel Lederman, William F. Maloney, and Luis Servén (Washington, D.C.: World Bank, December 2003), that the gap in living standards between Mexico and its trading partners remains high, with highly "unequal" effects on individuals, regions, and sectors.

2. All economic sources, including the World Bank and the U.N., agree on this fact. See Angus Maddison, *The World Economy: Historical Statistics* (Paris: OECD, 2001), for long-run statistics.

CHAPTER 3

The Public Debate on Outsourcing Is Misleading

The debate surrounding outsourcing has been framed in a singular way that is misleading: You are pigeonholed as either pro or con. This kind of rudimentary argument sweeps away a more sensible approach that could shape outsourcing to be truly mutually beneficial for Americans and citizens of developing countries. Indeed, the simplistic framing ignores reality. As with trade, the full effects of outsourcing are complex, with significant and unevenly distributed positive and negative aspects. Outsourcing generates winners and losers, and policymakers should focus on how to maximize the positive effects while mitigating the negative ones. Also, the ramifications of outsourcing are uncertain, but uncertainty doesn't fit the sound bites of politics. Instead, you are either a free trader or a protectionist; you believe in free markets or you are an economic isolationist.

The arguments are precisely so black-and-white because the corporations that benefit most from outsourcing view it as good lobbying strategy. And the strategy has been effective, for two reasons. First, by overstating the gains from outsourcing, companies can deflect attention from the damage it causes. And they present their statistics in seductive ways that make them appear plausible and authoritative. Second, the singular focus on the benefits of outsourcing resonates with the elites—editorial boards, academics, and politicians—who want to believe that globalization will solve

America's economic problems. These elites wield disproportionate influence on policy, so they are much more important to sway than the general public, and because they are predisposed to the positive message, the strategy is an easy sell.

Unfortunately, the debate is not just an academic exercise; it has real consequences. The Founding Fathers designed gridlock into the American policy-making process. As a result, it is more difficult to pass new legislation than it is to block it. So by casting outsourcing as overwhelmingly positive with few or no negative effects, corporate lobbyists have effectively blocked any bills that would mitigate outsourcing's devastating effects on average Americans.

The debate has also misdirected our attention toward arguing the merits of outsourcing—is it a problem or a boon?—instead of tackling the problems created by outsourcing. For example, what advice and support do we give people who are displaced by outsourcing? Where are new jobs going to be created? How do we create better jobs? What should young people study when high-paying occupations seem to be moving overseas? Even if the United States had the political *will* to face these problems, no one has good solutions. While there is great uncertainty about outsourcing, everyone should be focused on ensuring the best outcome.

What Experts Say About Outsourcing

As noted in Chapter 1, President Bush's chief economic adviser, Gregory Mankiw, in February 2004 expressed the conventional wisdom about offshore outsourcing when he said that it is just another form of trade and probably good for the U.S. economy in the long run. He raised quite a stir when he made those comments rather nonchalantly, because they indicated his indifference toward the trend. The Republican Speaker of the House, Dennis Hastert, sent Dr. Mankiw a public letter admonishing him about his statement. And Mankiw, on leave from his teaching position at Harvard, qualified his statements slightly. But make no mistake: Most economists agree with Dr. Mankiw's assessment.

Recurring Themes: Outsourcing Is Good for the United States and Is Inevitable

Studies of outsourcing seem to repeat the same explanations of why it is necessary and why it is good for the economy. Critics are dismissed as dinosaurs—as "protectionist" and "isolationist" and therefore lacking faith in free markets. But not all of these pro-outsourcing arguments are logical or consistent, which reflects the uncertainty of the outcomes of outsourcing. Let's examine these themes.

The first theme is that American human capital—meaning the knowledge and skills of American workers—is inadequate. Reasons often given for outsourcing include (1) American workers don't have sufficient skills, owing in part to our poor education system; and (2) there are not enough young people studying science and engineering in college, or enough high-skilled workers generally. Of course, this argument ignores the fact that many of the Americans displaced by outsourcing excelled at their jobs and have graduate degrees in computer science or engineering from the very best schools. With record levels of unemployment for computer scientists, the economy is not absorbing the ones we have, so there is no point in graduating more.

The second theme is that outsourcing is somehow inevitable. According to this, (1) companies must be able to hire offshore because they are under intense global competition; (2) not using outsourcing has cost U.S. workers even more; (3) outsourcing is an inexorable law of nature; and (4) companies have to outsource to get access to local markets. The theme of inevitability disregards the fact that many companies engaged in outsourcing are experiencing record profits. They are not outsourcing because they have to, they are outsourcing because they *can*.

A third set of themes paints outsourcing as benign or even beneficial to the U.S. economy. Some reports claim that the number of jobs moving overseas is so miniscule as to be meaningless, and that good-paying jobs are waiting to be had, requiring a simple upgrade of a skills set. They say that the number of jobs lost to outsourcing is minimal compared to the normal "churn" in the economy, explaining that millions of people change jobs every year. The assumption is that the churn of jobs is more important than net job creation. Now, churn may have some merit in terms of measuring

job shifts by American workers, voluntary or involuntary, but it ignores the abysmal rate of reemployment of displaced workers (65 percent). So the churn argument in the absence of other data is simply obfuscation.

In a fourth theme, many outsourcing proponents suggest that the U.S. economy somehow automatically creates new jobs, and that displaced white-collar workers will land on their feet, just as blue-collar workers supposedly did in the dismal 1980s. Others often state that (1) outsourcing creates more jobs than it destroys, because insourcing gains outweigh losses from outsourcing; (2) outsourcing is a form of trade that, by theory, is always mutually beneficial; and (3) productivity gains and technological changes are the primary reasons for job loss, and these changes are good, as they increase the overall efficiency of our economy. In particular, the proponents say that 6.4 million jobs are insourced in the American economy. All this means is that 6.4 million workers are employed by companies that have foreign headquarters. This is far different from offshore outsourcing, where U.S. jobs are destroyed in favor of cheap foreign labor. For instance, the insourcing advocates would have you believe that when Daimler-Benz of Germany purchased U.S. automaker Chrysler, hundreds of thousands of jobs were instantly "insourced." Similarly, when major conglomerate Tyco International moved its headquarters from the United States to Bermuda to avoid paying U.S. taxes, hundreds of thousands of jobs were instantly "insourced." Of course, no new jobs were created by these paper actions. How proponents can equate this "job gain" to the substitution of foreign labor for American labor is hard to fathom, but it shows you the lengths to which they are willing to go to fight for their cause. Simply put, there is no reason to focus on the location of a company's headquarters anymore. The key is whether American workers are employed and getting paid decent wages.

Another theme of the outsourcing advocacy community is to compare the current exporting of jobs to the perceived threat posed by the rise of Japan in the 1980s, and then interpret history in an opportune way. For example, the American Electronics Association, the nation's largest technology industry association, says that even though Congress was under pressure in 2004 to enact protectionist legislation, it wisely chose to avoid doing so.[1] Of course, this is a surprising reading of the history of industrial policy in the 1980s, especially in the electronics industry, since voluntary

quotas were instituted and substantial subsidies were given to "protect" their industry.

Along these lines, most reports display faith in relatively straightforward remedies for the ill effects of outsourcing. The proponents suggest that (1) the "winners" of outsourcing can simply compensate the "losers"; (2) retraining programs will help displaced workers to easily find new jobs; and (3) more investment, innovation, and technology by the U.S. government will restore our technological advantage.

Pro-Outsourcing Studies

There have been literally dozens of pro-outsourcing studies issued by corporate lobbying groups. Most of the studies are self-referential, or simply rehash, or cite the same findings, which are always positive. So we will briefly mention three of the more important ones to provide a flavor of what the studies say. (For a detailed analysis and critique of these three key studies, see Appendix B.)

● *The ITAA Study.* In March 2004, a month after Mankiw's comments and at the height of the public discussion on outsourcing, the Information Technology Association of America (ITAA), a wealthy and influential lobbying group, was anxious about Congress's growing doubts about outsourcing. They paid Global Insight, a Massachusetts-based economics consulting firm, to conduct a study of outsourcing. Global Insight forecast that twice as many jobs would be created than would be destroyed as a result of outsourcing. While acknowledging that outsourcing would destroy more American IT jobs than would be created, the ITAA study claimed that many jobs would be created in other sectors, and that outsourcing would offer many other economic benefits, such as lower inflation and higher GDP.

● *The Mann Report.* Dr. Catherine Mann, a Fellow at the prestigious Institute for International Economics (IIE) in Washington, D.C., has written perhaps the most important study on outsourcing so far—important not necessarily because of its contents but because of its timing and the way that it has supported the outsourcing advocacy coalition. Her study was released in December 2003, just before the public debate on outsourcing peaked. Unlike the ITAA study, the Mann Report's major finding is that

outsourcing IT services will actually create many more American IT jobs than it will destroy. IT services costs will go down owing to outsourcing, unleashing immense productivity gains that will lead to more and better jobs for American IT workers.

• *The McKinsey Report.* The study that has had the second-greatest impact on the debate over outsourcing was completed by McKinsey Global Institute, an arm of the influential international management consulting firm McKinsey & Co. Like the Global Insight study, McKinsey relies on numbers to bolster the appearance that the study is definitive. McKinsey itself markets outsourcing services to potential clients, so it painted a rosy picture of outsourcing as a win-win situation for everybody. The key findings are that companies will save tremendous amounts of money by outsourcing; the U.S. economy will gain from outsourcing; and eventually even most American workers will benefit.

These studies all find the obvious: that companies will improve their economic efficiency by cutting costs. They ignore other important variables, such as the distributional effects—who wins and loses—and impacts on innovation and national security. They also lead you to believe that it is possible to predict what will happen in the future and that outsourcing will be overwhelmingly positive as long as policymakers don't get in the way.

Table 3-1 summarizes the main findings of the most important U.S. reports so far on outsourcing. As you can see, no report yet provides a comprehensive look at how outsourcing is affecting our economy, let alone why or what can be done about its detrimental effects.

Open Proponents of Outsourcing

Company executives, shareholders, and consulting firms clearly are benefiting from outsourcing. So it is understandable that they present outsourcing in the best light, even going so far as to distort the facts to serve their purposes.

Proponents of outsourcing generally try to confuse matters by using subtle tactics. For example, they will say that cheap labor isn't the only reason that companies are exporting jobs—that they are interested in serving local markets overseas. They divert attention away from wage differentials

Table 3-1. Major reports and findings on outsourcing.

Source	Date	Key Assertions	Sponsor
American Electronics Association	March 2004	Rehash of existing arguments in favor of outsourcing.	Industry
Business Roundtable	March 2004	Same as American Electronics Association.	Chief Executives
Dr. Catherine Mann, Institute for International Economics	December 2003	IT services costs will go down due to offshoring, unleashing immense productivity gains that lead to more and better jobs for U.S. IT workers. More support for displaced workers is needed.	Industry
Dr. Robert Atkinson, Progressive Policy Institute	June 2004	Offshoring is causing real problems, but we need to innovate our way out of it. More support for displaced workers is needed.	Democratic Leadership Council
Economic Policy Institute	June 2004	Debunks many of the offshoring advocacy reports, particularly on insourcing.	Labor Unions
Electronics Industry Alliance	May 2004	Proposes ways in which U.S. can maintain technological leadership by greater investments in education and technology infrastructure.	Industry
Global Insight	March 2004	IT offshoring will create more jobs in non–IT sectors in the U.S. economy that will more than offset losses in the IT sector.	Information Technology Association of America
McKinsey Global Institute	August 2003	U.S. companies save money, and the U.S. economy is a net beneficiary by 12 to 14 cents for each dollar that is offshored. Some workers lose but they can be easily compensated, and we should adopt policies to support displaced workers.	McKinsey & Co.
U.S. Chamber of Commerce	April 2004	Similar to American Electronics Association report.	Industry

and focus instead on the potential for expanding markets abroad. They are factually correct that cheap labor is not the only motivation for outsourcing, but in most cases of white-collar outsourcing, cheap labor *is* the overwhelming reason for outsourcing.

Almost the entire IT services industry in India, for instance, is set up for export. The domestic Indian market is miniscule, on the other hand, and far less profitable for U.S. companies seeking a larger market. Perhaps it will eventually grow, but no one expects it to be substantial anytime soon, and it is implausible that it could be even a secondary factor in outsourcing business choices. As we know from our experience with Mexico, workers who earn a few dollars a day cannot afford to purchase products made with U.S. labor.

The proponents of outsourcing far outweigh those who are alarmed by the phenomenon. Few people in positions of power seem to be taking the trend seriously; in fact, many see it as a positive trend. The governments and businesses of developing countries are obviously in favor of actions that offer their citizens more jobs. The Indian government, including former Prime Minister Vajpayee, and NASSCOM, the Indian software services organization, have stated that outsourcing makes simple economic logic and is a reflection of how free trade should work. Using textbook economic theory, they give the standard answer—that is, that outsourcing creates cheaper goods for American consumers. Moreover, they say, U.S. corporations are taking advantage of cheaper labor costs in India. Clearly, there are strong interests involved, in India and in the United States, in promoting further outsourcing.

U.S. Corporations as Advocates of Outsourcing

As noted earlier, U.S. corporations claim that outsourcing is a positive-sum game for the American economy. For the most part, corporations, including the many that have actually outsourced jobs, have tended to be quite tight-lipped about it. Most of the pronouncements have come from industry associations. The associations generally claim that outsourcing increases economic efficiency and growth, which will lead to more jobs in the long run. They also point out that American consumers have shown no interest in the actual source of the product or service, so that corporate decisions

to outsource simply reflect consumers' wishes for the lowest prices.

The U.S. Chamber of Commerce released a report attacking the "myths" surrounding outsourcing and stated that opponents of outsourcing were simply ignorant in terms of its economic benefits. The American Electronics Association (AEA) and the Computer Systems Policy Project, associations of high-tech companies, repeated the attack. The EIA (Electronics Industries Alliance) took a slightly more moderate tone, arguing that while outsourcing is positive, policymakers should continue to support innovation research. The upshot of these reports and the motivation behind them is to derail any ideas of an active policy stance on outsourcing because these organizations see outsourcing as a boon to America's economic competitiveness.

Corporate executives have also entered the fray. Craig Barrett, CEO of Intel Corporation, has been quite vocal in attacking the U.S. educational system and warning of the competition that Americans face from India, China, and Russia. He has railed against what he perceives as misguided U.S. policies, such as subsidizing agriculture instead of high-technology research, that make the situation worse, and he suggests that the United States subsidize broadband and wireless infrastructure investments—which, not surprisingly, would increase demand for Intel's products. He admonishes workers, saying that they have no right to believe that their jobs are secure and that the government should not meddle in outsourcing decisions.[2] This situation is ironic, since Intel was one of the companies that came to Washington, D.C., in the 1980s to ask for help in developing the U.S. semiconductor industry, which was losing market share to Japan. That help turned into protection for the industry via voluntary quotas and subsidies.

During the summer of 2004, when these companies felt that they had weathered the outsourcing storm, their lobbying interests shifted to other matters, such as convincing Congress to stop the SEC from forcing companies to expense stock options. In short, they promote the virtues of free trade when it is convenient for them.

Mainstream Economists

The points outlined above, as well as the claim that outsourcing is not a serious cause for concern, are echoed by mainstream economists hailing

from both political parties. Jagdish Bhagwati, an internationally famous economist from Columbia University (and a Democrat), has stated in several editorials that outsourcing is a "natural" economic phenomenon that is part of a normal economic development of the U.S. economy. The cost savings of outsourcing will lead to greater U.S. economic efficiency. Outsourced Americans will find new jobs in parts of the U.S. economy that grow. In a *New York Times* essay called "Why Your Job Isn't Moving to Bangalore," Bhagwati argues that Mankiw was just stating the "simple truth" that outsourcing is beneficial to the U.S. economy.[3] In the same piece, Bhagwati claims that there is "little evidence of a major push by American companies to set up research operations in the developing world." The reality is, as we demonstrate later, that many high-technology companies are doing just this, and developing countries are trying to attract those types of jobs.

Robert Reich, former Secretary of Labor under President Clinton, and Alan Greenspan, current chair of the Federal Reserve, have also dismissed outsourcing as a long-term threat. Greenspan believes that the key to American jobs is simply that we have workers who are more capable. Thus, the answer to outsourcing questions is to increase budgets for the retraining of workers. Ben Bernanke, Greenspan's colleague on the Federal Reserve Board, repeats these sentiments, but adds that by reducing costs, outsourcing actually improves the competitiveness of America's exports. Curiously, Bernanke does not mention the fact that outsourcing also affects the other side of the ledger—namely, that it creates imports that substitute for national production of goods and the jobs that go with that production.

Politicians

Politicians on both sides of the Atlantic have expressed their support for outsourcing. In the U.K., Prime Minister Tony Blair said that British companies will benefit by letting British jobs move to China and India. In another nod to how influential McKinsey consulting is, he cited their report as showing that "contrary to every instinctive reaction, such methods are not merely necessary for business to survive, but can increase the provision of jobs. . . ."[4] The Secretary of the Treasury for the Bush Administration, John Snow, said, "[Outsourcing] is one aspect of trade, and there

can't be any doubt about the fact that trade makes the economy stronger."[5] In an attempt to tap into the pride of the nation, President George W. Bush portrayed anyone questioning the current outsourcing policy as someone who doesn't believe in Americans' ability to compete.[6]

Media

Perhaps what is surprising is the supportive stance taken on outsourcing by members of the media. The *New York Times* and the *Washington Post* have supported the positive assessments of outsourcing, as have many other editorial boards around the country. Thomas Friedman, a *New York Times* columnist and best-selling author, downplays as "few" the jobs that are affected by outsourcing. He also states that the benefits to India in terms of job creation and economic growth will help U.S. security concerns in South Asia. There have been only a few voices in the media wilderness that are critical of outsourcing, such as Lou Dobbs of CNN, Jodie Allen of *U.S. News & World Report,* and Bob Herbert of the *New York Times.*

Consulting Firms

Consulting firms and think tanks like IIE have passed themselves off as neutral. In fact, Catherine Mann's key study on outsourcing was funded by industry.

McKinsey Consulting has a financial interest in promoting outsourcing: If the outsourcing market increases, McKinsey will benefit by selling more outsourcing consulting services to companies. McKinsey has additional interests in outsourcing. They have had NASSCOM, the Indian Software Services Industry Association, as a long-standing client and have jointly issued a number of reports on the Indian IT industry. For these reasons, it would be surprising if the McKinsey Report did not come to the win-win conclusion.

Critics of Outsourcing

There is a growing number of voices that criticize outsourcing. The arguments have generally not attacked the analytic reports directly. Most of the effort has been to convince people that outsourcing creates real and signif-

icant problems. A microcosm of this effort was an exchange between Paul
Craig Roberts, former Assistant Secretary of Treasury under President
Reagan, and Jagdish Bhagwati that was published in the *Wall Street Journal*
in the spring of 2004. Roberts expended considerable effort trying to
explain why outsourcing is a problem, and Bhagwati simply dismissed the
idea of outsourcing's negative impact as a nonissue.[7]

Other critics, such as CNN's Lou Dobbs, have focused on the stories
of individuals who have been displaced by outsourcing and the record trade
deficits that are unsustainable and damaging to America's future. Dobbs
has been vilified by the pro-outsourcing crowd and in many policy elite circles, but instead of addressing his questions head-on, the proponents of oursourcing have marginalized his comments by attacking him personally. In
one particularly distasteful remark, a prominent journalist went so far as to
claim that Dobbs was possessed by a demon.

Then there is a large and growing group of American workers who
have been negatively impacted by outsourcing and are mad as hell. Lastly,
but certainly not least, the AFL-CIO has been a strong and important crit-
ic of outsourcing. The AFL-CIO provides important links for workers to the
political process and especially to the Democratic Party.

Unfortunately, the major problem with the policy debate is that it is
overwhelmingly one-sided. There are very few worker-oriented think tanks
that have the resources to fight the lobbying onslaught by the pro-outsourcing advocates.

Concerned Politicians

Some politicians who are from areas that have been devastated by job losses
to oursourcing, as well as hit by the slow economic recovery in general,
have been guarded in their pronouncements. As noted earlier, Dennis
Hastert, the Republican Speaker of the House, sent a letter to Mankiw asking him to retract his cavalier statement. This does not imply that the generally pro-business Republicans are against outsourcing, but simply that
they recognize, as can the corporations involved in it, the explosiveness of
the issue in key states such as Ohio and Pennsylvania.

Certain Democratic Party leaders have taken what appear to be
stronger stands on outsourcing. Chuck Schumer, Democratic Senator

from New York, wrote a *New York Times* editorial expressing concern about mainstream economic explanations of outsourcing. Senators Hillary Clinton (also of New York) and Tom Daschle (South Dakota), who lost his seat in the 2004 election, introduced legislation that required companies to provide 90 days' notice to employees whose jobs were to be outsourced. Massachusetts Senator John Kerry also introduced legislation that would require companies to disclose to customers the location of foreign call centers.

The outsourcing issue had important reverberations in the 2004 presidential race. Vice Presidential candidate John Edwards made the issue a prominent feature of his primary campaign. Democratic Presidential candidate John Kerry called outsourcing a threat to the economy and unveiled a proposal to change the current tax code, which allows companies that earn revenues abroad to defer their taxes if they keep the monies abroad.

Similarly, there has been a proliferation of political activity on the state and local levels regarding outsourcing. Thirty-three states have some legislation restricting outsourcing. Perhaps the most prominent case took place in New Jersey, which has actually outsourced call centers for support given to local welfare recipients! Given that the purpose of welfare is to get Americans back to work, this was seen as an especially egregious use of public funding. These very jobs could have been preserved for local residents, thus aiding taxpayers by reducing welfare rolls. However, the reform legislation to mandate U.S. sourcing for New Jersey public services was successfully stalled by corporate lobbyists.

The source of some politicians' concerns is the very real pain of those people whose jobs have been outsourced. This is discussed more fully in Chapter 7.

A Handful of Economists

A few prominent economists have taken a critical view on outsourcing. Famous economist Paul Samuelson, 1970 Nobel Laureate in Economics, and Brad DeLong, former Assistant Secretary of the Treasury under President Clinton, have expressed concern regarding the downward pressure on wages and the long-term impact of outsourcing. Samuelson, who practically devised modern trade theory himself, went so far as to call out

certain economists, such as Bhagwati, for passing on "polemical untruths" about the actual gains from trade, and said that anyone who believes that outsourcing does not exert wage pressure on U.S. workers must believe in the tooth fairy.[8]

Paul Craig Roberts was one of the first economists to break from the orthodoxy by writing a series of scathing editorials on outsourcing in which he has said that outsourcing is "lethal for America's future." Joseph Stiglitz, another Nobel-winning economist, has expressed concern about the negative impacts of outsourcing on U.S. workers.

Organized Labor, Workers, and the American Public

Labor unions have become the main organized enemies of outsourcing, with the AFL-CIO having featured the issue on its homepage. WashTech, the Washington State unit of the Communication Workers of America, has developed a special Web site on outsourcing and has sponsored a number of studies and rallies. WashTech has also played a key role in helping to disclose outsourcing information that companies would prefer to keep quiet.

A number of workers have taken matters into their own hands. Many have become grassroots activists, with some even running for Congress themselves. Besides a host of individual efforts opposing outsourcing, as discussed in Chapter 7, several antioutsourcing activist groups have been created. Many of these groups are listed in the Bibliography. Of course, according to the polls, the American public strongly opposes outsourcing, as you would expect.

Proponents' Reaction to Critics

The reaction by proponents of oursourcing to any questions regarding its benefits has been swift and certain. The proponents want to discredit the opposition before it can gain any headway, especially among policymakers.

Cries of Protectionism

One line of attack used by outsourcing proponents has been to tar all opponents of outsourcing as "ignorant" or "protectionist." Among economists, the label *protectionist* refers to someone who still lives in the Dark Ages in

terms of economic knowledge. Most economists have based this conclusion on the major economic event of the twentieth century, namely the Great Depression, which was sparked by a wave of reciprocal protectionism. Because economists have linked U.S. free trade policies to the worldwide economic growth of the 1960s, they believe that free trade is the only path to prosperity.

A more serious reading of history reveals some doubts about whether free trade per se was responsible for the economic growth in the 1960s. Among other things, European and Japanese economies were recovering quickly after the war, and had high demand for both capital and goods but limited domestic capacity. Moreover, the United States, during the Vietnam era in particular, was running very high budget deficits and buying products from all over the world. Because this was an era of fixed exchange rates based on the dollar, our exports were not affected. That is no longer the case. Last but not least, as discussed in Chapter 2, there is no such thing as free trade. If free trade alone were responsible for growth, we would not have experienced the stagflation of the 1970s, the recession of the early Reagan years in the 1980s, or the current malaise.

Outsourced Workers Will Get Other Jobs

The basic historical facts don't stop outsourcing advocates from dismissing all arguments against it, however. For instance, Daniel Drezner, in an article in *Foreign Affairs* titled "The Outsourcing Boogeyman," equates people who believe that outsourcing causes unemployment with those who believed the sun revolves around the Earth. He goes on to say that they are merely "scapegoating foreigners."[9]

Of course, outsourcing does in fact cause unemployment, which is undisputed even by nearly every outsourcing advocate (except, perhaps, Drezner). What proponents hope is that workers who are unemployed because of outsourcing will be quickly reemployed—which to date no proponent has actually shown to be true, since they haven't actually looked at what happens to outsourced workers!

Federal Reserve Chairman Greenspan states that millions of jobs are created and lost every month. Therefore, the displacement of a few hundred

thousand jobs is part of the natural churn of job creation and losses. But Greenspan is confusing the churn of those moving in and out of jobs with the net number of jobs in the economy.

Rosy Forecasts Based on Selective Statistics

Another problem is that the economic statistics cited by outsourcing proponents are often selective and misleading. For example, the McKinsey report uses employment data up to 2001, which favors their conclusion. Global Insight's forecasting model is subject to the same guesswork present in most economic models that claim to predict the future. Catherine Mann's report relies on the previously rosy Bureau of Labor Statistics (BLS) occupational outlook forecasts, which were created before the dot-com bust.

Proponents frequently mention the BLS's mass layoff statistics, which were released in June 2004. The BLS estimated that only 2 percent of the jobs lost in the first quarter of 2004 were from outsourcing. But any objective analysis of how the data were gathered reveals that this number vastly understates the effects of outsourcing.

First, companies must self-report the information, and as we know they are reluctant to reveal that they are outsourcing. Second, there are a number of options they can select when responding to the question about why the jobs were destroyed, many of which overlap with outsourcing. Lastly, these statistics are limited to companies that have fifty or more employees and lay-offs of fifty or more employees, which means that the data-gathering misses a large number of outsourcing activities. True to form, outsourcing proponents swiftly jumped on the BLS data as proof that outsourcing's effects are insignificant, not bothering to check whether the data were accurate.

Ignoring the Complete Picture

Pro-outsourcing analyses simply ignore key statistics that are important for any true discussion of outsourcing. These statistics include:

- The staggering unemployment rates within hard-hit sectors
- The inability to map trend lines for an emerging phenomenon
- The effects of outsourcing on innovation and security

- The lack of study or concern for the substitution effects of bringing foreign workers to the United States on guest-worker visas
- The downward wage pressure from outsourcing, as featured by critics
- The abysmal reemployment rates for displaced workers
- The basic limitations of data available on outsourcing and its effects

Even if we had the political will to address outsourcing in the ways that the proponents suggest, their recommendations simply don't work.

Conclusion

If we seem overly critical of the pro-outsourcing advocates, it is because we have truly been amazed at the lengths they are willing to go to throw away any semblance of objectivity in their analyses, which are sloppy and selective. Whenever one line of their argument is refuted, they simply move on to another one. And in some cases they have even resorted to ad hominem attacks on critics instead of rational analysis.

The people who have been impacted by outsourcing are intelligent and articulate. Many economists claim that this is the only reason that outsourcing is receiving any attention, meaning that it is much ado about nothing. They say that no one cared much when blue-collar workers lost out as manufacturing went offshore in the 1980s because those folks were not as educated. But this kind of rationale is remarkably out of touch. First, it is a poor reading of what was actually done in the 1980s to help stop the manufacturing exodus. Second, it's true that the United States didn't do enough to help the blue-collar workers who were adversely affected. But that doesn't mean that nothing should be done to help white-collar workers: *Two wrongs don't make a right.*

Before getting to what can be done, we need to understand better exactly how much outsourcing is happening, why it is happening, and how it is happening. Let's move now to providing the comprehensive and objective view that has so far been missing from this debate.

Notes

1. Carrie Kirby, "Group Says U.S. Overreacting to Outsourcing: Tech Association Urges Congress to Delay Protectionist Measures," *San Francisco Chronicle* (March 24, 2004).

2. Jane Larson, "Competing Is Key, Says Intel CEO," *Arizona Republic* (June 5, 2004).

3. Jagdish Bhagwati, "Why Your Job Isn't Moving to Bangalore," *New York Times* (February 15, 2004).

4. Patrick Wintour, "U.K. Can Benefit from Jobs Heading to India, Says Blair," *The Guardian* (March 23, 2004).

5. Liza Porteus, "Outsourcing Targeted in 2004 Campaign," *Fox News* (March 31, 2004).

6. Ibid.

7. Timothy Aeppel, "Offshore Face-Off: Moving Jobs Overseas Can Cut a Company's Costs; But Is It Bad for the U.S. Economy? Two Economists Debate the Issue," *Wall Street Journal* (May 10, 2004).

8. Steve Lohr, "An Elder Challenges Outsourcing's Orthodoxy," *New York Times* (September 9, 2004).

9. Daniel W. Drezner, "The Outsourcing Bogeyman," *Foreign Affairs* (May/June 2004).

Outsourcing of High-Wage Jobs

The increasing loss of high-wage, white-collar, and high-tech jobs to offshore outsourcing in the past few years has taken Washington by surprise. These were the jobs that were thought to be immune from low-wage competition. Outsourcing alone doesn't explain the loss of jobs in white-collar sectors, and especially in the high-tech sector, but it is an increasingly important source of job loss and will only grow in significance.

Since neither economic theory nor Washington policymakers anticipated this phenomenon, there are no reliable statistics on the loss of jobs. Exacerbating the lack of official statistics is the fact that the companies that are moving jobs offshore are keeping the process under wraps, in the hope of avoiding negative publicity. However, some investigative work can begin to bring together the various pieces into a picture that suggests how serious this outward flow has become and what exactly is the nature of the positions that are moving overseas, as well as provide insight into why companies are so eager to shift work to overseas locations.

How Much Outsourcing Is Happening?

Identifying the precise number of jobs being outsourced overseas is difficult, for two primary reasons. First, the federal government does not collect

data on jobs shipped overseas. Second, companies are reluctant to reveal which jobs they have shipped overseas and ask their overseas outsourcers to keep quiet about the deals. Companies are so secretive that they are even unwilling to speak at off-the-record meetings organized by policy think tanks—even refusing to send representatives to attend the meetings. These meetings are specifically off-the-record in order to elicit frank and open discussion among various stakeholders, but in the many meetings that we have attended over the past few years, only two companies have spoken openly about their outsourcing plans. Even the organizers of such meetings have been surprised by how few companies are willing to attend.

This lack of a window into corporate planning makes policy design and formulation much more difficult. Without access to corporate executives' minds, the best way to gain insight into what is happening and what will happen over the next few years is from "independent" observers—namely, consulting firms that have corporate clients—and from company announcements.

Current Estimates of Job Losses

The report that jump-started the debate on offshore outsourcing and has had the most influence with business planners and policymakers was done by John McCarthy of Forrester Research, Inc., a consulting firm. McCarthy predicted that approximately 3.3 million white-collar jobs and $136 billion in wages would move overseas by 2015. It should be noted that the report was released in November 2002, before *offshore outsourcing* was a household phrase among managers. In a subsequent report, released in May 2004, McCarthy increased the long-term prediction slightly to 3.4 million but said that the near-term exodus over the next two to three years would be much faster than earlier predicted, with 830,000 jobs leaving by the end of 2005.[1]

A summary of McCarthy's predictions is included in Table 4-1. The report predicts that the exodus of computer occupations will happen earlier and deeper than other types of jobs, but that the computer field is hardly alone. Jobs moving overseas include a wide range of occupations, such as architecture, accounting, engineering, information technology, and call-center operators. This report and its numbers have been cited so frequent-

Table 4-1. Projected numbers of U.S. jobs to be moved offshore, by profession.

(To low wage countries such as China, India, Russia, and the Philippines.)

Profession	2003	By 2005	By 2010	By 2015
Art, Design	2,500	8,000	15,000	30,000
Architecture	14,000	46,000	93,000	191,000
Business	30,000	91,000	176,000	356,000
Computer	102,000	181,000	322,000	542,000
Legal	6,000	20,000	39,000	79,000
Life Sciences	300	4,000	16,000	39,000
Management	3,500	34,000	106,000	259,000
Office	146,000	410,000	815,000	1,600,000
Sales	11,000	38,000	97,000	218,000
TOTAL	315,000	830,000	1,700,000	3,400,000

Note: Numbers have been rounded.

Source: Near-Term Growth of Offshoring Accelerating, Forester Research, Inc., May 14, 2004.

ly that many people believe it is a precise forecast rather than simply an educated guess. In some ways, with the amount of publicity that the Forrester report has drawn, it has become something like a road map for company managers, and may be a self-fulfilling prophecy.

A flurry of other reports were issued by research firms that compete with Forrester, including A.T. Kearny, Deloitte, Gartner, and McKinsey. Gartner upped the ante by predicting that one-half million, or 10 percent, of U.S. IT jobs would move offshore by the end of 2004.[2] Others such as Deloitte Consulting have focused their efforts on financial services firms, like Citigroup, JP Morgan Chase, and Fidelity, and they estimate that as many as 2.3 million U.S. jobs in banking and securities may move overseas.[3]

The figures in these reports should be taken with a grain of salt, since they are at best educated guesses and at worst biased advocacy pieces. As with most emerging phenomena, no good forecasting models exist so no one can predict with any reasonable certainty what will happen. In fact, the reports themselves are usually rather sparse documents, devoid of methodology, with simple tables of predictions. For example, the Gartner report is only four pages long.

The other reason to be cautious is that these research firms also sell consulting services on how to move work overseas; consequently they have a built-in bias to encourage outsourcing efforts. As more work is outsourced overseas, these research firms stand to gain more business. However, these firms exert a strong influence on U.S. corporate management. They can often shape managerial strategy for an entire industry because they are believed to be on the cutting edge. Corporate managers, afraid of being left behind, may adopt a research firm's pronouncements because they have no better window on their competitors' strategy. In fact, many of these same research firms contributed to the excesses of the dot-com bubble by forecasting ridiculously high revenue growth in Internet commerce.

The Kinds of Jobs That Are Vulnerable

Some academics and think-tank fellows have identified occupations that are particularly vulnerable to offshore outsourcing. Cynthia Kroll and Ashok Deo Bardhan, from the University of California at Berkeley, have estimated that a staggering 14 million positions, or nearly one in nine of all U.S. jobs, are vulnerable to being outsourced overseas, the majority of which are back-office jobs.[4] The results of the Kroll and Deo Bardhan study are shown in Table 4-2.

Rob Atkinson, a senior fellow at the Progressive Policy Institute, a think tank established by the business-friendly "New Democratic" wing of the Democratic Party, has estimated that a similar number (12 million jobs) are vulnerable. Atkinson notes that 54 percent of those jobs pay more than the median wage, which by definition means that high-wage occupations are especially at risk.[5]

Professor Martin Kenney and his colleague Rafiq Dossani have traveled numerous times since early 2003 to India, where many non–IT white-

Table 4-2. Projected numbers of U.S. jobs vulnerable to offshoring, by occupation.

Sectors	Employment 2001	Average Annual Salary 2001
All Occupations (Total U.S. Employment)	127,980,410	$ 34,020
Occupations at Risk of Outsourcing		
Office Support*	8,637,900	$ 29,791
Computer Operators	177,990	$ 30,780
Data Entry Keyers	405,000	$ 22,740
Business and Financial Support**	2,153,480	$ 52,559
Computer and Math Professionals	2,825,870	$ 60,350
Paralegals and Legal Assistants	183,550	$ 39,220
Diagnostic Support Services	168,240	$ 38,860
Medical Transcriptionists	94,090	$ 27,020
Total in Outsourcing Risk Occupations	**14,063,130**	**$ 39,631**

Percent of All Occupations 11.0%

Notes: Data are from Bureau of Labor Statistics Web site.
*Office Support aggregates data from 22 detailed Office and Administrative Support categories.
** Business and Financial Support aggregates data from 10 detailed Business and Financial Occupations.

Source: Ashok Deo Bardhan and Cynthia Kroll, "The New Wave of Outsourcing," Fisher Center for Real Estate and Urban Economics, University of California at Berkeley. Fisher Center Research Reports, Report #1103 (November 2, 2003).

collar jobs have been outsourced. They went to study the Business Process Outsourcing (BPO) phenomenon, and as a result they predict that some 700,000 customer service and corporate back-office jobs will move from the United States to India by 2008.[6]

Even architecture services are moving offshore. HLW International, a New York–based architectural firm, designs office complexes for

upstate New York in their facilities in Shanghai, China. The Chinese architects use videoconferencing in lieu of face-to-face meetings and are able to design to "local" building codes.[7] And tax breaks are not enough to keep even call-center positions. After getting $3.85 million in tax breaks from the state of Florida, the lure of cheaper labor spurred Capital One to shift 1,100 credit-card call-center jobs to India and abandon five buildings and 550,000 square-feet of office space.[8] Reuters Group shifted six of its financial reporting jobs to India in early 2004, which it followed later in the year by cutting twenty editorial positions in the United States and Europe and hiring sixty people in India to replace them.[9] These relatively small outsourcing ventures obviously were successful because Reuters subsequently announced it was making Bangalore the company's primary information-gathering hub. It is hiring 1,500 workers in its Bangalore office, the equivalent of 10 percent of the company's total workforce.[10]

How Outsourcing Snowballs

The financial services industry provides an interesting case of how offshore outsourcing snowballs from IT to other occupations. The industry is information-intensive and has long been a cutting-edge customer for IT services because of its unique set of information security needs. In a 2004 survey of forty-three top financial services institutions, Deloitte Consulting found that the companies had on average increased their offshore personnel 500 percent, from 300 to 1,500 workers, between 2003 and 2004 and that 80 percent of that increase went to India.[11]

The pace seems to be accelerating rapidly in the financial services. In fact, pent-up demand in this sector is so great that many Indian IT firms now specialize in IT and BPO work, especially for financial services. Mastek, an Indian offshore outsourcer, earned 42 percent of its 2004 revenue from financial services, up from 22 percent the year before.[12] A *CFO Magazine* survey of 275 finance executives reveals that 64 percent of the firms that already outsource offshore are planning on increasing the number of jobs they send abroad, indicating that they are happy with the results. Also, according to the survey, 47 percent of the offshored jobs were high-paying, with salaries of more than $50,000.[13]

As companies become more comfortable with outsourcing IT overseas, they begin to see the possibility of shifting related tasks, such as loan processing. Companies that offshore are establishing facilities, building intangible knowledge on how to do business overseas, and tapping the local labor pool. It can only be expected that they will increasingly move more functions overseas.

The Number of Outsourcing Companies Is Rapidly Growing

A quick scan of news articles, press releases, and the Internet makes it abundantly clear that the number of companies announcing expansions of their overseas operations is accelerating. Lou Dobbs's Web site lists hundreds of companies that are "Exporting America"—his phrase for offshore outsourcing and the title of his recent book on the subject.[14] WashTech, a labor union established by the Communication Workers of America in Washington State, hosts the "Offshore Tracker," a Web site that tracks company announcements of overseas expansions (http://www.techsunite.rg/offshore/). The Bibliography for this book gives the addresses for these and other important Web sites.

Many companies are either not hiring in the United States or are downsizing their domestic workforce. Nearly every major technology company, including Microsoft, Intel, Hewlett-Packard/Compaq, Yahoo, Google, IBM, Electronic Data Systems (EDS), and Computer Sciences Corporation (CSC), is expanding its workforce abroad. In a bold move, Siemens, the German industrial conglomerate, announced that they were moving most of their 15,000 programming jobs from the United States and Western Europe to China, India, and Eastern Europe. Even smaller specialized engineering firms like Brecis Communications are moving all of their design verification and software development from the United States to India. The company designs advanced electronic chips for the latest Internet devices.[15]

The U.S. media, until recently, had not been paying close attention to the global job shift. For instance, on June 17, 2003, the *Economic Times of India*, a leading Indian financial newspaper, announced that EDS was opening its first BPO center in India, with about 500 jobs. A company executive was quoted as saying, "This is part of our best shore strategy wherein

we are not only looking at India but several other countries within Asia."[16] The very next day, the American press reported that EDS was laying off 2 percent of its workforce, or approximately 2,700 people.[17] In fact, in March 2003, we received inquiries from the Indian press about our thoughts concerning the coming backlash from U.S. workers, about four months before anyone in the U.S. press was thinking seriously about it. Table 4-3 shows a small sample of companies expanding their offshore workers while downsizing in America.

Government Services Are Offshored, Too

It's not only private companies that are outsourcing white-collar jobs. Federal, state, and local governments have taken part in the outsourcing of government services. There are few estimates in this area, but a study showed that just about every state government has offshored at least some of its work, oftentimes unwittingly.[18] In many cases, companies are not required to inform states if the work is being completed overseas. For example, the state of Washington determined that about 150 contracts contained at least $50 million worth of offshore outsourcing.[19]

Government procurement is at the heart of many offshore outsourcing controversies. The issue is often framed as, "Should tax dollars be used to create jobs offshore when there are so many unemployed Americans?" The outsourcing advocates argue that the answer is obviously yes because it is cheaper. However, this kind of debate only scratches the surface.

U.S. government procurement rules are complex and take into account a large array of noneconomic criteria that limit competition. For example, advanced technology work for the Defense Department is often limited to U.S. companies, such as the Navy's supercomputer purchase from IBM, because this serves national security goals such as preserving U.S. leadership in the supercomputer field. (Of course, it is somewhat ironic that IBM is able to present itself as a U.S. company when it means getting billions of dollars in U.S. government contracts, but calls itself a global company when it wants to export jobs.)

But nonsecurity objectives also shape the U.S. government procurement policies. For instance, many contracts are set aside for small and disadvantaged businesses (precertified by the government) so that only they

Table 4-3. Examples of companies announcing expansion overseas and downsizing in the U.S.

Company	Offshore Country	Offshore Expansion	Downsizing in U.S. & Western Europe
EDS	Multiple Low-Cost	20,000[1] (by 2006)	20,000
IBM	India	5,000	3,000[2]
3Com	China	1,000[3]	
Autodesk[4]	China	?	650
Siemens[5]	China, India, and Eastern Europe	15,000	15,000
Hewlett-Packard[6]	Low-Cost Countries	4,400	2,000
Bank of America[7]	India	1,500	12,500
Capital One[8]	India	1,100	1,100
Intel[9]	India	1,000–3,000	4,000

Sources:
1, 3. David Zielenziger, "Reuters Summit-Tech Cos Focus on Asia to Expand Jobs," www.Reuters.com (February 27, 2004).
2. Bulkeley, William M., "IBM Now Plans Fewer Layoffs from Offshoring," *Wall Street Journal* (July 29, 2004).
4. Carrie Kirby and John Shinal, "Offshoring's Giant Target: The Bay Area, Silicon Valley Could Face Export of 1 in 6 Jobs—Worst in the Nation," *San Francisco Chronicle* (March 7, 2004).
5. S. Srinivasan, "Most Siemens Software Jobs Moving East," Associated Press (February 16, 2004).
6. Dean Takahashi, "HP Results Solid in 4th Quarter: Revenue Growth Strong; 2,000 More Job Cuts," *San Jose Mercury News* (November 20, 2003).
7. Stella M. Hopkins, "BofA Expands into India Outsourcing: Up to 1,500 People May Be Hired at New Facility," *Charlotte Observer* (May 9, 2004).
8. Robert Trigaux, "Capital One: The Political Drama," *St. Petersburg Times* (July 29, 2004).
9. Aliza Earnshaw, "Intel Holds Job Fairs for 'Redeployed' Employees, While Hiring Overseas," *Portland Business Journal* (August 26, 2002).

can bid on them. The rationale is that this special treatment increases business ownership and employment in traditionally underrepresented groups. Offshore outsourcing, however, may significantly and severely distort the intended impact of such procurement regulations. U.S. firms that win U.S. government business because they have small and disadvantaged business status could turn around and perform all of that work offshore.

A Lack of Government Monitoring

Despite this growing trend toward offshore outsourcing, the U.S. government has made little effort to monitor the flow of jobs overseas. The U.S. Commerce and Labor Departments have no system for tracking the number of jobs moving overseas, and there are no plans for implementing one. In early 2004, Congressman Frank Wolf, a long-serving Republican from the Virginia suburbs of Washington, D.C., asked the Commerce Department to study the problem. The department's report is hampered by the paltry funds appropriated by Congress for the study; the $335,000 was enough to do only a cursory examination of the problem and a rehash of existing data.

What is desperately needed is original data collection and research. Some people in government claim that they lack the resources to collect the data, which is remarkable considering how much the federal government spends ($130 billion annually) on research and development. Only a few million dollars are needed to conduct the research needed to help develop a better sense of what is happening. Fortunately, there is recently passed legislation, also sponsored by Congressman Wolf, that appropriates $2 million to conduct such a study.

In the first quarter of 2004, the Bureau of Labor Statistics (BLS) added two questions on offshore outsourcing and offshoring to their Mass Layoffs Statistics survey of employers. As a result, the BLS found that 4,663, or just 2 percent of the layoffs during the first quarter of 2004, were due to companies moving work overseas, either offshoring or offshore outsourcing. The offshoring advocates were ecstatic, pointing out that the jobless recovery had nothing to do with moving work overseas. There are a few problems with using this statistic, though.

- The survey asks for layoff events that include more than fifty people at a time, which captures only a small percentage of the actual layoffs in any given time period, since most layoffs involve fewer than fifty people.

- The data were collected at a time when companies were avoiding bad press concerning outsourcing, so it is likely that they changed their practices and began laying people off in a more surreptitious manner, by ones and twos.

- The survey offered many options for reasons for the layoffs, including increased competition, loss of sales, etc. Many of these reasons could overlap with outsourcing, but respondents could only select one reason.

- The BLS report cannot pick up hiring that takes place offshore in lieu of hiring that would have, prior to outsourcing, taken place in the United States.

Companies Keep Secrets

Adding to the data-collection problem are company policies and practices that limit disclosure of their offshoring activities and plans. In hopes of limiting employee backlash, companies are keeping their labor "rebalancing" plans secret. Oftentimes they are not disclosing these plans to domestic employees, and when they do, companies institute clauses in severance packages that force employees to be silent about their impending termination.

Even if the employees don't have a specific contractual restriction forcing them to be silent, many fear that if they do speak out they will be blacklisted by industry and have significant problems in getting a new job. For instance, many technology workers have been willing to speak off the record with us, but they refuse to speak with reporters. This situation is particularly acute in occupations where unemployment rates are very high and the stakes for potential job opportunities are that much higher. In many cases, U.S. employees have been forced to train their overseas replacements.

Even when workers do know that their jobs are being exported, they have little alternative than to accept it. We personally know several

American engineers whose divisions have been shipped overseas. Most of these engineers have been laid off, but in some cases a few workers were offered the opportunity to relocate to the new country. This sort of offer may appeal to a few American workers—until they find out that they will be paid wages equivalent to the native workers.

The Upward Trends in Offshore Outsourcing

To get a sense of how fast the trend toward offshore outsourcing is expanding, you must examine the relative growth rates among IT companies here and abroad. As shown in Table 4-4, revenues for the three major Indian IT companies are growing whereas, U.S. IT majors have shrinking revenues. It is pretty clear that the Indian-based IT firms, which are on the leading edge of outsourcing, are gaining market share from their U.S. rivals and are hiring much more vigorously than their U.S. rivals. This has in turn forced U.S. IT firms to adapt and actually adopt the Indian IT services model of maximizing offshore production—selling to U.S. customers by using labor in India. In another sign that the times favor offshore outsourcing, Tata Consultancy Services, the largest Indian IT firm, was able to raise more than $1 billion in cash in an initial public offering in July 2004, something that would be unthinkable for a U.S.-based IT services company.[20]

In an ironic twist, outsourcing advocates point to increased insourcing by companies such as Indian-based outsourcer Infosys, which announced the creation of a new subsidiary in the United States called Infosys Consulting, and which plans to hire up to 500 U.S. sales consultants over the next three years.[21] The problem for U.S. workers, though, is that those consultants were hired to sell an offshore business model, in which the vast majority of work is done overseas—so, if Infosys Consulting is successful, more work will actually move offshore. Since the bulk of jobs in any IT project include the people who do the programming and technology work, not the salespeople, the net effect for the U.S. workforce will be increasingly negative the more successful Infosys Consulting is. In this case, the insourcing may create one U.S. sales job, but cause ten U.S. programming jobs to be sent overseas.

Furthermore, top executives from major high-tech companies indicate that they plan on expanding their hiring in India and China but not in the

Table 4-4. Growth rates of offshore outsourcing vs. onshore IT companies.

Company Stock Symbol	Revenue Growth
INFY (India)	38.3%
WIT (India)	29.3%
SAY (India)	10.8%
EDS (US)	-0.2%
CSC (US)	-0.7%
AMSY (US)	-16.6%

Source: Authors' analysis of company annual reports submitted to U.S. Securities and Exchange Commission.

United States. The view from India is that more and more Fortune 500 companies are anxious to move work there. U.S. company managers feel that if they aren't offshoring, then they may be at a competitive disadvantage.[22]

Here is what we do know for sure about offshoring and offshore outsourcing:

- Most objective observers believe that the absolute number of jobs that have been relocated overseas by August 2004 is relatively small compared to what is to come, except in a few first-mover occupations such as IT.
- These same unbiased observers believe that we are at the beginning of a paradigm shift in the ways that jobs can be exported—something the consulting firms call an "irreversible mega trend."[23]
- The practice of offshore outsourcing is becoming institutionalized in many companies, which have created new job titles such as Global Supply Coordinator and International Project Coordinator.
- MBA programs at top schools like University of Indiana and the Sloan School of Management at MIT are teaching future business executives how to better manage offshore projects.[24]

The Next Wave of Jobs to Go Abroad

IT jobs have been the first white-collar jobs to move overseas. However, they are not the only types of jobs that have moved, and they are likely to be a harbinger of an increasing array of jobs to be exported. Nandan Nilekani, the CEO of one major Indian offshore outsourcer, Infosys, puts it bluntly when he says that any job that can be delivered over a wire will be offshored.[25] This is certainly too optimistic (from his standpoint), but his prediction indicates the potential breadth of offshore outsourcing. There are important policy and practical reasons we need to understand for which jobs will be exported, which ones will stay, and which new ones will be created here. Policymakers are making decisions that impact what types of jobs Americans will be able to fill—decisions such as increasing the number of students studying engineering by financing expansion of university programs. Students face the daunting task of deciding which occupations to pursue and which ones to avoid.

The evidence indicates that a wide array of positions, at a range of experience, and with varied education and technical skills levels are beginning to be sent overseas. Not all jobs will be sent overseas, but it is difficult to identify the categories of jobs that will go and the ones that will stay. The offshored jobs don't fit the traditional patterns that we are accustomed to, such as low-wage and low-skill jobs.

Even seemingly offshore-safe jobs such as medical doctors are not immune. For example, Massachusetts General Hospital has been sending X-ray and MRI images to radiology physicians in India for initial screening, and 3-D images that highlight problem areas are sent back to U.S. physicians. And an estimated 35,000 U.S. tax returns are processed in India. High-end special effects work for the Hollywood blockbusters *Men in Black* and *Independence Day* were outsourced to India.[26] Lawyers and their support staff are not immune, either. Hildebrandt International is offering the services of offshore lawyers at one-fifth the cost of an American lawyer.[27]

Personal Information Is Exported As Well

The radiology example above brings up an important aspect of offshoring work: sensitive information. You might believe that jobs that handle personal financial and medical records—the kind of data individuals would

most want to keep private—would be off-limits to offshoring. Once again, offshoring defies the conventional wisdom, as an increasing amount of sensitive personal data is sent overseas.

A series of articles by David Lazarus of the *San Francisco Chronicle* shed light on how sensitive data can be exposed and how companies can unwittingly offshore work because multiple layers of outsourcing conceal it. For example, the University of California at San Francisco Medical Center, like most hospitals, outsources its medical transcription work—a $20 billion-a-year business nationwide. In this, doctors dictate information on their patients into a tape recorder; the patient information then needs to be transcribed from tape to typewritten form, which is a labor-intensive process, in order to build the patient's medical records. UCSF outsourced their transcription to a vendor in Texas. That vendor in turn outsourced the work to an underemployed medical doctor in Pakistan, who was willing to do the transcription at a fraction of the price it would have cost in the United States. So, the Texas vendor acted simply as a broker, unbeknownst to the university.

Everything was running smoothly—quality work, delivered on time—until the Texas contractor stopped paying the Pakistani doctor. When she complained to the contractor about nonpayment, she received no reply. Incensed about getting stiffed for work that she already completed, she sent a message directly to the hospital administrators, threatening to publish the hospital's private medical records on the Internet unless she was paid immediately. Hospital officials were aghast when they received the message, and they eventually resolved the problem, but not before much embarrassment.[28] Even jobs that handle sensitive information are being offshored, sometimes with the knowledge of the companies and sometimes not. In many countries, if personal information is leaked or stolen overseas, it is difficult, if not impossible, to get law enforcement help. A number of conferences were held in 2004 to consider the legal ramifications of offshoring private information, and companies are trying to address these concerns.

Even the Good Jobs Are Disappearing

As discussed earlier, there are very few good data sources on the types of jobs being exported. Some experts, like Catherine Mann, have argued that

only low-level positions will move offshore, but the facts don't support her hypothesis.[29] Microsoft has a major research center in China and is on-site, offshore-outsourcing some of its highest-level software positions, such as software architects, to India-based Satyam and Infosys.[30] And the "father of the Pentium" chip, Vinod Dham, has launched a Silicon Valley venture-capital firm whose entire business model is built around offshore outsourcing. The idea is to have a completely offshore workforce, with just the executives sitting in their glass offices in Silicon Valley.[31] This is particularly remarkable since venture-capital companies fund high-risk start-ups that are trying to bring the most advanced technology to market. Intel is adding 600 additional engineers to its R&D operations in Russia, more than doubling its base of 400 engineers.[32]

A few quick searches on the Monster job search Web site in India, www.monsterindia.com, shows that many positions require advanced technical degrees. Below is a sample of an advertisement retrieved from Intel's operations in India.

Job Title: RF Simulation Engineer   (Job# 274125)

Position Description: In this position you will build various antennae, RF channel, and PHY/MAC models for various RF technologies; and simulate platform noise impact. You will also interact closely with internal wireless product groups to develop solutions to enhance RF performance in notebooks.

Qualifications: This position requires an M.S. or Ph.D. in Electrical Engineering with experience in mobile notebooks, WPAN, WLAN, WMAN, WWAN, and platform noise.

You must also possess:

● Experience building various antenna, channel, PHY/MAC models, prototypes, test systems; and simulating the impact of multiple radios that are integrated into notebooks.

● Fluency in writing simulations of advanced communications systems.

Some have argued that the positions moving offshore are not the type of work Americans would like to do. For instance, in software development, they claim that the testing and maintenance tasks that have been moving offshore are mundane and uninteresting. An out-of-work U.S. software programmer may differ with this opinion, but those who argue that only low-level work is moving overseas are missing two key trends.

First, engineering design, and even research and development, is moving offshore. This is not low-level, but rather some of the most interesting, important, and cutting-edge technology work. Many companies have announced new facilities in China, Singapore, Russia, and India that house high-level functions like research, design, and development. In describing the rationale for raising its R&D investment in China to $100 million, a chief technology officer of France's telecom giant Alcatel said, "Our goal is to develop China as an R&D center not just for China, but for the rest of the world."[33] Texas Instruments has had an R&D facility in Bangalore, India, for more than ten years, and General Electric Medical Systems also performs R&D at its Bangalore facility.

Second, companies in countries such as India and China are not satisfied with doing low-level work. In fact, the major Indian IT firms—Infosys, TCS, Wipro, and Satyam—are competing with and beating U.S. IT firms EDS, Accenture, CSC, and IBM for large jobs. Indian generic drug maker Ranbaxy has partnered with British-based pharmaceutical company GlaxoSmithKline to lower the costs of and speed up drug research and to conduct clinical trials. With laboratories that meet U.S. Food and Drug Administration standards, India is poised to capture many of the emerging biotechnology jobs.[34] In Chapter 8, we discuss the ways these countries are attracting such jobs. The idea that the United States will shed its low-level labor-intensive work and workers will just move up the skills ladder is sorely misleading, since even high-level work is moving offshore.

Offshore Outsourcing in Other Developed Countries

The United States is not the only country grappling with the labor-export issue. Controversy is also swirling in Europe and Australia. Indeed, companies in the United Kingdom and Australia are able to take advantage of

the large numbers of English-speaking workers available in India. In fact, Prime Minister Tony Blair publicly supported the offshore outsourcing of British jobs, citing the McKinsey Global Institute study as proof that this outsourcing would "increase the provision of jobs" in Britain.[35]

In an attempt to stop a plan to move thousands of jobs to India, Lloyds TSB in the U.K. is being sued by a customer on behalf of its unions that oppose offshore outsourcing. The suit has been filed on the grounds that the movement of these jobs would violate the U.K.'s data privacy laws.[36] HSBC, a major British bank, announced that it was moving 7,500 jobs from the U.K. to India and Malaysia, at a time that it posted record profits of $12.8 billion.[37]

Australian trade minister Mark Vaile made public remarks fully supporting the offshoring of even government contracts. Leaders from the opposition Labour Party called the government's position a disaster for local businesses.[38] In an attempt to deflect any public backlash, Australian Prime Minister John Howard's spokesman offered no comment when asked about his thoughts on his trade minister's comments.[39] The deal that started the controversy was an offshore outsourcing agreement between telecommunications company Telstra and IBM. After initially denying that any jobs would be exported, Telstra later admitted that 450 positions would go to India as part of the deal.[40]

In Germany, companies are threatening to move jobs to lower-cost Eastern European countries in order to extract concessions from labor unions. Siemens stopped plans to move 2,000 jobs from Germany to Hungary after its labor unions agreed to longer working hours.[41] DaimlerChrysler is using similar tactics, threatening to move work from Stuttgart to South Africa, in order to gain concessions from labor unions.[42] Germany's SAP AG is the largest Enterprise Resource Planning (ERP) software company, and it plans on increasing its staff in Bangalore by 170 percent, to 3,000 programmers, making it the largest development center outside of Germany and comprising 10 percent of its overall workforce.[43] ERP software is used by nearly every Fortune 1000 company as its core business software, so even European offshore outsourcing includes high-level work.

Where the Jobs Are Heading

India has received the widest attention, but it is hardly the only destination for offshoring. India has some distinct advantages, many of which were acquired by adopting specific government policies, such as:

- A low-cost, high-skilled English-speaking workforce
- A large diaspora population in the United States that helps make business connections
- Active and friendly government policies
- The economies of scale and efficiencies gained by being the first country to attract a large number of these jobs

India has been able to capitalize on the last factor to capture ever larger and more sophisticated work. Companies are comfortable working in India because they have already done so successfully or they know other companies who have. Additionally, the business deal-making process has become more regularized and standard. That is, the business matchmaking infrastructure—brokers and contract lawyers—is in place for large deals in India in a way that they may not be in other offshoring contenders such as Romania. Table 4-5 lists countries that are destinations for offshore outsourcing projects and a sampling of the types of work being outsourced.

CIO Magazine, a leading publication for IT executives and managers, suggests the following criteria for companies to ponder when they are trying to choose a country to locate some of their IT outsourcing: geopolitical risk, English-speaking, and price.[44] They rank India as the number one destination, but consider China and Russia up-and-comers, with large numbers of low-cost and highly skilled workers. U.S. firms trying to diversify their risk are also looking to near-shore options such as Canada and Mexico—countries with stable governments and established business practices and relationships.

Other countries are learning from India's experience and are beginning to market their natural advantages, such as having the same time zone as the United States, or they try to acquire advantages by improving their telecommunications infrastructure. For example, China has made it a national priority to train many more people to speak English, setting the

Table 4-5. Outsourcing destination countries and example projects.

Country	Company Sending Jobs	Type of Work
India	Multiple	IT, BPO and Engineering
China	Multiple	Manufacturing, Software, Engineering
Argentina	Humphrey & Partners Architects[1]	Creating 3-D Computer Drawings
Ghana	Affiliated Computer Services[2]	Data Entry
South Africa[3]	IBM	BPO
Canada	TIG Insurance Co.[4]	Computer Programming
Mexico	Multiple	Manufacturing, Call Centers
Romania	Multiple	Computer Programming
Russia	Intel	Research Engineers

Sources:
1. Katherine Yung, "Job Security Hopes Fading: Offshoring, Automation and More Are Leaving Workers Unsure How to Adapt," *Dallas Morning News* (June 26, 2004).
2. Mark Horvit, "Exporting Jobs: Offshoring Transforms the Global Workplace," *Fort Worth Star Telegram* (June 19, 2004).
3. "IBM Prefers South Africa as Backup for Outsourcing," *ComputerWeekly* (August 4, 2004).
4. Yung, "Job Security."

goal that most Chinese will speak English in twenty years.[45] India's advantage is great (as discussed further in Chapter 8), but many Indian companies are concerned about potential Chinese competition, to the point that major firms Infosys, Wipro, and Tata have established operations in China.[46]

The degree to which highly skilled workers in India have been underemployed in their own domestic economy is astonishing. Ghanaian businesspeople were recently shocked to learn that their white-collar labor costs are actually higher than those of Indian workers. Another interesting com-

parison is the difference in the typical education between a U.S. and an Indian call-center operator. In the United States, a call-center operator generally has a high school degree, but in India many of them have MBAs.

It is clear that even though India is the current destination of choice, many more countries are beginning to target these jobs and industries and a vast—seemingly endless—supply of low-cost and high-skilled workers will become available for Western companies. While some economists, such as Jagdish Bhagwati, argue that the overseas talent pool is severely limited, they seem to ignore how fast developing countries will adapt to the new opportunities presented by outsourcing. Also, as companies become as comfortable doing business in Ukraine as they are in India, certain things are likely to happen:

- More companies will outsource more tasks.
- High-skilled wages will remain low.
- Companies will force different country governments to compete with one another for those jobs by offering tax incentives, free training, and other incentives.

In this sense, it seems unlikely that offshoring will be reversed. However, how the United States reacts to and addresses this new aspect of globalization is still an open question. Before tackling that question, let's examine in detail why offshoring is occurring.

Notes

1. Ed Fraunheim, "Q&A: The Facts on Offshoring," www.cnetnews.com (August 11, 2004).

2. IEEE-USA Press Release, "500,000 US IT Jobs Projected to Move Overseas by Year-end 2004; IEEE-USA Sees Continued Loss in U.S. Economic Competitiveness, National Security" (July 21, 2003).

3. Saritha Rai, "Financial Firms Hasten Their Move to Outsourcing," *New York Times* (August 18, 2004).

4. Cynthia Kroll and Ashok Deo Bardhan, "The New Wave of Outsourcing," Research Report, Fisher Center for Real Estate and Urban Economics, University of California at Berkeley (Fall 2003).

5. Robert D. Atkinson, "Understanding the Offshore Challenge," Policy Report, Progressive Policy Institute (May 24, 2004).

6. Sanford Nowlin, "San Antonio: Call Center Friendly?" *San Antonio Express* (July 10, 2004).

7. Peter S. Goodman, "White-Collar Work a Booming U.S. Export," *Washington Post*, p. E1 (April 2, 2003).

8. Robert Trigaux, "Capital One: The Political Drama," *St. Petersburg Times* (July 29, 2004).

9. "Reuters Offshore Experiment," *BusinessWeek* online, March 4, 2004, and Griff Witte, "Reuters to Move Editorial Jobs from U.S. and Europe to India," *Washington Post* (August 10, 2004).

10. "Reuters to Make Bangalore Biggest Information Hub," www.Reuters.com (October 7, 2004).

11. Saritha Rai, "Financial Firms Hasten Their Move to Outsourcing," *New York Times* (August 18, 2004).

12. Ibid.

13. Don Durfee and Kate O'Sullivan, "Offshoring by the Numbers: Results of Our Survey of 275 Finance Executives at a Broad Range of Companies," *CFO Magazine* (June 1, 2004).

14. Lou Dobbs, *Exporting America: Why Corporate Greed Is Shipping Jobs Overseas* (New York: Warner Business Books, 2004).

15. Robert Keenan, "Brecis Trims Engineering Staff, Turns to Offshore Development," *CommsDesign* (February 3, 2004).

16. "EDS Plans to Expand BPO Ops to Chennai, Gurgaon," *Economic Times of India* (June 17, 2003).

17. David Koenig, "EDS Says It Will Cut 2,700 Jobs, Sell Some Assets," Associated Press State & Local Wire (June 18, 2003).

18. Phillip Mattera, "Your Tax Dollars at Work . . . Offshore: How Foreign Outsourcing Firms Are Capturing State Government Contracts," *Corporate Research Project of Good Jobs First* (July 2004).

19. Brad Shannon, "Workers Anxious as Jobs Head Overseas: Millions Spent by Washington's State Agencies on Work Done Offshore," *The Olympian* (August 1, 2004).

20. "India's Software Giant Starts Taking Orders Ahead of IPO," Associated Press (July 29, 2004).

21. Carrie Kirby, "Indian Outsourcing Firm to Set up Fremont Unit, Infosys

of Bangalore Plans High-End Consulting Division in U.S.," *San Francisco Chronicle* (April 9, 2004), p. C1.

22. "IT Professionals 'Losing Appetite' to Work Overseas," *Press Trust of India* (July 26, 2004).

23. Sanford Nowlin and Travis E. Poling, "U.S. Jobs: Next Stop, India," *San Antonio Express* (September 21, 2003).

24. Christopher S. Stewart, "Outsourcing Joins the M.B.A. Curriculum," *New York Times* (March 28, 2004).

25. Kerry A. Dolan and Robyn Meredith, "The Outsourcing Debate: A Tale of Two Cities, Who Loses and Who Gains from U.S. Jobs Moving Overseas?" www.Forbes.com (March 30, 2004).

26. Amol Sharma, "India Winning Higher-Status Jobs from U.S.," *Christian Science Monitor* (June 18, 2003).

27. Anthony Lin, "Law Firms Offered Outsourced Support Staffs," *New York Law Journal* (June 7, 2004).

28. David Lazarus, "A Tough Lesson on Medical Privacy: Pakistani Transcriber Threatens UCSF over Back Pay," *San Francisco Chronicle* (October 22, 2003), p. A-1; and "Pakistani Threatened UCSF to Get Paid, She Says," *San Francisco Chronicle* (November 12, 2003), p. B-1.

29. Catherine L. Mann, "Globalization of IT Services and White Collar Jobs: The Next Wave of Productivity Growth," Policy Brief 03-11, *International Economics Policy Briefs*, Institute for International Economics (December 2003).

30. Greg Levine, "Gates: Microsoft to Boost China R&D," www.Forbes.com (July 1, 2004); and Steve Lohr, "High-End Technology Work Not Immune to Outsourcing," *New York Times* (June 16, 2004).

31. Matt Marshall, "Executives in Valley, Workers Offshore: Newpath Ventures Pushes Strategy for its Start-ups," *San Jose Mercury News* (May 16, 2004).

32. "Intel Looks to Russia to Build R&D," *Financial Times* (May 24, 2004).

33. Abe De Ramos, "The China Syndrome: U.S. Companies Are Beginning to Outsource Technology Research and Development to India and China. Will a Meltdown in Tech Jobs Follow?" *CFO Magazine* (October 15, 2003).

34. Andrew Maykuth, "India's Drug Firms Aim to Compete with Giants," *Philadelphia Inquirer* (May 4, 2004); and Geoff Dyer, "How India

Hopes to Reshape the Drug World," *New York Times* (August 17, 2004).

35. Patrick Wintour, "U.K. Can Benefit from Jobs Heading to India, Says Blair," *The Guardian* (March 23, 2004).

36. "Lloyds Faces Legal Challenge to Outsourcing," www.Reuters.com (August 18, 2004).

37. Jill Treanor, "HSBC Cuts to the Core," *The Guardian* (July 26, 2004).

38. Simon Hayes and James Riley, "Vaile Greenlights Offshoring," *Australian IT* (August 17, 2004).

39. Julian Bajkowski, "PM at Odds with Ministers over Offshoring Government IT Jobs," *Computerworld*, Australia edition (August 17, 2004).

40. David Crow, "More Consider Passage to India," *The Australian Financial Review* (July 14, 2004).

41. "Siemens and Unions Strike Deal," *International Herald Tribune* (June 25, 2004).

42. "Daimler, Workers Strike Wage Deal," Associated Press (July 23, 2004).

43. S. Srinivasan, "SAP to Add 1,900 Programmers in India: The Business Software Vendor Will Invest Another $24 Million and Add the Programmers by the End of 2006," *InformationWeek* (August 3, 2004).

44. Todd Datz, "Outsourcing World Tour," *CIO Magazine* (July 15, 2004).

45. William J. Holstein, "Office Space: Armchair M.B.A.; How a Technology Gap Helped China Win Jobs," *New York Times* (July 18, 2004), p. 9.

46. Sarith Rai, "India Taps China's Reserve of Technological Talent," *New York Times* (November 2, 2004).

CHAPTER 5

Why Companies Are Moving Jobs Overseas

In the last chapter, we reviewed the extent to which offshore outsourcing is accelerating over time and across different kinds of jobs in the U.S. economy. A phenomenon as big as this outsourcing—an "irreversible megatrend," as consulting firms call it—develops for many reasons. This chapter will identify the key reasons for offshore outsourcing. Some of these reasons change over time, but many are compelling and probably will persist. Understanding the reasons behind offshore outsourcing will provide a clearer idea about what can be done about it.

Reason #1: Cost and Salary Differences

First and foremost is cost. Highly skilled, educated labor is far cheaper in many developing countries than it is in the United States. The savings in labor costs can be as high as a factor of 90 percent, though when one counts the additional burdens of management and coordination across thousands of miles, the net advantage is probably closer to 30 percent. For example, outsourcers charge $30 an hour for the services of a programmer in India, whereas they charge $120 for a programmer in the Midwest. That results in a savings of 75 percent, but does not include the extra burdens placed on the customer in communicating his needs to the programmer in

India, which when accounted for would reduce the net savings to 30 percent.

Another business model—on-site offshore outsourcing—is used by companies to take advantage of U.S. immigration regulations. This model, which is used by many Indian IT services firms, brings the cheap foreign workers into the United States on H-1B and L-1 guest-worker visas. For example, software architects, on guest-worker visas, can be hired from on-site offshore outsourcers such as Satyam, at $90 per hour, which is about $60 per hour less than the going rate for an American software architect.[1] That's a net cost saving of 40 percent for customers, and there are no issues of additional coordination costs since the foreign worker is on-site.

The substantial cost savings span different occupations and skill levels. Indian engineers earn anywhere between $5,000 and $8,000 per year, and accountants less than that. On the Business Process Outsourcing (BPO) side, a typical data entry clerk in Accra, Ghana, earns between $4 and $6 a day! And there are thousands of responses for each job ad placed by employers.[2] For high-level research, the cost savings are also tremendous, with science and engineering PhD graduates in developing countries commanding a $12,000 per year salary.[3] A recent survey by *CFO Magazine* found that 90 percent of those companies engaged in offshore outsourcing achieved some savings, and in this time of heavy cost cutting, companies will choose savings over maintaining their own workers.

Why is high-skilled labor so much cheaper in other countries? Part of the reason is the abundance of excess labor in those countries, but another important reason is that the workers can afford to be paid less because their cost of living is significantly lower. Table 5-1 shows the salaries for engineers with equivalent standards of living in various countries. The factor being multiplied in the second column is purchasing power parity (PPP), a cost-of-living measure created by economists to show the differences in price that are not captured by exchange rates.

Many observers have long understood that exchange-rate conversions do not account for the true differences across countries. In a tongue-in-cheek attempt to explain the concept of purchasing power parity, *The Economist* magazine has a regular feature it calls the Big Mac Index, to show the costs of a McDonald's Big Mac in different countries. For exam-

Table 5-1. Salary requirements for engineers with equivalent standards of living.

Country	Purchasing Power Parity (PPP)	Salary
U.S.	(1.0) * $70k	$70,000
Hungary	(0.367) * $70k	$25,690
China	(0.216) * $70k	$15,120
Russia	(0.206) * $70k	$14,420
India	(0.194) * $70k	$13,580

Source: World Bank's International Comparison Program, *World Development Indicators,* World Bank Group, Washington, D.C., 2002, Table 5.6.

ple, a Big Mac in the United States costs $2.90, but it costs $1.26 in China and $4.90 in Sweden.

Returning to the table, a Russian engineer earning $14,420 can live an equally good life as an American engineer with a $70,000 salary (multiply $70,000 by the Russian–U.S. PPP factor of 0.206).

PPP is only a rough estimate, since not all goods and services are available in every country. However, it can tell us a lot about how fast wages in India, say, might begin to rise as outsourcing increases. Some people speculate that wages for Indian engineers will skyrocket soon, but the enormous PPP disparity should act as a buffer on those salary demands. While their engineering services will be exported, their own cost of living, which is based on the products and services that they purchase on a regular basis, will remain very low. For example, when we were in Bangalore in 2003, we could hire a taxi for a full day, including driver, gas, and unlimited mileage, for an amazing $10. That should provide some insight into how cheap labor is, since gas is more expensive in India than the United States. So, it is unlikely that Indian workers will demand much higher salaries because their cost of living will remain low. As discussed earlier, there is a huge surplus of highly educated workers who are ready, willing, and able to step in for any worker who asks for too much, and India has an enormous share of its 1 billion plus population under the age of 25. There have been reports that wages for programmers in India rose at a 10 to 15 percent rate in the

past year, but those gains are on top of such a low base that it would take many years of growth for wages to equal wages in the United States or Western Europe.

China has a similar oversupply of skilled labor. In spite of an economic boom in China and offshore outsourcing, recent college graduates are struggling to find work, and starting salaries for new graduates dropped by 40 percent between 2002 and 2003.[4] Even if salaries in India and China do rise slightly, those increases will be offset by decreasing management and coordination costs. Companies will become much more efficient at coordinating outsourcing projects, which will increase their net savings.

Increasing Pressure to Outsource

The cost savings have been so great that Silicon Valley venture capitalists—companies that provide seed funding for the most advanced start-up technology companies in exchange for an equity stake and some managerial control—are requiring their fledgling organizations to have an offshore outsourcing plan before the venture capitalists hand out the next round of funding.[5] So, even with start-up companies, generally with small staffs, offshore outsourcing is becoming an imperative.

CEOs of major corporations do not escape the pressure from capital markets to outsource, either. Top executives of publicly traded companies (those companies that are traded on the stock exchanges) report their performance on a quarterly basis to shareholders and financial analysts. They hold telephone conference calls to share the information. This provides executives an opportunity to highlight the positives of their stewardship of the company in the past quarter and also enables the financial analysts to ask questions and indirectly to put pressure on executives.

Financial analysts rate whether a company is doing well or not, and report this to their clients, and often to the public. They play an important role in shaping investors' opinions on how a company is doing, which determines which direction the stock price will take. Since executive compensation is correlated directly with the stock price, corporate managers are very eager to please analysts. Lately, analysts are asking probing questions about companies' outsourcing plans. The analysts believe that companies can cut costs significantly, and if a company does not outsource some of its work offshore, its stock price will be punished.

Boston Consulting Group (BCG) released a report in May 2004 that takes the pressure to outsource a step further by claiming that it is "imperative for companies to offshore" as much work as possible or face extinction.[6] The group sells consulting services to companies on how to outsource, so the report is part of their marketing strategy to drum up more business by scaring managers into exploring offshoring with them. The tragedy is that managers often look to management consulting groups like BCG and McKinsey for advice. Many executives did earlier stints in one of these management consulting firms, so from their point of view, following BCG's advice is a no-lose strategy. If BCG is right and offshore outsourcing does save the company a lot of money, then the executives come out smelling like roses. If, on the other hand, BCG is wrong and the outsourcing is more peril than promise, then managers can feel secure that most competitors also chose to offshore, and they can blame the strategy on BCG.

Other Cost Factors

It is obvious that U.S. engineers cannot afford to compete on price with overseas engineers—or, as Paul Kostek, past chairperson of the American Association of Engineering Societies, put it:

> As an engineer who has had to reinvent myself a dozen times during a 24-year career in order to stay competitive, I have to ask myself if an overseas competitor in Belarus, Beijing, or Bangalore possesses the same skills that I do, and if proximity isn't important, and if they'll work for $800 a month, then why hire me at $8,000 a month? It's a question that is increasingly hard to answer. For the next generation considering a career in engineering, it will be even harder.[7]

There is one area concerning costs where the United States may actually be able to compete with other countries. While there are great discounts for salaries in places like India, real estate development and office space upgrades often cost just as much as they would in the United States. Some small towns in the United States are hopeful that they may be more

competitive for call centers compared with countries like India. Though the wage differential is greater, they may have an advantage in real estate costs, not to mention the additional advantage of geographic proximity.[8] Some observers are calling this the *rural sourcing option*, and it has been promoted by Senator Hillary Clinton.

Reason #2: Domestic Outsourcing as a Strategy

Over the past decade, managers have been taught to focus business efforts only on their core competencies and to domestically outsource all functions or processes that are not considered as providing a strategic advantage. (Note that we are using the phrase *domestic outsourcing* to refer to what is generally just called outsourcing in the business literature—that is, buying goods or services from suppliers rather than handling them in-house.) The motivation for this strategy was driven by different reasons in different companies and industries.

In the auto and other heavy industries, domestic outsourcing was chosen in part because supplier companies, which were generally smaller, were less likely to be unionized and often paid lower salaries and benefits. In other large businesses, the motivation was to introduce competition to in-house departments and employees to drive productivity gains. The perception was that the in-house accounting staff was lazy because they knew that accounting had to be done and it could only be done by them. Furthermore, in-house services were expected to be unresponsive to in-house customers.

Major Fortune 500 companies are often organized in separate divisions around product lines but share common headquarter services like accounting. Since the accounting department knew that all of the divisions had to use their services, they were often not very customer-friendly or responsive. So company managers figured out that threatening to domestic-outsource functions like accounting would force in-house accountants to become more responsive or risk losing their jobs. Many companies forced this competition by allowing their business divisions to go outside the company to hire accounting vendors.

In other cases, company managers believed that domestic outsourcers could do better work at cheaper prices than in-house staff. For example, many small businesses outsource their payroll functions to specialized com-

panies like Paychex, Inc. Economists have been describing the gains from specialization since the days of Adam Smith and his portrayal of the imaginary pin factory. The idea is that a company that specializes in payroll processing can probably do payroll processing at a much lower cost than a company that makes ball bearings. It probably makes sense, then, for that ball bearing manufacturer to purchase its payroll processing from Paychex rather than hire office workers to do it in-house.

In still other cases, large and older companies chose to domestic-outsource as a technique to downsize its own staff. Many established businesses had internal policies that made it difficult and expensive to lay off workers unless it was done en masse, as part of a restructuring effort. Restructuring, more truthfully called downsizing, was much easier to do if the whole department's functions were outsourced. The domestic outsourcing company then had the luxury of cherry-picking the employees it wanted to keep. In the words of Congressman Peter Defazio (Democrat from Oregon), "We've seen a number of companies contract out work [domestically] to pay lower wages" and those contract firms pay lower or no benefits.[9] This kind of restructuring provides public relations cover for many firms that are more sensitive to bad publicity, such as companies that win billions of dollars in U.S. government contracts. And in the current wave, it enables companies to disavow responsibility when their former staffs are laid off by the outsourcer and the jobs are then exported.

Domestic Outsourcing Is Now Easier

A set of enabling technologies and management strategies made domestic outsourcing more realistic and cheaper during the 1990s. Managers began to take an engineering approach to business processes and to break down each process into discrete, modular tasks. So, insurance companies would break down their claims processing into smaller, discrete pieces. This follows directly in line with Frederick Taylor's scientific management approach of the early twentieth century that transformed piece-part manufacturing into mass production.

In the late twentieth century, information technology enabled managers to break down processes that were essentially information in nature into discrete pieces that had standard interfaces with the next piece of the

process. This was often called *business process reengineering*, or BPR, by management consultants. With these pieces and standard interfaces, there were now "pinch-points" where companies could pinch off a set of tasks and outsource them instead of doing them in-house.

Government Domestic Outsourcing

Even the federal government has entered the outsourcing game by taking jobs that are held by civil servants and contracting them out. Many people simply do not realize that the vast majority of money spent by the federal government is for work performed by the private sector. Some of the most important work is still done by the 2 million civil servants; however, Congress and the Bush Administration spurred a new initiative—called A-76, in government-speak—whereby those jobs held by civil servants are now put up for bid to private contractors.

By law, a person has to be a U.S. citizen to get a federal civil service job. By contracting the work out to the private sector, that restriction is lifted, and the work can even be shipped overseas. Legislation originally introduced by Senators Craig Thomas (Republican from Wyoming) and George Voinovich (Republican from Ohio) was enacted in 2004, which prevents any work that has been privatized by the A-76 process to be done in the United States for at least one year. The legislation was passed in response to concerns about critical government functions moving overseas. It was added to a larger spending bill that was signed by President Bush on January 23, 2004 [P.L. 108-199].[10] States and municipalities have adopted similar privatization approaches to save money, contracting out services such as customer support for social welfare benefits and IT support.

Moving the Work Offshore

For all of these reasons, domestic outsourcing has become big business, and ever more companies, such as IBM, are positioning themselves to be outsourcers. So, what does this have to do with sending work offshore?

First, most of the tasks that are outsourced do not require geographic proximity, so they are naturally the types of jobs that can be done remotely, within the United States or outside it. Second, outsourcing specialists are better poised to move work offshore. As outsourcing companies become

larger and capture a larger share of tasks that were done internally, they gain efficiencies through economies of scale and it becomes more economically realistic for them to move work offshore. They can spread the international coordination costs over a much larger volume of business. If we think of the payroll-processing example above, it is unrealistic for the ball bearing manufacturer to move its internal payroll processing staff overseas, but it makes economic sense for an outsourcer like EDS, which has a large number of customers and therefore a larger operation, to move a portion of its staff overseas. In fact, most customers do not realize that some of the work they are purchasing is being done offshore.

Reason #3: Better or Unique Talent Overseas

Some people, particularly in industry, argue that there is a shortage of technically trained U.S. workers, and that that situation drives employers to seek talent overseas. They claim that they cannot find the talent in the United States, so they are forced to take their operations to where the talent is. This line of reasoning is highly questionable. From 2001 to 2004, IT workers have experienced the worst labor market in the United States, ever. Unemployment rates for IT occupations have been persistently at record levels, and wage rates are coming down significantly. There is obviously no shortage of U.S. IT workers, and there is no indication that U.S. high-tech workers are less skilled than their foreign counterparts, some of whom were educated in the same U.S. institutions.

Industry lobbyists point to the large number of engineers that India and China graduates every year in arguing this as the primary reason they are sending work there. Of course, they don't say that India has been graduating large numbers of engineers for decades, but hardly any company was sending work there, even five years ago. For some reason, this "lack of U.S. talent" argument resonates with many people, but it is specious at best, because there are plenty of well-qualified underemployed or unemployed U.S. engineers, and for decades there has been an oversupply of talented workers overseas.

We have some personal experience with overseas talent. Our late father earned his engineering degree in 1954 from a prestigious university in Bombay, but was unable to find a good position in his own country after graduation. He was finally able to find a job, but only after using family

connections. And the job wasn't very challenging and didn't pay very well. This is even more remarkable, since it was only seven years after India gained independence from Great Britain in 1947. One would think that a country with the needs and aspirations of India could have utilized a talented engineer, but it did not, and our father left for better work opportunities in Europe and later Canada and the United States. His talent was used to help rebuild Europe in the aftermath of World War II instead of his own country. And his story is not uncommon. Many highly skilled engineers left their own countries because they were just not being absorbed by the economies of these developing countries. This labor exit push may now be ebbing a bit, as outsourcing offers more opportunities for talented individuals to stay at home.

Corporate executives also seem to have a low opinion of American workers when comparing them to Chinese workers, whether they are factory-level workers or mid-level engineers. As one semiconductor executive put it when talking about why Chinese workers are so dedicated to their $122 a month jobs (even willing to work during holidays): "It's not easy to get a job over here. They are very, very hungry."[11]

Reason #4: No Penalty for Destroying U.S. Jobs

Companies operating in the United States are shifting work offshore more rapidly than companies operating in the E.U. and elsewhere because they experience little or no cost when they destroy U.S. jobs. Most U.S. white-collar workers are categorized as "at will" employees, meaning that they are employed at the will of the employer, and the employer can lay them off at any time, for any reason, as long as they do not violate laws against discrimination. Over time, companies have become smarter about how to wield this power and have been able to shed workers in an efficient manner. Some larger firms still provide severance packages and outplacement help, such as job-training assistance and resume-writing consultation, but these costs are minimal compared to the potential savings they will reap from outsourcing the work offshore.

Wall Street analysts applaud the destruction of U.S. jobs as a cost-cutting move, which helps the bottom line. It is viewed as a sign of strength rather than a weakness, so the capital markets reward U.S. job destruction,

especially if it is done to shift work to cheaper overseas labor. For example, Carly Fiorina, the CEO of HP, was applauded by Wall Street when she announced that the company was going to outsource at least 2,000 jobs overseas.[12] The analysts seem unconcerned by the possibility that offshoring may actually hurt companies in the long run by creating competition overseas and eroding their technological innovation and creative capabilities. But Wall Street is known for favoring a short-term outlook.

Negative Publicity

The major "cost" to companies that are destroying U.S. jobs has been bad publicity. In our many conversations with corporate lobbyists and public relations directors, one common refrain is that the news media has "overhyped" the outsourcing story and unfairly targeted their companies as bad guys.

Thomas Donohue, the president of the U.S. Chamber of Commerce and one of the most powerful lobbyists in Washington, promotes offshore outsourcing as a way to increase employment in the United States and dismisses worker anxiety simply as "whining" by a small number of unemployed.[13] It is ironic that *CFO Magazine*, which is targeted at top financial managers, conducted a poll of 275 finance executives and found that only 11 percent of the people Donohue represents agree with his job growth theory. A majority (61 percent) of those surveyed thought that offshoring will lead to a net reduction in jobs in the United States.[14]

The industry lobbyists are particularly vitriolic when it comes to Lou Dobbs, who has made offshore outsourcing almost a nightly story on his television show and has written a book on the series titled, "Exporting America: Why Corporate Greed Is Shipping American Jobs Overseas."[15] We have had numerous meetings with influential industry and university lobbyists who say that Dobbs has lost his mind.

Despite what they perceive as negative publicity, companies are sending work overseas at an unabated pace. For instance, the *CFO Magazine* poll found that only 13 percent of the financial executives perceived public backlash as a risk to their outsourcing plans.[16] At "how-to" outsourcing conferences, a major information research firm asked its participants how many of them will slow their offshore outsourcing because of bad publicity, and the response was: Almost universally none.

Even IBM, which has received a disproportionate amount of negative publicity on its offshore outsourcing activities, decided to go on the offensive and unveiled a "kinder, gentler" set of internal policies. They claimed to have a new policy to try to place in other parts of the company those U.S. workers displaced by outsourcing. But IBM didn't do this just because of bad publicity. The primary motive was to save money: It is cheaper to place an internal worker in a new position than to recruit someone from outside. IBM is not by any means slowing down their outsourcing plans because of negative publicity.[17] And an executive from major outsourcer Cognizant said that he thought the political focus on offsource outsourcing had diminished and it was back to business as usual.[18] This sentiment mirrors our own recent interactions with business lobbyists, who are much more at ease with offshore outsourcing, figuring that they have weathered the storm of controversy.

Workers at an Extreme Disadvantage

Individual workers are on an unequal footing compared to the corporate managers and lobbyists, whose extremely deep pockets are only part of the advantage they enjoy in shaping the public dialogue. We have spoken to hundreds of workers who are afraid to talk publicly for fear of getting blacklisted in their industry. Most of the types of jobs that are being exported are nonunion, and the employees are "at will." There is no individualized or collective contract between employer and employee, so companies such as GE and Dell have become increasingly sophisticated in taking advantage of opportunities to dismiss employees for more or less nondiscriminatory reasons. This lack of bargaining power also means that employees are at the mercy of employers' wishes, even if it means having to train their own replacements.

That is one of the reasons that labor unions have been trying to organize grassroots technology workers through campaigns like www.TechsUnite.org. Labor union organizers such as Marcus Courtney, of Washington State's Communications Workers of America, have been active in the offshoring debate, hoping to recruit new union members from the ranks of disaffected and displaced IT workers. Courtney formed an organization called WashTech (www.washtech.org), which boasts tens of thousands of subscribers to its e-mail listserv.

As has been well reported, union membership in America has been on the decline and it is unlikely that widespread unionization of IT workers is anywhere on the horizon. For example, even though the union at IBM—Alliance@IBM—has increased its ranks from 5,000 to 6,000 members in 2004, it still represents only about 4 percent of the 141,000 U.S. workers at IBM.[19] And of the 6,000, only about 450 are full dues-paying members. The rest are subscribers. WashTech has been extremely effective as one of the workers' lone voices to the media. They have been able to obtain and leak to the media internal documents that embarrass IBM and Microsoft.[20, 21] Unfortunately, they operate on a shoestring budget and are no match for the millions of dollars that companies pour into public relations and lobbying. In fact, there are rumors that U.S. companies allocated $100 million to advance their interests in the debate over offshore outsourcing, and that reporters who write stories unfavorable toward the corporate position are—targets for intimidation.[22] After all, reporters work for newspapers and magazines that are dependent on advertising revenue from many of those same companies.

Business lobbyists also have the major advantage of preparing their arguments well in advance because they know what type of outsourcing projects the companies plan on executing. In fact, one business lobbyist told us that they had been preparing for the offshore outsourcing backlash as early as 2001 because they knew where the company was headed.

In the end, there is no substantial organization that represents the interests of American workers. This vacuum is something that needs to be filled, and we provide some ideas on how to do it in Chapter 9, when we discuss policy recommendations.

No Government or Media Pressure

Companies are under no pressure from the federal government or the editorial pundits to slow down the offshoring process. George W. Bush's Secretary of Labor, Elaine Chao, when asked about weak job creation, dismissed the job numbers as of minimal importance by saying, "The stock market is, after all, the final arbiter."[23] This is a remarkable statement from a Secretary of Labor, whose singular purpose is to look out for and help U.S. workers. But the perspective is bipartisan. Robert Reich, Secretary of Labor under the Clinton Administration, has also enthusiastically endorsed

offshoring in editorials. One, plainly titled "High-Tech Jobs Are Going Abroad! But That's Okay," makes it abundantly clear that Reich is unconcerned about the impacts of outsourcing.[24]

As mentioned earlier, at the unveiling of the 2004 edition of the Economic Report of the President, chief economic adviser to the president, Gregory Mankiw, nonchalantly remarked that outsourcing was just another form of trade and is probably good for the U.S. in the long run. He did not see the issue requiring any further discussion or attention.

Many media pundits, such as George Will and Tom Friedman, have joined the offshoring band-wagon.[25] Editorial boards at many major newspapers, such as the *Washington Post*, are also singing the praises of offshoring and promoting Mr. Mankiw's "don't worry, be happy" approach to it.[26] Both columnists and editors dismiss the corresponding destruction of U.S. jobs as a trivial matter. These pundits and editorial boards play an important role in shaping public opinion, and also in putting pressure on policymakers. And this process provides cover for those politicians that support offshoring and blunts the arguments of policymakers who express concern.

Reason #5: U.S. Tax Incentives

Though they are not really discussed in public, many economic statistics on investment show huge amounts of money going to undisclosed locations or to small offshore islands, such as the Caymans, where they are filtered through anonymous and tax-free accounts to their final destinations. This allows corporations and rich individuals in the United States and Europe to largely avoid paying taxes. Moreover, through their lobbying efforts over the years, U.S.-based multinational corporations convinced Congress to pass legislation that allows them to indefinitely defer any taxes due on profits earned overseas. However, the catch was that the deferral was good only until they repatriated those profits to the United States, when they would be taxed at the normal corporate rate of 35 percent. So, companies have been deferring their earnings for so long that they have built up an estimated $400–$600 billion worth of profits sitting offshore.[27]

Not content with the deferral benefit, companies have successfully lobbied Congress to provide a moratorium on taxes for one year so that they

can repatriate the money to the United States and pay only a 5.25 percent rate on it. How's that for a deal? Wouldn't you love to be able to have the ability to earn income and pay virtually no taxes on it? Unfortunately, as individuals we don't have the millions of dollars to lobby for that kind of privilege. And how did the companies justify this corporate welfare windfall? Ironically, by arguing that it would enable them to use those hundreds of billions of dollars to invest in the United States and create jobs for Americans. JP Morgan Chase Bank reported that the tax moratorium would create 400,000 jobs.[28] The thinly veiled threat is that they will keep those monies overseas and invest in other countries, and create jobs there instead of in the United States if they don't get the added tax break.

In an attempt to reach out to the corporate CEOs after his ill-advised comment that they were "Benedict Arnolds" for offshoring jobs, Democratic presidential candidate John Kerry proposed that we give the companies their moratorium (at a tax rate of 10 percent) and even lower the corporate tax rate from 35 percent to 33.25 percent, but the proposal came with a hitch. Companies would agree to give up their ability to defer taxes on any future foreign earnings. Of course, the proposal made a resounding thud in the corporate community. Why? Because the corporate lobbyists figured they could have their cake and eat it too by lobbying for a better deal on their own, which would give them the moratorium at a lower rate of 5.25 percent with no other conditions. And they were successful in late 2004. So, they get the lower tax rate and are able to defer taxes on future income indefinitely. When the timing is appropriate, they will lobby for another moratorium in the future using the same arguments. Why give up free money when you don't have to?

Reason #6: Technological Change

At the height of the dot-com bubble, IBM ran a television commercial featuring a worker driving a car in the desert, with his manager as passenger. The manager asked his employee what the hell they were doing in the desert and why they purchased land there for the company's next facility, since it was in the middle of nowhere. The employee said two words: "the Internet." The manager realized right away what his employee meant: The Internet had made geographic location unimportant. While the commercial could

easily be dismissed as part of the dot-com hype, it was prescient in many ways, albeit it might have been more appropriate if they had been driving through one of the emerging IT centers in the developing world, such as in Bangalore, India.

Improvements in telecommunications technologies—the emergence of the Internet and lower long-distance telephone costs—have made it economically feasible to outsource offshore. For instance, SmartPrep, an offshore tax-return processor, scans tax documents in the United States and sends them electronically to its staff in India. The Indian tax preparers then input the data into a tax preparation software package. Because of advances in computing and networking technologies, these files, which would have been prohibitively large in the recent past, are now sent in the blink of an eye. Security technology advancements also enable the company to control access to information. For example, offshore employees are not able to print out any of the documents that they prepare.

Sophisticated collaborative software overlaid on the Internet makes geographic co-location less important. For example, PlaceWare software allows people to conduct a "WebConference," at which participants can make presentations remotely and demonstrate software. Cheap telephony and videoconferencing technologies also provide a substitute for face-to-face meetings, as in the case of HLW, which has a number of architects in Shanghai doing design work for buildings in upstate New York.[29] More sophisticated software is available to facilitate the management of engineering design across companies and countries.

The development of software technologies and the standards necessary to share work across companies and computer platforms has been supported by the U.S. Department of Defense (DoD) for more than twenty years. The DoD purchases most of its equipment, which has increasingly been designed on computer-aided engineering software. Since it comes from many suppliers, it became necessary to ensure that multiple suppliers and the DoD could all collaborate in specifying designs and sharing information. For instance, DoD underwrote the development of VHDL, a standard software language for digital electronics design.

These technologies have spilled over into the private sector to enable more seamless integration of work across multiple companies in the semiconductor value chain. Because the standards are widely adopted, they have

facilitated the modularization of work and the ability of companies higher up the value chain to outsource more work.

Increased Standardization

A combination of technology maturity and the desire to collaborate across companies has forced greater standardization in computing technology. Natural monopolies often emerge in the IT industry because of the necessity for customers to collaborate. For instance, the real breakthrough in use of the Internet was its standardization rather than its superior technologies. So, the increased standardization and consolidation in hardware, with the PC desktop becoming ubiquitous, and more importantly in software sectors—such as Enterprise Resource Planning (ERP) and the Microsoft Office Suite—have changed customer tastes and made outsourcing more feasible and cost-effective. In other words, suppliers no longer have to support a separate computer platform for each of their customers.

Standardization also shifts competition pressures from differentiation to cost. In the case of IT, companies previously gained strategic advantage—differentiation—from their competitors by implementing a specialized system. Now, IT customers have moved from customized and proprietary systems to standard ERP platforms because they no longer believe that IT can provide a strategic advantage. These standard platforms provide cost savings because they are easier to upgrade and don't require specialized knowledge. In sum, there are two technology-related trends that promote outsourcing in software.

First, standardization has led to lower aggregate demand and a shift in balance of power from software vendor to customer. Customers are now demanding that software vendors compete on price rather than unique abilities, which plays directly in the hands of business models that maximize offshore production.

Second, an IT worker can learn one of the three standard ERP products and no longer has to write custom code. The standard software packages make it easier for Indian or Chinese software programmers to learn the software that a large number of customers will use. This also means that service providers need less face-to-face interaction, which directly supports the notion that a larger share of each software project can be done offshore.

Slower Pace of Change

This draws us to a larger trend, one that many may find counterintuitive: Information technologies are actually changing at a slower pace. During the decade of the 1990s, multiple major technological paradigm shifts hit at about the same time. A single technological paradigm shift drives customer demand and a particular kind of IT labor demand. The multiple shifts occurring at the same time drove customer demand and IT labor demand to unthinkable heights. The paradigm shifts included a move from mainframes to PC–based client-server system architectures, functional-based programming languages (C) to object oriented (C++ and Java), the Y2K bug, and ERP software. And of course, the biggest change was the adoption of the Internet.

Customers began to adopt the new technologies created by the paradigm shift in order to acquire strategic advantage or to keep up with their competitors. On the labor side, workers were learning new technologies on the job. Because it was new, the customer didn't fully understand how the technology worked and needed significant hand-holding during implementation, which required customized migration plans and heavy face-to-face interactions.

All of this drove IT labor demand beyond its capacity. U.S. corporate managers, feeling the pressure to implement the latest technologies because they didn't want to be left behind, poured hundreds of billions dollars into IT. The lack of capacity in the United States opened up the opportunity for offshore locations to capture U.S. business. It's important to keep in mind that this was due more to a lack of capacity than a desire to cut costs.

In the past four years, however, there has been no major technological paradigm shift, and, as expected, demand for IT has waned. As technologies have matured, companies have shifted their attention from implementing the latest technology to cost cutting. Meanwhile, the capacity that was created overseas during the boom is now well poised to offer the right set of standard services at a much lower cost. Lastly, intermediary companies—brokers, if you will—have sprouted up to reduce the transaction costs of doing business with offshore outsourcers. They connect the low-cost workers in developing countries to the developed-country customers.

Reason #7: Access to Emerging Markets with Proactive Policies

The relatively recent entrance of more than half the world's population into market economies—the collapse of the Soviet Union, and China and India's economic liberalization—has been offered as another reason for off-shoring. While this rationale has been overplayed by many, there are two important and connected effects to discuss, one with respect to workers and the other with regard to corporate strategy.

Major companies view India, and especially China, as critical future markets. They believe that if they do not have a presence in China, they may miss out on the coming consumer boom. While the market may be relatively small now, it is growing much more rapidly than are developed-country economies. Even though many companies are not making money by selling to the Chinese market now, they believe that they must have a presence there. As detailed in Chapter 8, the Chinese government has been skillful in leveraging access to its market by requiring foreign companies to set up production facilities in China.

We have all heard the phrase "brain drain," whereby the best and brightest from developing countries left for greener pastures in developed countries. One of the reasons that they left was the lack of good opportunities at home. So, why didn't companies set up facilities in India in the 1980s to tap this cheap and highly skilled talent? They probably faced ownership and other restrictions. But with liberalized investment rules, multinational companies are more comfortable building facilities in India and leveraging the cheap talent.

A new and portentous trend is building. U.S. businesses are so anxious to scale up their overseas labor pool that they are not even bothering with the normal hiring process, instead preferring to purchase established foreign businesses. For instance, IBM purchased the Indian company Daksh in April 2004, and in the process instantly gained 6,000 Indian workers.[30] The reverse trend, of Indian-based IT companies purchasing U.S. businesses may also happen, but the motivation of these Indian companies will be to gain U.S. customers, not hire American workers. For example, Indian IT giant Wipro purchased the energy management line of American Management Systems in 2002.[31]

Some of the incentives and regulations that developing countries have used to attract jobs and industries are discussed in Chapter 8. New Dell Computer CEO Kevin Rollins addressed an audience in Tokyo in July 2004, where he said that it was imperative for Dell to accelerate growth in key countries like China and Japan, and that growing jobs in those countries was simply a matter of good business strategy.[32]

Reason #8: Easier with Experience

As companies become more comfortable moving work overseas, and they achieve some cost savings, they will move even more work for even greater savings. But there is more at play than just the cost savings gained by offshoring. Existing overseas operations actually attract additional work for noneconomic reasons. Manufacturing managers have been decentralizing research and development (R&D) and moving it closer to the production processes over the past decade. It is only natural that as production has gone overseas, it has attracted engineering design work and even higher-level R&D.

For example, Delphi, a major automobile parts supplier, has a large assembly-line operation in Ciudad-Juarez, Mexico, employing workers earning about $4,800 a year. Subsequently, in order to have geographic proximity to their assembly plants, Delphi established a technical center nearby, which employs 1,700 engineers and design experts.[33] So the lower-skill jobs (assembly) act as an attractor to high-skill jobs (engineering).

Reason #9: U.S. Immigration Policies

By bringing in lower-cost foreign labor, many of the leading outsourcing companies utilize U.S. immigration policies to grow their businesses. These firms have been the first movers in offshore outsourcing because they had strong operations offshore and could get access to U.S. clients through the immigration regulation loopholes—that is, there is a strong correlation between offshore outsourcing and H-1B and L-1 visa use. This in turn exposed a large number of foreign workers to U.S. business practices, who have now returned to their native land to manage the business developed by offshore outsourcing. They know both sides of the business: the U.S. client interaction and how to manage operations in their native country.

Because of their lower cost basis, these offshore outsourcing firms are forcing traditional U.S. IT services firms to adopt their business model: a lean U.S.-based staff and a large offshore staff. Our research shows that a number of offshore outsourcing firms have stretched the guest-worker visa regulations (H-1B and L-1) to gain competitive advantage in the U.S. market. This exploitation of lax U.S. visa regulations has actually accelerated the offshore outsourcing because the costs of outsourcing are kept artificially low through these visa loopholes.[34]

By 1998, the H-1B had become essentially an IT worker visa, and the bulk of these workers came from India. The tie to IT was strengthened by the large Indian presence in the Silicon Valley. Considering the strength of the Indian higher education system, including several world-class Indian Institutes of Technology, the English language of the students, and the links to the Indian diaspora here, this result is understandable. In fact, parallel with the growth of offshore outsourcing has come the development of an Indian "Silicon Valley" around the southern city of Bangalore.

While the H-1B was initially exploited by U.S. firms to take advantage of cheap Indian labor, ironically it increasingly appears that Indian firms are able to outcompete U.S. firms by underbidding them. There is a knowledge transfer factor at play here also; as H-1B and L-1 workers take their knowledge of U.S. customers back home with them, they are able to more smoothly do the work from abroad. Workers with H-1B experience in the United States are in great demand in the Indian labor market.[35]

It is not just our research that shows how important on-site offshore outsourcing is to Indian IT companies; their representatives say it themselves repeatedly. Kiran Karnik, head of the Indian software services industry association NASSCOM, says, "Any constricting of the [U.S.] visa process . . . is bad for the industry" because 40 percent of the work involves their use.[36]

Phiroz Vandrevala, an executive at Indian IT heavyweight Tata Consultancy Services, was asked by a major Indian business magazine about the cost advantages that TCS gains through the visa programs. The question was, "Ability to hire professionals on lower wages is a competitive advantage for TCS and other Indian IT majors, but what do you do when this is seen as a threat in the U.S.?" Mr. Vandrevala's response was, "Our wage per employee is 20 to 25 percent less than U.S. wage for a similar employee. . . . This [labor arbitrage] is a fact of doing work on-site. It's a

fact that Indian IT companies have an advantage here, and there's nothing wrong in that." He goes on to say that while the offshore share of work is increasing, he anticipates that what TCS needs for more H-1Bs and L-1s will increase as business in general goes up. TCS boasts that their client list includes eight of the top ten U.S. Fortune 500 companies.[37]

The visa programs facilitate the "knowledge transfer" from U.S. to overseas workers. Intel brings in some of its foreign workers on L-1 visas to be trained by American staff so that they can take that knowledge back to their home offices in India, China, and Russia.[38] While Intel claims that this process does not cause American layoffs, the result is that American workers are being asked to transfer their individual intellectual capital to potential future competitors. In the current atmosphere, it would be no surprise that Intel may export those Americans jobs in the future.

There have been countless stories about U.S. workers unwittingly training their foreign replacements, who happened to be in the United States on guest-worker visas. In other cases the workers knew they were training their replacements and had to do it or else forfeit severance and unemployment benefits. The future looks bleak as a powerful coalition of interests tries to use free-trade agreements to further weaken the few safeguards that American workers still have. What's more, elites that represent U.S. corporate interests, such as the Institute for International Economics, have aligned themselves with the World Bank to argue that any kind of visa restriction is a nontariff barrier to trade.[39]

Reason #10: Corporate Strategy that No Longer Includes Workers

Some CEOs, such as Jack Welch, former head of General Electric (GE); Michael Dell, head of Dell Computer; and Carly Fiorina, of Hewlett-Packard, have been evangelists for offshoring. GE was one of the first firms to offshore work to India. Welch coined the famous "70-70-70" phrase within GE, saying that GE will outsource 70 percent of its work, 70 percent of outsourced work will be done overseas, and 70 percent of the offshore outsourcing will be done in India. Ironically, GE originally entered India with the hope that it could sell its products to that domestic market. Managers figured out very quickly that they would have difficulty penetrating the

Indian market and instead were better off using Indian labor for GE work sold elsewhere. In a fitting move, GE named the facilities in Bangalore the Jack Welch Research Center, after the vigorously pro-outsourcing CEO.

Companies like Dell and GE have institutionalized the practice of ranking employees and firing those that rank lowest. This forces employees to compete against one another, and it highlights the current management attitude toward workers. They no longer view workers as stakeholders in the company. Now, the only two groups that matter in company decision making are company executives and large shareholders. Workers are considered just one more input in the production process, and if they can be replaced by new technology or cheap overseas labor, then they should be.

One industry lobbyist explained to us that offshoring is equivalent to companies' globalizing their supply chain for labor, implying that exporting jobs was the same thing as importing a pencil. Or as Craig Barrett, CEO of Intel, put it while explaining why he was so outspokenly in favor of outsourcing: "Companies like Intel have a responsibility to their shareholders to hire the best talent available," no matter where it is, and that no U.S. job is safe and secure.[40] And it isn't a matter of an Intel or a Microsoft being forced to move jobs overseas because the company is losing money, since these companies are making so much money that Microsoft recently had $60 billion in cash it didn't know how to spend. These are highly profitable businesses that can afford to pay first-world wages. Yet they destroy these jobs not because they are forced to but because they can.

This is a far cry from the situation just a few years ago, when many companies included workers' interests in their calculations. Company managers used to be embarrassed when they announced layoffs; now they are celebrated. Many have argued that this "flexibility" makes U.S. companies more competitive and is necessary because of globalization, a process that corporate executives have been championing. Corporate executives work in their best self-interests, and shareholders have recognized this. They have tried to align executives' interests with shareholders' interests by offering greater stock compensation. In one corporate scandal after the next, you've seen how executives make decisions that pump up stock prices in the short run by dismissing workers. "Chainsaw" Al Dunlap, former CEO of Sunbeam, may be the best case in point.

One might hope for a return to the good old days of employer-worker

loyalty, but that doesn't seem feasible. The reality for workers is that only if their interests align with those of the corporate executives will the company act on their behalf. Business practices are often imitative, since no one wants to be left behind in an industry trend. And the same is true for offshore outsourcing: Managers are now aware of it as a possibility, and more importantly they perceive it as something they must do because their peers are doing it. The practice is becoming institutionalized at so many companies with a new job title—Global Supply Coordinator—that describes a new cadre of managers responsible for figuring out how best to move work overseas and how best to manage it when it gets there.

Outsourcing is driven by two stakeholder groups: shareholders and upper management. The company executives are acting rationally by trying to cut costs and improve their bottom lines. However, their actions are not necessarily meeting the interests of their own U.S. workforce; in fact, one can argue that this process is counter to what many of their own employees would prefer. So, the companies clearly no longer consider the interests of U.S. workers, including their own U.S. employees.

At a press conference in January 2004, eight computer-company CEOs expressed this new fact of life quite clearly. While defending the companies' "right" to move as much work offshore as they please, Carly Fiorina, the CEO of Hewlett-Packard, said in response to concerns about the impact on American workers, "There is no job that is America's God-given right anymore. We have to compete for those jobs."[41] She created a firestorm by seeming so uncaring to the plight of U.S. workers, but her statements are echoed in most boardrooms across the country. Because so many company executives believe that offshore outsourcing is good for them and their shareholders, we are at only the very beginning of a much larger trend as companies attempt to shift as much work as possible offshore.

Conclusion

Have U.S. firms opened a Pandora's box by creating their own future competition? Managers in U.S. companies will have to figure out how to establish effective operations offshore and/or contract relationships with third parties. How will they protect sensitive data and proprietary company information? How do they, on the one hand, appease equity analysts by claim-

ing that they are cutting costs by moving offshore and, at the same time, keep the news from their U.S. workers, who might get quite angry and begin to organize? For U.S. policymakers, the issue is how to measure the scale and scope of the offshore movement and, most importantly, how it might impact the U.S. labor market and innovative capacity. Will kids shy away from pursuing engineering careers because of poor career prospects? How will a smaller pool of U.S. technical professionals impact the United States's ability to innovate for economic growth and military security?

Another crucial issue involves how the United States will compensate domestic workers displaced by the offshore outsourcing trend. Most agree that the losers in trade should be compensated, but the reality is that this is much more difficult than most economists and politicians understand. First, it is difficult to actually identify who has been affected by offshoring, especially when companies are misrepresenting what they are doing. Many workers are sworn to secrecy as a condition of receiving their severance packages. Even if we could identify the displaced workers, how do we determine the appropriate compensation? Can a forty-five-year-old engineer with a master's degree realistically retrain to become a nurse? We are inching toward a point where all U.S. workers are temporary contractors/consultants. Industry's mantra has been to show agility when it comes to hiring and firing workers. It was only in 1992 that IBM laid off its first employees, yet what was once a big deal has become routine. Some U.S. workers actually benefited from the absence of loyalty between employer and employee during the boom times of the late 1990s. They switched positions, and received signing bonuses and stock options. That boom time masked the real, radical changes going on in U.S. employment. Now workers need to view themselves as free agents, working for themselves and not the company. This will lead to potentially greater rewards for a few workers and surely greater risk for all workers.

This change is ironic, since we have heard so much about the "knowledge economy" and how important "human capital" is to economic growth. We now have a human capital paradox whereby worker knowledge is terribly important but companies have a great disincentive to invest resources in those workers: Why should a company train a worker who will leave or be laid off in short order? This larger trend is going to have profound effects on American workers and society, as well as on workers in developing coun-

tries and developing societies. It calls into question much of the conventional wisdom of the elites in Washington and academia.

Unfortunately, most of the proponents and analysts of offshore outsourcing do not address the fundamental problem: What do you do with all the idle U.S. workers, and what impact will offshore outsourcing have on our capacity for future high-tech innovation and work? In the next two chapters, we begin to look at some of the deeper impacts that offshore outsourcing is beginning to have on the U.S. economy.

Notes

1. Steve Lohr, "High-end Technology Work Not Immune to Outsourcing," *New York Times*, June 16, 2004. While $90 per hour would nominally translate into an annual salary of $180,000 if someone worked 2,000 hours per year, contract workers will only net a fraction of this amount. Contract workers typically do not bill an entire year's worth of business. They spend part of the year marketing their services and part idle, which is the risk they take. Also, they pay for any benefits out of the nominal rate, so the translation from nominal billing rate to an equivalent salary requires significant discounting.

2. Mark Horvit, "Exporting Jobs: Offshoring Transforms the Global Workplace," *Fort Worth Star-Telegram* (June 19, 2004).

3. Robyn Meredith, "China Wants Brains, Not Just Brawn," www.Forbes.com (June 30, 2004).

4. "Poor Payers to a Degree," *The Economist* (June 10, 2004).

5. Matt Marshall, "VC's Offshoring Push Goes into Overdrive: Everett Prods Start-ups to Turn to Labor Abroad as Cost-Strategy," *San Jose Mercury News* (May 16, 2004).

6. Paul Blustein, "Implored to 'Offshore' More: U.S. Firms Are Too Reluctant to Outsource Jobs, Report Says," *Washington Post* (July 2, 2004), p. E1.

7. Paul Kostek, "Can You Compete with an $800-a-Month Engineer?" *Puget Sound Business Journal* (August 29, 2003).

8. Ryan Chittum, "Call Centers Phone Home: Small-Town Economics Lure More Companies to Outsource in Remote Corners of the U.S.," *Wall Street Journal* (June 9, 2004), p. B1.

9. Jeff Kosseff, "Not All That's Outsourced Gone Abroad: Some Analysts Fear that Domestic Outsourcing Poses as Big a Threat to U.S. Jobs as

Offshoring, A View Reflected in Unemployment Data," *The Oregonian* (June 15, 2004).

10. William P. Dizard, "New Law Limits Offshoring of A-76 Work," *Government Computer News* (January 29, 2004).

11. Dawn Gilbertson, "ON Semiconductor Stays a Step Ahead in China: Phoenix Chipmaker Blazed a Trail Inland Toward Cheaper Labor," *Arizona Republic* (August 2, 2004).

12. Dean Takahashi, "HP Results Solid in 4th Quarter: Revenue Growth Strong; 2,000 More Jobs to Be Cut," *San Jose Mercury News* (November 20, 2003).

13. Rachel Konrad, "Donohue Endorses Outsourcing of Jobs," Associated Press (June 30, 2004).

14. Don Durfee and Kate O'Sullivan, "Offshoring by the Numbers: Results of Our Survey of 275 Finance Executives at a Broad Range of Companies," *CFO Magazine* (June 1, 2004).

15. Lou Dobbs, *Exporting America: Why Corporate Greed Is Shipping American Jobs Overseas* (New York: Warner Books, 2004).

16. Durfee and O'Sullivan, "Offshoring by the Numbers."

17. William M. Bulkeley, "IBM Now Plans Fewer Layoffs from Offshoring," *Wall Street Journal* (July 29, 2004).

18. Robert Trigaux, "Capital One: The Political Drama," *St. Petersburg Times* (July 29, 2004).

19. William M. Bulkeley, "New IBM Jobs Can Mean Fewer Jobs Elsewhere," *Wall Street Journal* (March 8, 2004).

20. Lohr, "High-end Technology Work."

21. Jeff Nachtigal, "Microsoft's India Workforce Doubles: Internal Documents Detail Contract Employee Work Agreements," *WashTech News* (July 28, 2004).

22. John C. Dvorak, "Scams, Lies, Deceit, and Offshoring," *PC Magazine* (April 28, 2004).

23. Tom Raum, "Bush Economic Team Under Fire, Hands New Ammo to Democrats," Associated Press (February 19, 2004).

24. Robert B. Reich, "High-Tech Jobs Are Going Abroad! But That's Okay," *Washington Post* (November 2, 2003), p. B3.

25. George Will, "The Economics of Progress," *Washington Post* (February 20, 2004); Thomas Friedman, "Software of Democracy," *New York Times*, March 21, 2004, "Secret of Our Sauce," *New York Times*

(March 7, 2004); and "Small and Smaller," *New York Times* (March 4, 2004).

26. "Political Timing, Outsourced," *New York Times* (February 17, 2004); and "Mr. Mankiw Is Right," *Washington Post* (February 13, 2004).

27. Greg Griffin, "Offshore Money Machine," *Denver Post* (May 4, 2004).

28. Ibid.

29. Peter S. Goodman, "White-collar Work a Booming U.S. Export," *Washington Post* (April 2, 2003), p. E1.

30. Abigail Rayner, "IBM Deal Boosts Presence in India Despite U.S. Anger," *London Times* (April 8, 2004).

31. Ibid.

32. "New Dell CEO Wows to Increase Jobs Worldwide," AFP (July 27, 2004).

33. Mark Horvit, "Delphi Among Firms Sending Engineering, Research Work Out of U.S.," *Fort Worth Star-Telegram* (June 22, 2004).

34. Ron Hira, "U.S. Immigration Regulations and India's Information Technology Industry," *Technological Forecasting and Social Change*, 71, No. 8 (October 2004), pp. 837–864.

35. Ibid.

36. "Nasscom Fears More Visa Restrictions Against IT Pros," *Press Trust of India* (May 24, 2003).

37. Shelley Singh, "U.S. Visas Are Not a TCS-Specific Issue," *Business World India* (June 30, 2003).

38. "U.S. Tech Workers Training Their Replacements," Associated Press (August 11, 2003).

39. Fakir Chand, "World Bank to Take up Visa Curbs Issue at WTO," www.Rediff.com (May 23, 2003); and Aaditya Mattoo and Sacha Wunsch, "Preempting Protectionism in Services: The GATS and Outsourcing," *Essential Reading from the Institute*, the Institute for International Economics (January 2004).

40. Jane Larson, "Competing Is Key, Says Intel CEO," *Arizona Republic* (June 5, 2004).

41. Carolyn Lochhead, "Economists Back Tech Industry's Overseas Hiring; Workers Deny U.S. Lacks Qualified Staff," *San Francisco Chronicle* (January 9, 2004).

CHAPTER 6

The Far-Reaching Effects of Outsourcing on the U.S. Economy

Offshore outsourcing in the services sector is a major shift in how our economy operates, and it will have serious impacts on the trajectory of economic growth, national security, the distribution of income, and the workforce. These impacts will be both positive and negative. When the business owners and consultants who are moving jobs overseas claim that their actions will have a clear net positive, they are merely fortune telling. It should come as no surprise that they are rabidly in favor of offshore outsourcing, since they (or the corporations for which they work) stand to be big winners in the short run. But will the United States be better off?

Offshore outsourcing has a major negative downside in that many people, groups, and communities will be adversely affected. The phenomenon has created major suffering for many Americans (see the next chapter), and as this outsourcing continues to spread, Americans will demand action. On the positive side, the hope is that offshore outsourcing will help lift U.S. economic growth and development by lowering the input costs of services and expand and open new markets abroad. If American businesses become more competitive, they may have a better chance to survive against wholly owned, lower-labor-cost competitors such as in China. There may be positive consequences from increased trade and rising living standards in developing countries. However, there are a number of areas of uncertainty. In

short, we simply don't know yet how this shift in business operation will affect U.S. competitiveness and our national innovation system.

The Long-Run Impacts on Economic Efficiency

Mainstream economists tell us that offshore outsourcing will have a positive effect on the economy in the long run because of its resulting improved economic efficiency—that is, companies will be able to deliver services more cheaply, and consumers will benefit through lower prices. The U.S. economy further benefits when those companies reinvest the extra profits gained by offshoring for expansion in the United States.

The logic is quite straightforward: If you can buy something cheaper than making it yourself, then you should buy it. Let's say that you have the option of hiring someone to clean your house for $8 an hour or of taking time off from work to do it yourself. Which would you choose? If you are paid more than $8 an hour, then you would choose to hire the cleaning person. From an economist's point of view, this is a more efficient allocation of resources (in this case labor): More is produced with the same set of scarce resources—your time and money.

So, why shouldn't companies buy software services from India at half-price? From an economic efficiency point of view that considers only price, it is the proverbial no-brainer. Unfortunately, in the real world things are a bit more complicated. The economic efficiency argument assumes that those U.S. workers who would have been producing that software are now redeployed to work on other things, known as the *full employment assumption*. In the words of the outsourcing advocates, the displaced U.S. workers are "freed up" to do better, higher-paying, and more interesting work. But if the U.S. workers are instead idle, then the economic efficiency argument falls apart; the U.S. economy will actually be worse off than if the company had used U.S. workers. On the other hand, the company will *always* be better off by purchasing the foreign work, regardless of whether their former American workers are redeployed, since they have no responsibility for the U.S. workers. So you can understand why companies are so anxious to use cheap foreign labor, regardless of its impact on the U.S. economy.

Even if the U.S. workers eventually find new work, it is not clear that the U.S. economy as a whole will always be better off. For example, schol-

ars Ralph Gomory and William Baumol have shown that even when the basic economic models are used, trade does not always make both trading partners better off.[1] In fact, they show that trade can result in a net positive for one country and a net negative for the other. Yet, most international trade is based on an idea of comparative advantage—basically that each nation should specialize in the goods it produces best; through trade, each country is better off as overall world production is more efficient. However, there are many problems with this outdated notion of trade. For one thing, comparative advantage says nothing about the distribution of gains from trade. While world efficiency should be theoretically improved, the efficiency may be captured by some countries and not others. Who gains from international trade may depend very much on whether the countries are the ones producing the high-quality, high-wage goods or the high-quantity, low-skilled commodities of international trade. Moreover, the simplistic idea of comparative advantage doesn't accommodate the fact that countries can acquire an advantage through investments in infrastructure, education, and industrial policy.

Some Companies Benefit from Exporting Jobs

Large U.S. companies have been represented in Washington by a number of lobbying organizations, including the Business Roundtable, U.S. Chamber of Commerce, and in the high-technology sector, by the Information Technology Association of America, Electronics Industry Alliance, American Electronics Association, and Computer Systems Policy Project. All of these organizations have come out strongly in favor of their companies' unfettered ability to export U.S. jobs and have no interest in taking responsibility for the consequences to their employees. The near unanimity of the large-corporation community is somewhat surprising on the face of it, but one has to understand that the lobbying organizations represent the interests of the CEOs, executives, and shareholders. They do not represent the workers' interests.

The large companies have come out in favor of outsourcing because the executives stand to gain and the boards of directors, which represent shareholders, expect that offshore outsourcing will help boost profits and stock prices, as discussed in Chapter 5. The windfall gains from the trans-

fer of work offshore will be shared by executives, shareholders, and consumers. Their lobbyists would have you believe that all of the cost savings are passed on to consumers. However, none of the companies that outsource services work offshore in what industrial organization specialists would call "competitive markets." They all exist in something closer to an oligopoly, or a market with just a few sellers and limited competition, which means that some of the cost savings are siphoned off for executives and shareholders on their way to the consumers.

You can understand why so many CEOs have taken a determined stance on outsourcing: It affects their own fortunes directly. They are not compensated based on the number of workers they have, but on how high they can pump up the stock price and on profits they can achieve. The intense pressure for short-term return on investment has even run roughshod over the previous management philosophy of investing in human and corporate resources to ensure long-term competitiveness and profitability. There may be some downsides for these companies, though, as employee morale drops considerably because of outsourcing. For instance, as we discussed earlier, IBM claimed that they stopped the policy of forcing their U.S. workers to train their replacements—known as *knowledge transfer*—citing that it contributed to poor morale.

A second group of companies are laughing all the way to the bank— the consulting companies that are setting up the offshore outsourcing deals. As mentioned in Chapter 3, these consultants may be advising companies how to move offshore or, in some cases, doing the transition work themselves. They include McKinsey & Co., Forrester Research, Gartner, Deloitte Consulting, A.T. Kearney, and many others. It should be no surprise that these consulting groups also happen to be the ones putting out reports in favor of offshore outsourcing, trying to persuade policymakers that it is a good thing.

A third group of companies benefiting from outsourcing are the foreign firms that are winning more business at home. Those companies now have opportunities that they never dreamed of before. They can act as outsourcers or as direct suppliers to all of the sparkling new facilities being built overseas by the large U.S. multinationals. The commercial real estate market is booming in Bangalore.

But Other Companies Lose

Although the overwhelming support for offshore outsourcing has come from CEOs and lobbyists who represent companies, not all companies will benefit from it, and not all support it. In the manufacturing sector, the American Manufacturing Trade Action Council (AMTAC), an industry association that represents U.S. apparel and textile companies and other manufacturers, has been a vocal opponent of the type of globalization that the larger manufacturing companies, represented by the National Association of Manufacturers (NAM), support. AMTAC even sponsored a highway billboard campaign that included the words, "Lost Your Job To 'Free Trade' & Offshoring, Yet?" These billboards were posted in South Carolina, a state with heavy manufacturing job losses.

Not every company executive views offshore outsourcing as good, but the voices of the opponents are muted in Washington by the greater interests and influence of large multinational companies. Jack Davis, a self-described "lifelong Republican" and small manufacturer employing seventy-five people in Akron, New York, was so exasperated with inaction by Washington to the hemorrhaging of jobs overseas that he switched parties and decided to run for Congress against a powerful Republican incumbent, Tom Reynolds. Davis's prior ties to the Republican Party run deep; he had been a large contributor to Reynolds and Bush/Cheney over the past few years. But about his determination and rationale for running and spending $1.2 million of his own money, Davis says, "I'm willing to sacrifice my fortune, my time, and maybe my life, too. . . . Free trade is destroying American industries, jobs, and the middle class, and I have to do something about it."[2]

The truth is that many U.S. companies stand to lose business as a consequence of outsourcing offshore. It is a hot topic at real estate conferences, for instance. Many in the commercial real estate industry believe that as white-collar jobs move overseas, demand for office space in the United States will diminish—at a time when office vacancy rates are very high anyway. One industry analyst estimates that demand for about 50 million square feet of office space will shift overseas every year. To put that figure into perspective, the central business district of Tampa, Florida, has about 7 million square feet of space.[3] Another analyst predicts that over the next twelve years, 500 million square feet, or the equivalent of about 17 per-

cent of the nationwide supply of office space, will be vacated as companies move operations overseas. They predict that lower demand will result in higher vacancy rates and lower property values.[4]

Others predict that markets that have heavy concentrations of financial services firms, such as Manhattan, San Francisco, Boston, and Charlotte, will be especially hard hit. In addition to the direct impact on real estate companies, smaller companies—from restaurants to photocopy services—that supply support services to company operations and their workers will be adversely affected.

The Impacts on U.S. Labor Demand

We can distinguish three types of work that are done offshore.

- Tasks being done by U.S. workers that are being directly transferred because of lower costs overseas.
- New tasks that prior to offshore outsourcing would have been done in the United States, but instead are done overseas. These are the tasks that don't show up in direct job exportation, but instead as depressed labor demand in the United States.
- Brand new tasks that would never have been done in the United States before offshoring occurred.

We are in a period of transition, in which many companies have just discovered the benefits of offshore outsourcing, so they are anxiously scrambling to substitute cheaper foreign labor for American labor. The direct transfer of work overseas is growing much faster than the overall labor demand within most companies, so U.S. workers are becoming expendable. For instance, IBM is eliminating U.S. jobs even though their worldwide workforce is growing; Siemens ICN announced that they are shifting nearly all of their IT services work, thus its 15,000 workers, from the United States and Western Europe to low-wage countries in Eastern Europe and Asia.[5] Companies have euphemistically referred to this process as "rebalancing" the workforce.

A variation on the direct transfer of work is when an offshore outsourcer takes business and market share away from U.S. domestic out-

sourcers. In the IT services industry, we see that offshore outsourcers such as Infosys and Cognizant are gaining market share very rapidly from outsourcing firms that operate domestically, and they are also expanding their workforce overseas.

The second kind of transfer, which is much more subtle, happens when jobs that would normally have been created in the United States are instead created overseas. This kind of offshoring will have a large impact that is more difficult to track and predict. Companies that have new growth in sales for their products expand their overseas labor pool in lieu of expanding their U.S. workforce. So, companies such as Google, Microsoft, and others support their growth by building new facilities and staffing them overseas. Or companies that would normally replace U.S. workers who leave for better opportunities or retirement instead opt for overseas labor. The impact on the U.S. workforce from this indirect transfer of jobs will be less observable, but it will have a dampening effect on U.S. labor demand.

Lastly, some offshoring will create new jobs that would never have existed in the United States. For example, high-labor-intensive work may be feasible only with cheap overseas workers. An example may be electronic archiving, such as computer-scanning of a newspaper's articles, converting them into text-searchable documents and archiving them for electronic retrieval. This process still requires a large amount of labor because automated computer scanning makes mistakes and requires human review, so it would be prohibitively expensive to perform this in the United States. This kind of work likely has no effect on U.S. labor demand, but it is the exception rather than the rule.

Companies justify their overseas expansions by saying that they need to service the local market. For example, car companies establish plants in China to sell to the Chinese market. This action may be the result of government incentives or regulations, comparative transportation and distribution costs, access to raw materials, and/or the benefits associated with being close to their customers. The latter is sometimes called *localization*, whereby a company modifies its product so that it can meet local tastes, norms, or language requirements. For example, tax-preparation software needs to be modified to meet a country's tax laws and language, and it makes sense to use people familiar with those laws and language. But in many cases, the claim of localization is just that—a claim. The vast majori-

ty of IT and BPO facilities being established in India are there to service North American and Western European markets, not the local market.

Advocates would have you believe that consumers are the major beneficiaries of outsourcing because they will pay less and be able to buy a wider variety of goods and services. Because of lower labor costs, goods and services *will* be cheaper, but as shown earlier, the savings from cheaper labor are split among the executives, shareholders, and consumers. Of course, those workers who are displaced owing to outsourcing will surely have diminished ability to consume those goods and services.

Will Offshore Outsourcing Lead to Expansion of Overseas Markets?

Proponents of offshore outsourcing argue that as the economies of developing countries grow, there will be increased opportunities for U.S. companies to sell their produces—that they are not only opening up markets but also creating new ones. They go on to say that if U.S. companies are unable to utilize overseas talent, they will no longer be competitive with foreign companies. One of the underlying questions that is not asked by these companies is whether they are improving their own competitive advantage or potentially creating future competition for themselves by outsourcing the work.

Offshore outsourcing does not always work the way companies expect it to work. For example, in 1980, IBM domestically outsourced the microprocessor for its PC to Intel and the operating system to Microsoft. And the two companies that have benefited most from IBM's decision are Microsoft and Intel. In fact, IBM recently sold its PC line to a Chinese company. Likewise, as work is outsourced overseas, will the next generation of innovative companies be located overseas?

Outsourcing advocates also argue that salaries in developing countries will rise rapidly as more and more work moves offshore, generating greater demand for labor. What those same advocates do not acknowledge is that no one really knows how soon that shift will happen. There are a tremendous number of underutilized workers (excess supply) in those developing countries. Many people with college degrees in technical disciplines, like engineering, are currently working in call centers, answering phones, for example. And in addition to underutilized workers, many new colleges have

been created, producing ever more English-speaking workers ready to compete for jobs. The other factor that most of these offshoring advocates do not acknowledge is the incredible gap in the cost of living for workers in the United States versus India or China.

As we discussed in Chapter 5, it costs less than one-fifth the amount of money to live just as well in India or China as it does in the United States. In other words, workers demand lower salaries in India in part because of excess supply, but also because their cost of living is considerably lower. This means that the United States is unlikely to benefit from any significant increase in wages as Indian workers gain new spending power. They will be much more likely to purchase their own cheaper products. Considering the huge and growing population in many developing countries, if we count on wages to even out globally, that means lowering American workers' standard of living closer to that of workers in these developing countries, rather than bringing them up to our level.

There also is no guarantee that U.S. companies will continue to gain from outsourcing. Indian IT companies Tata Consultancy, Infosys, and Wipro are all much more profitable than their U.S. competitors, and they are gaining market share in the United States. Table 6-1 shows that Indian IT services firms, which specialize in offshore outsourcing and on-site offshore outsourcing, are much more highly valued and profitable than their U.S. counterparts. For instance, EDS is twenty times the size of its competitors Infosys and Wipro, but it has a lower market capitalization. EDS's CEO, Michael Jordan, recently publicly declared that his company must use offshore labor in order to compete with companies that have offshore delivery models.[6]

In countries such as China, it is Chinese—not foreign—companies that are supplying most of the domestic market. As Chinese and Indian companies' competitiveness continues to grow, U.S. companies have no assurance that their market share in these emerging economies will grow to offset losses at home. As an example, our data indicate that Indian firms are generally more competitive in their own markets than U.S. ones would be.

Outsourcing advocates also ignore the argument that they are destroying the buying power of consumers in their most lucrative market—the United States—by destroying jobs here and putting downward pressure on wages. The mutually beneficial relationship between a highly productive

Table 6-1. Creating competition—offshore outsourcing IT services firms valued much higher than U.S. firms.

Name	Country HQ	Market Capitalization (U.S. $ millions)	Trailing Twelve Months Sales (U.S. $ millions)	Price to Sales	Sales Growth % 1 Year	Net Profit Margin 5-Year Average %	Effective Tax Rate 5-Year Average %
Infosys Technologies Limited (ADR)	India	$12,135	$1,164	10.42	40.96	28.7	14.01
Wipro Limited (ADR)	India	$10,512	$1,395	7.53	36.37	19.5	13.42
Electronic Data Systems	US	$8,633	$21,834	0.40	0.55	3.6	35.87
Computer Sciences Corporation	US	$8,107	$14,949	0.54	30.15	3.4	30.55
Affiliated Computer Services	US	$6,404	$4,106	1.56	8.43	8.2	38.64
Cognizant Technology Solutions	US	$3,215	$465	6.92	60.74	13.7	31.23
Satyam Computer (ADR)	India	$2,892	$620	4.67	23.34	2.7	14.02
Perot Systems Corp.	US	$1,431	$1,618	0.88	9.65	4.2	54.37

Source: Reuters News Services (August 29, 2004).

workforce and an entrepreneurial business sector that is the foundation for America's prosperity seems to be crumbling. Behind the arguments made by the economists and businesspeople that everyone will gain, there are problems that they either paper over or ignore.

Will More Jobs Be Created?

Even the macroeconomic data expose the hubris of offshoring advocates that we will be better off in the long run. But, of course, we live in the short run. If offshore outsourcing happens when economic activity is creating a large number of jobs, its negative impacts are much smaller, but still important, than when few jobs are being created. Indeed, historical precedent shows that job creation tracks the economy's output. As GDP expands, more jobs are created. Figure 6-1 shows the total number of nonfarm jobs versus the net number of workers in the labor market in the United States from 1984 to 2004. In other words, the U.S. economy had about 93 million jobs in 1983, which grew to 132 million in 2004. That means 39 million net new jobs were created in a two-decade span, but as is obvious from the figure, job creation does not follow a smooth path over time.

During a recession there is job destruction, and during expansion there is job creation. Figure 6-2 shows GDP versus nonfarm jobs, 1984 to

Figure 6-1. U.S. job creation vs. labor force, 1984 to 2004.

Source: U.S. Bureau of Labor Statistics (August 29, 2004).

2004. It clearly shows how the recession, defined as at least two consecutive quarters of declining GDP during the late 1980s and early 1990s resulted in some job destruction. However, the relatively mild recession of 2001 resulted in greater job destruction and an extremely prolonged slump in job creation. This latter job destruction was first explained as a bursting of the stock market bubble and then as a result of the 9/11 attacks. However, the economy had robust GDP expansion in 2002 and 2003, but a continued job-creation drought during this time. This paradox took economists by surprise, and in 2003 they began to call it a *jobless recovery*—while some politicians were calling it a "job-loss recovery."

Also, keep in mind that about 1.8 million net new workers enter the United States's workforce every year as children reach working age and immigration outweighs the number of people entering retirement as shown in Figure 6-1. That means that the U.S. economy needs to create 1.8 million new jobs annually just to stay even with population increases and maintain the same job prospects for workers. So, it should be no surprise

Figure 6-2. U.S. job creation vs. real GDP, 1984 to 2004.

Sources: U.S. Bureau of Labor Statistics and U.S. Bureau of Economic Analysis (August 29, 2004).

that there is extreme anxiety for workers; they already know what the statistics show very clearly—that the United States is not creating enough jobs for those who want them, and workers who are displaced by offshoring face the worst labor market in the past two decades. They are not being reabsorbed into the economy.

And even where there has been some job creation, the job quality was lower. Over a period covering the end of 2003 and the early part of 2004, lower-wage jobs grew 50 percent faster than higher-wage ones, and 14 percent of the new jobs were as temporary work.[7] So, instead of the ideal outsourcing scenario promoted by offshoring advocates, whereby both Indian and U.S. workers are employed, a more common scenario presents the U.S. worker who trained his foreign replacement visiting the unemployment office or working as a temp or lower-salaried contract worker. As Economics Nobel Laureate Joseph Stiglitz put it when discussing the negative impacts of international trade, "If society as a whole isn't able to create new jobs, what you've done is move people from . . . jobs to unemployment."[8]

The offshore outsourcing theory would hold up better, but not perfectly, if the United States were not running such a large trade deficit. If India, China, and all other countries imported more goods and services from the United States, then labor demand in the United States would increase, and at least some of those idle U.S. workers would have a better chance of getting a job. What makes Mankiw's statement all the more remarkable is that he knows that actual job creation has been more than 5 million below his own predictions, and yet he summarily dismissed the negative effects of offshore outsourcing. And others peg the job creation deficit at as much as 7–9 million.

Americans know that the job market is poor. Some 82 percent believe that it is a bad time to be looking for work, and one in five are afraid that someone in their household will be laid off.[9] Americans also have strong negative sentiments about offshore outsourcing. According to a survey of worker sentiment conducted by Hudson Highland Group, a professional staffing firm, 66 percent believe that offshore outsourcing is bad for the economy and 50 percent advocate government policies to penalize companies that move operations offshore.[10]

Where Is the Recovery for Labor?

Economists have been befuddled by the fact that all the macroeconomic numbers are positive: We are supposedly out of a recession, but the labor market has yet to recover. This is readily apparent in Figure 6-2, where GDP has been growing fast but job creation is tepid at best. One illustration of this soft job market has been the shift in bargaining power from labor to corporations. This has manifested itself in corporations' capturing the lion's share of gains from the most recent economic recovery. From the end of the recession in 2001 to the first quarter of 2004, corporate profits grew 62.2 percent while labor compensation grew only 2.8 percent over the same time. On the basis of past recoveries since World War II, we would expect a much more balanced sharing of the spoils of increased economic production, with corporations taking on average 13.9 percent and workers getting 9.9 percent. And most of the labor compensation in this recovery was due to increased employer health-care costs and required pension liability payments, so workers' net buying power has actually diminished.[11]

Some have argued that the unemployment rates of 2003 and 2004 were historically low and do not justify the level of anxiety that workers are experiencing. They say that worker anxiety is manufactured by the media and is a result of unrealistically heightened expectations created during the boom years of the late 1990s. However, net job creation is a better measure of the labor market than are unemployment rates. Unemployment rates miss the large numbers of workers who drop out of the unemployment statistics because they get discouraged and cease looking for work, because of the long duration of their unemployment, and because some have accepted substandard employment out of desperation (the so-called underemployed). For instance, many white-collar professionals have become independent consultants, but they may not bring in steady business. Others have been given permanent part-time status so their employers can avoid paying health care and other benefits. So, recent measures of unemployment rates have systematically underestimated the actual softness of the labor market. It is also important to look at the effects of this softness on individual occupations; labor markets in fields like IT are being disproportionately depressed by offshore outsourcing.

The GDP growth/jobs creation mystery has been the subject of much discussion in economic circles. Some have argued that the GDP data may be overstated, thus better explaining the sluggish job creation, because it doesn't properly account for outsourcing. This idea was addressed by the government's Bureau of Economic Analysis, which hasn't been able to support or refute the notion.[12]

Looking to the future, some proponents, like Global Insight, the economic consulting firm hired by IT industry lobbyists, have argued that offshore outsourcing will actually create a net increase in the number of jobs.[13] Chief Financial Officers—key corporate decision makers when it comes to hiring—believe just the opposite: that offshoring will have a net negative impact on the number of jobs in the United States.[14] Suffice it to say, no one truly knows what the net impact on the number of jobs will be. While the pundits debate the causes and speculate about the future, millions of Americans continue to search for decent employment.

The Impacts on Types of Occupations and Education

Offshore outsourcing has already had a devastating impact on certain occupations and regions. In terms of occupations, information technology (IT) was the first professional-services sector targeted by offshore outsourcing and has been the hardest hit to date. IT is also the area with the longest experience in outsourcing. However, as noted earlier, there are signs that offshore outsourcing is starting to affect other sectors, including accounting, financial analysis, insurance processing, and various types of call centers.

Even occupations that one would think should be immune from offshore outsourcing are moving abroad. For instance, Reuters news service has moved some business reporting and editorial functions overseas. In fact, just about any work involving computers has been moving overseas. More alarming is the observation that top professional service positions, and not just the "grunt work" jobs, have been shifted offshore. These include jobs in architectural design, engineering, consulting, and medical services, such as radiology.

Software Programmers and Engineers Receive Scant Assistance

As the first technology jobs have been moved offshore, there have been significant ripples already felt throughout the software and engineering community. Software programmers and engineers are trying to identify which types of jobs might be safe from offshoring so that they can specialize in them. Others are dropping out of the professions altogether and searching for alternative careers. Still others are organizing themselves into unions to protect their professions from offshore competition. It remains to be seen whether these efforts will be successful.

Many software programmers have been denied the government assistance that other workers are able to get when their jobs are lost because of international trade. In the 1960s, Congress established the Trade Adjustment Assistance program to offer job training and extended unemployment assistance to workers adversely impacted by trade agreements. But Jim Fusco, a software programmer, was denied help from the program because the Labor Department does not consider software a "product," an eligibility requirement established by law.

This limitation has not been lost on certain lawmakers, however. In 2002, Senate Democrats proposed to expand the TAA eligibility to cover more service workers, including software programmers, but those efforts were killed by House Republicans, who argued that the program was already too costly.[15] A similar bill to extend TAA benefits to service sectors was introduced in 2004, but it died because there was no way to pay for the program, given the rising federal deficit. Even for those who have received TAA help in retraining, many workers are still struggling to find jobs in a poor labor market. Gordon Miller went back to school for a second MBA after his engineering job was exported by HP to Singapore in 2001. But he hasn't been able to find a job, and says, "If we don't have the higher-level jobs to retrain to, then the retraining is not effective." And many displaced workers who *are* qualified to receive TAA assistance are denied because of a lack of funds.[16]

Education No Longer Serves Its Students

In occupations that have been impacted the most, educators are anxious to examine how globalization and offshore outsourcing will affect the job

prospects for the students they teach. Education, like other areas, has been sideswiped by changes in technology.[17] The rise of distance education providers, like Jones International and the University of Phoenix as well as more established institutions such as the University of Maryland, have ratcheted up an already accelerating international competition for students. The development of Web-based course instruction and the possibilities for video teleconferencing are reducing the strong historical advantages that U.S. institutions and trainers had in attracting the best students from around the world.

The U.S. reaction to this crisis in education has been tepid on a national level. The U.S. system of higher education suffers from a Byzantine set of rules on accreditation that vary by state and were designed to lower the value of foreign credentials in the U.S. job market. These rules are rapidly becoming outdated, as the rest of the world moves toward clearer standards, such as is the case for the European Union. Moreover, U.S. institutions are increasingly opening branches abroad. The United States seems to lack a clear strategy for adapting to these and related changes in higher education.

Indeed, globalization has become the hot topic among engineering deans and department heads at colleges across the country.[18] Enrollments and even applications for enrollment have dropped precipitously in electrical engineering and computer science, the two technology disciplines that have been among the first to move overseas. Engineering educators in the United States are considering changes to the curricula to ensure that their graduates are employable. Their ideas include adding courses that emphasize teamwork, including so-called soft skills such as management and leadership, and teaching technical skills that cannot be easily compartmentalized and outsourced.

And engineering is not alone. Enrollments in computer science are down 20 percent nationwide, while enrollments in management information systems departments within business schools are down even move. And some individuals who have just graduated with degrees in computer science feel betrayed. Phuc Ly, a recent graduate of UCLA, thinks he wasted his time studying computer science and is headed to Japan to teach English because of a poor job market for his knowledge.[19]

So, as engineering and computer science educators grapple with the

realities of offshoring and offshore outsourcing, it is less clear what educators in other at-risk fields are doing. Universities are often the slowest institutions to change, so it is no surprise that faculties have not reacted to the trends. Unfortunately, because companies are so reluctant to reveal which jobs are being sent offshore and which ones are staying, educators are left to speculate about what skills they should be teaching.

What Will Be the New and Better Occupations?

Most economists agree that because of increased offshoring, the United States will have a different set of occupations. That means that certain occupations will disappear altogether and others will change significantly. Unfortunately, the best that these economists, including Alan Greenspan, can tell us is that they hope the new mix of jobs will be better than the old and will require more education and higher skills. The picture they paint is of simple, low-level work moving overseas and more sophisticated and interesting work available at home.

As *Washington Post* columnist Steve Pearlstein points out, if corporations actually were planning for this shift, then you would expect them to be investing heavily in the skills development of their U.S. workforce as they off-loaded their lower-level work. But, in the words of George Mason University President Alan Merten: "For the most part, companies are now unwilling to make serious, long-term investment in their employees."[20] This view has been supported repeatedly by corporate executives that we've met who are happy if their employees are training as long as it's on their own time and dime. They say that the most important criterion in hiring is finding someone who can "hit the ground running," who doesn't need any training and can contribute to the bottom line from day one.

Recent trade data don't support the notion that the United States will maintain its high-technology jobs. In the second half of 2003, for the first time ever the United States ran a trade deficit in its high-technology products, which calls into question the premise that U.S. workers will just move on to the next big thing.[21] In fact, in its latest employment projections, the U.S. Bureau of Labor Statistics cites offshoring as one of the reasons IT occupations will grow much slower than expected just two years ago. While the bureau does not specify how much of a downward factor offshoring is on the projections, you can expect that its negative effects will continue to grow.

As shown in Tables 6-2 and 6-3, the jobs that will be created in lieu of those IT jobs are generally much lower paying positions, and only three of the top ten are technology-related positions (Table 6-2), compared to eight of the top ten just two years ago (Table 6-3). Only five of the ten fastest-growing occupations pay better than the average occupation, as opposed to eight of the ten in the prior prediction. Most of the fast-growing jobs also share another characteristic: They generally require face-to-face interactions that are difficult to offshore. In the latest released projections, the BLS believes that almost 1 million fewer IT jobs will be created over the next ten years. Figure 6-3 shows the drop in projections.

Table 6-2. Ten fastest-growing occupations, 2002–2012.

Rank	Occupation	Employment		Change		Median Pay
		2002	2012	Number	Percent	
1	Medical assistants	365	579	215	59	$24,169
2	Network systems and data communications analysts	186	292	106	57	**$59,113**
3	Physician assistants	63	94	31	49	**$65,665**
4	Social and human service assistants	305	454	149	49	$23,857
5	Home health aides	580	859	279	48	$18,241
6	Medical records and health information technicians	147	216	69	47	$24,523
7	Physical therapist aides	37	54	17	46	$20,966
8	Computer software engineers, applications	394	573	179	46	**$72,529**
9	Computer software engineers, systems software	281	409	128	45	**$76,232**
10	Physical therapist assistants	50	73	22	45	**$36,608**

Notes: Better-than-average pay occupations shown in boldface. The median pay for all occupations was $28,400.

Source: Bureau of Labor Statistics (2004).

Table 6-3. Ten fastest-growing occupations, 2000–2010.

Rank	Occupation	Employment		Change		Median Pay
		2000	2010	Number	Percent	
1	Computer software engineers, applications	380	760	380	100	**$72,530**
2	Computer support specialists	506	996	490	97	**$39,437**
3	Computer software engineers, systems software	317	601	284	90	**$76,232**
4	Network and computer systems administrators	229	416	187	82	**$56,056**
5	Network systems and data communications analysts	119	211	92	77	**$59,114**
6	Desktop publishers	38	63	25	67	**$31,595**
7	Database administrators	106	176	70	66	**$58,198**
8	Personal and home care aides	414	672	258	62	$16,453
9	Computer systems analysts	431	689	258	60	**$64,168**
10	Medical assistants	329	516	187	57	$24,170

Notes: Better-than-average pay occupations shown in boldface. The median pay for all occupations was $28,400.

Source: Bureau of Labor Statistics (2004).

So, the new mix of occupations that created after the offshoring boom are not guaranteed to be better. Computer software engineers have a median wage of about $70,000 per year, and computer support specialists are paid about $40,000 per year. These are obviously jobs that pay more than the average job in America. When those jobs are gone, will we be able to easily create new ones that provide similar opportunities for workers? Keep in mind that the BLS formulated its projections before the large wave of offshore outsourcing occurred, so it is likely the projections highly underestimate the number of jobs that can easily be shipped overseas.

Figure 6-3. Computer occupation growth diminishes.

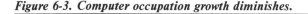

Decrease in # of jobs forecasted by BLS 2002–2012 projections vs. 2000–2010.

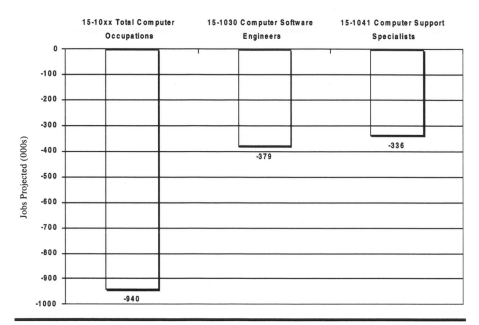

Source: Bureau of Labor Statistics (2002 and 2003).

Our primary institution for providing retraining services to laid-off workers is the community college system. These institutions develop customized courses to train workers for whatever jobs might be in demand. In the past, displaced manufacturing workers retrained as computer professionals. In the last couple of years, community colleges have been emphasizing nursing and other health-related professions, but who knows what the need will be in the future? The community colleges have been effective in providing practical training for their students for entry-level positions. It seems unlikely, however, that the current education infrastructure will be able to support retraining for the types of jobs that experienced workers with master's degrees in computer science will want. A highly skilled technical professional whose job is outsourced may scratch by as a cab driver, or even prosper as a real estate agent, but both the individual and the country suffer from the lost opportunity to utilize those high-tech skills.

Some Financial Services Jobs Are Threatened

As discussed in Chapter 4, financial services jobs are also vulnerable to off-shore outsourcing. Tax preparation appears to be the first accounting tasks that will be moving offshore. The Big Four public accounting firms, which service the vast majority of U.S. publicly traded companies, already have a global footprint and are well poised to expand the amount of offshoring they do and increase their overseas workforce. A number of accounting out-sourcing firms, such as Outsource Partners International (OPI), SurePrep, Mphasis, CCH, and Xpitax, are already offering tax preparation and are tar-geting other accounting functions such as financial reporting, accounts receivable, accounts payable, billing, collections, travel expenses, and pay-roll. OPI will process an estimated 10,000 tax returns in 2004.[22] Because they certify the results of publicly traded firms, accountants play an impor-tant public role in the regulated financial markets of Wall Street. Indeed, the public depends heavily on their integrity, which becomes all too appar-ent when it fails, as in the case of Enron.

In response to increases in accounting outsourcing (domestic and off-shore), the American Institute of Certified Professional Accountants (AICPA), the professional society that oversees the profession, is devising new rules for its members to follow. It proposes that the accounting firm with direct contact with the customer has a responsibility for the integrity and quality of the work done, maintaining the confidentiality of client infor-mation, and notifying the client about outsourcing. Accountants currently have to disclose that work is being sent offshore only if their clients ask.[23] However, accountants have not been as adversely hit by offshore outsourc-ing as have IT workers, because any overseas losses are offset by increased labor demand stateside. New regulations like the Sarbanes-Oxley Act, passed after the Enron scandal and other accounting scandals, have forced so many companies to rework the way they report their financial statements that accountants are in high demand.

The Threats to U.S. Technological Capacity

While the country may indeed get back to full employment as the off-shoring advocates argue, it is not clear what types of jobs will exist and whether they will pay the same wages as the jobs that have been exported.

In fact, there are strong reasons to think that they will not. As Craig R. Barrett, CEO of Intel, has put it: "The U.S. no longer has a lock on high-tech, white-collar jobs."[24]

As you know, U.S. manufacturing has also been hit hard by offshore outsourcing. What you may not know is that this development has had important and serious consequences for American engineers, the people responsible for technological innovation, economic growth, and national security. Some people wonder whether manufacturing matters very much, since it accounts for only about 14 percent of the Gross Domestic Product. However, from a technological innovation point of view, manufacturing matters greatly. Nearly 41 percent of American engineers work in the manufacturing sector. The manufacturing sector also accounts for 62 percent of all research and development (R&D) and 90 percent of all patents in the United States. The prevailing management approach is to locate R&D as close to manufacturing production as possible. As manufacturing moves overseas, it is inevitable that both engineering work and R&D will follow.

America's economic competitiveness and national security are increasingly dependent on the superiority of our technology and technical know-how. Recognizing this fact, another argument that offshoring advocates make is that the jobs that will be created in the United States in the future will require even higher skills and pay even better wages than those that have been exported. There is a widespread belief—almost a blind faith—that as communications, semiconductor manufacturing, electronics, and other key technological capabilities are off-loaded to other countries, the United States will just move on to the next field, to the next "big thing."

Many observers, including government officials, argue that the next hot industry is going to be nanotechnology, and that nanotechnology is going to generate enormous economic benefits and create many new jobs. At this point, we can only speculate on the impact that nanotechnology will have on the economy and jobs, and hope that it will be as significant as some predict. However, the United States cannot be complacent, assuming that its past supremacy in technology development will continue. While there is a consensus that the most recent growth in wages and the economy was driven by technology—by technological innovation (i.e., being able to do new and innovative things because of technological advances)—the current exporting of jobs could well kill the seeds of future innovation.

Venture capital, the lifeblood of risky technology-rich start-up companies and of our future Googles and Yahoos, is also finding its way overseas. In 2004, most Silicon Valley venture firms shrank their funding. The few exceptions were firms that focused on India as an investment platform, where some venture firms are delivering 30 percent returns, while most U.S.-based funds are actually in the red.[25]

Even an established business like Boeing is having Japanese companies supply critical composite materials for the wings of its next generation of airplane, the 7E7 Dreamliner. Boeing insists that this makes good financial sense, and they are not concerned about loss of technology and unwittingly creating future competitors.[26] The future course of technological innovation is always uncertain, and many companies have made major blunders in outsourcing technology that they deemed unimportant.

The Brain Drain in Reverse

As a nation, the United States has benefited enormously from the so-called brain drain experienced by other countries. The best and brightest from all over the world have been attracted to America and the opportunities it affords them. Offshore outsourcing seems to have already changed that attractiveness for such people. The opportunities offered in their home countries are now much more appealing than they once were.

Moreover, offshore outsourcing is beginning to have a major effect on our own production of talent. As described earlier, the exporting of jobs is chilling the software profession. Job insecurity is extremely high, so many of our nation's brightest college students are shying away from studying technology disciplines. America's technology workers have been following the news of offshoring on a daily basis. They are no longer recommending it as a profession to their children, nephews and nieces, and other young people who are entering college. Enrollments in technology-related disciplines are down already, and all signs point to less interest in science and engineering by the best students of the future generation.

There are, furthermore, the spillover benefits from these industries and these jobs, and these benefits may no longer be assured. Future technology entrepreneurs are not born, they are developed. There are countless stories of technologists who learned the ropes while working for an estab-

lished technology company, only to head off later and begin their own successful companies. Intel got its start out of Fairchild Semiconductor. Ross Perot worked for IBM before starting EDS. The German software maker SAP was begun when its founders left IBM in Germany. Thomas Siebel, founder of Siebel Systems, once worked for Oracle. And vMoksha, a leading Indian IT firm, was founded by Pawan Kumar, who had worked for IBM Global Services in India. Many of the entrepreneurs who will start the technology companies of the future will get their feet wet in today's technology companies. It should be no surprise that if fewer technology workers are employed in the United States, there will be fewer technology entrepreneurs here in the future.

Further Concerns

There are other, less visible impacts that offshore outsourcing will have on innovation in America, such as who gets to set the standards for the next generation of technologies. Setting the technical standards is an increasingly complex process and is critical for technology business worldwide. The Chinese government is setting its own software standards for its next generation of wireless computers, mobile phones, and DVD players. Standards often have an impact on which companies succeed and the location of production.

Additionally, technology entrepreneurs have the right to own and reap the benefits of their hard work and innovative ideas. But, as has been the case with copyright infringement via music downloading and pharmaceutical copying, efforts to collect these benefits will increasingly fail as overseas companies steal the technology without granting compensation. The U.S. government has been trying to obtain multilateral and bilateral remedies through the WTO Trade Related Intellectual Property System and through free trade agreements signed with individual countries. But the problem will not be solved through international treaties alone; there needs to be corresponding implementation and enforcement of those rights. The history of Japan's technological development, whereby they copied much of our technology including electronics, is a lesson: As a way of gaining economic advantage, today's developing nations will feel less than motivated to enforce intellectual property laws. As more advanced technology is devel-

oped in developing countries, America will face new competitors who capitalize on weak intellectual property laws.

National Security Can't Be Outsourced

In this period of global terrorism, Americans are especially concerned about their security. Part of our national security policy for more than the past half-century has been to maintain a strong science and engineering workforce in the United States, thereby reducing economic vulnerability and producing leading-edge military technology at home. Indeed, we are secure in part because we have relied on our technological superiority. Our troops are the best trained, and many of our key industries are centered on defense. These industries include aerospace, information technology, materials sciences, and biochemistry. We have had the leading research universities in the world, and they have worked with our private and public sectors to lead the way in technological innovation.

But once our technological efforts are lost to foreign competitors, it will be difficult to maintain our edge. As more work moves offshore, the Defense Department and Department of Homeland Security will have to increasingly rely on providers of technology based in foreign countries that have no interest in helping the United States.

In the early 1990s, the U.S. military realized that it could no longer invent and develop all of the technology that it needed. It turned to the commercial sector for its new technologies—something called commercial off-the-shelf technologies (COTS). The private sector became a major bidder and provider of defense goods and services. But with increased offshore outsourcing, will the companies that the Defense Department relies on move their operations to other countries—perhaps to hostile nations? How will this affect our national interests? Our access to the technology? As a *Federal Computer Weekly* article put it: "Offshoring may make economic sense for the companies, but the security ramifications are starting to raise red flags for Congress, the Pentagon, and some vendors."[27] And according to the Government Accountability Office (GAO) the Defense Department is not prepared to handle the problems: "DOD acquisition and software security policies do not fully address the risk of using foreign suppliers to develop weapon system software."[28]

In an odd twist, government procurement rules may actually favor companies that use offshore labor, even if the costs are the same. Small companies, with minority or woman ownership, can apply to the federal government for certification as a "small disadvantaged business," known in procurement circles as 8(a) status; companies with 8(a) status then have preference in procurement decisions. Some 8(a) certified companies have an offshore business model and thus may be receiving preferential treatment over domestic companies. Is it in the best interests of national security to give *preferential* treatment to companies staffed with offshore labor?

Conclusion

Mainstream economists have focused on a single measure—economic efficiency—to explain why they believe that outsourcing is good for the United States. Understanding the economic efficiency argument is quite simple: Companies can hire highly skilled foreign workers at a fraction of the cost of U.S. workers. Large corporations are embracing offshore outsourcing because their company executives (the decision makers) stand to gain substantially by being responsive to their primary mission, improving shareholder value.

Unfortunately, this simplistic model of the economy ignores the real, devastating effects of offshore outsourcing. The economists assume that the U.S. workers who are displaced will quickly find better and more interesting jobs. Of course, we know instead that many workers will end up in lower-paying jobs or may not find work at all. Some occupations will disappear from the United States altogether, forcing those workers to find new careers. Additionally, educators will have to design new curricula so they can teach the skills that are not easily sent overseas. And offshore outsourcing negatively impacts technological innovation, the lifeblood of future economic growth in the United States. If we export our best software and engineering jobs, America will miss the next generation of innovations in nanotechnology, electronics, and biotechnology. Lastly, offshore outsourcing threatens America's technological leadership and national security. As our military becomes more dependent on technologies developed overseas, we incur significantly higher homeland security risks.

In sum, offshore outsourcing will have both positive and negative ram-

ifications for the United States, but the net effect is unknowable at this point. We do know that the positive and negative effects are not uniformly distributed: there will be both winners and losers as the phenomenon plays out. In the next chapter, we examine offshore outsourcing's impact on the relationship between workers and companies.

Notes

1. Ralph E. Gomory and William J. Baumol, *Global Trade and Conflicting National Interests* (Cambridge, MA: The MIT Press, 2000).

2. Richard McCormack, "David vs. Goliath: A Small Mfg. Company Owner Is So Concerned About Free Trade He's Running for Congress," *Manufacturing & Technology News.* 11, no. 16 (September 1, 2004).

3. Terry Pristin, "Overseas Job Shift Affects Office Market," *New York Times* (October 8, 2003).

4. Ray A. Smith and Alex Frangos, "When U.S. Jobs Go Abroad: Outsourcing Likely to Slow Office Rebound," *Wall Street Journal* (June 2, 2004), p. B4.

5. William M. Bulkeley, "IBM Now Plans Fewer Layoffs from Offshoring," *Wall Street Journal* (July 29, 2004); and S. Srinivasan, "Siemens to Move Most Software Jobs to Asia, Eastern Europe," Associated Press (February 16, 2004).

6. Paul McDougall, "EDS's Jordan: We Need Offshore Labor," *Information Week* (August 30, 2004).

7. Barbara Hagenbaugh and Barbara Hansen, "Low-wage Jobs Rise at Faster Pace," *USA Today* (June 29, 2004).

8. Alwyn Scott, "The Future of U.S. Workers: Nobel Laureate Looks at Jobless Recovery," *Knight Tribune Review* (January 7, 2004).

9. David R. Francis, "Job Security Becomes Job One at Home: As Layoffs Continue, Unemployment Is Expected to Climb Again This Week," *Christian Science Monitor* (April 2, 2003).

10. "American Workers Perceive Offshore Outsourcing as Threat to Economy, Not Themselves," press release, Hudson Highland Group (June 14, 2004).

11. Josh Bivens, "When Do Workers Get Their Share?" *Snapshot*, Economic Policy Institute (May 27, 2004).

12. Bureau of Economic Analysis, "Q&A's on Gross Domestic Product and

Outsourcing," www.bea.gov/bea/dn/GDP_outsourcing.pdf (August 3, 2004).

13. "ITAA/Global Insight Study Finds IT Outsourcing Results in Net U.S. Job Growth," press release, Global Insight, Inc. (March 30, 2004).

14. Don Durfee and Kate O'Sullivan, "Offshoring by the Numbers," *CFO Magazine* (June 2004).

15. Peter Loftus, "Laid-off Tech Workers Denied Govt. Job-Training Benefits," *Dow Jones News Service* (August 29, 2003).

16. Brent Hunsberger, "Dead Ends in a Downturn: Federal Efforts to Prepare Laid-off Workers for New Careers Help Only a Fraction of Those Who Qualify," *The Oregonian* (March 21, 2004).

17. See Anil Hira, "The Brave New World of International Education," *The World Economy* 26, no.6 (June 2003), pp. 911–931.

18. Ken Jenkins and Stephen Goodnick, "Globalization and Workforce Training in Electrical and Computer Engineering Education," *The Interface*, IEEE Education Society (August 2004).

19. Alex Pham, "Tech Bust Zaps Interest in Computer Careers," *Los Angeles Times* (July 20, 2004).

20. Steven Pearlstein, "Still Short of the Offshoring Ideal," *Washington Post* (March 12, 2004).

21. David R. Francis, "U.S. Runs a High-tech Trade Gap: Exports Fail to Keep Pace with Imports, Stirring Concern About a Key Fount of Jobs," *Christian Science Monitor* (June 2, 2004).

22. Carly Lombardo, "An Offshore Thing: Firms Are Looking to Outsource Other Functions Beyond Tax," *Accounting Technology* (November 2003).

23. Mark Horvit, "Not All Companies Secure Personal Data," *Fort Worth Star-Telegram* (June 25, 2004).

24. Steve Lohr, "Many New Causes for Old Problem of Jobs Lost Abroad," *New York Times* (February 15, 2004).

25. Matt Marshall, "VC Insider: Funding for Tech that Sees Through Clothes," *San Jose Mercury News* (August 10, 2004).

26. Imran Vittachi, "Boeing Outsourcing Gives Wing to Concerns," *Chicago Tribune* (December 21, 2003).

27. Matthew French, "The Outsourcing Hole," *Federal Computer Weekly* (July 19, 2004).

28. Government Accountability Office, "Defense Acquisitions: Knowledge of Software Suppliers Needed to Manage Risks," Report number: GAO-04-678, Government Printing Office (May 2004).

CHAPTER 7

The Human Face of Outsourcing: The Impact on Individual Workers and Communities

So far we have defined and documented the extent of offshore outsourcing and have suggested why companies are beginning to abandon their employees. We have examined the big picture—the overall effects of offshore outsourcing on the U.S. economy. Now let's zero in on the devastating consequences of this outsourcing for workers themselves and their communities.

The policy debate should never lose sight of the very real impact of offshore outsourcing on the prospects of American families and on the lack of guidance on how to minimize that negative effect. It is simply astonishing that anyone would buy the argument that shipping the country's best-paying and most technologically advanced jobs overseas without any plan for replenishment is always a good thing and has little or no negative ramifications. But this is precisely what the outsourcing advocates would like you to believe.

The offshore outsourcing of white-collar jobs is a fundamental shift in our economic structure that will have major impacts on many different people and groups. The impacts will be both positive and negative. But it is extremely important to note that those positive and negative effects are not evenly distributed—there are winners and losers in any economic change. Also, as we will see later in the book, there are few, if any, effective mecha-

nisms to help the losers. While the long-run outcomes of any major economic change are unclear, this situation should not proscribe us from acting to shape and react to ongoing changes. We can begin a more serious policy dialogue by examining those impacts that offshore outsourcing has already had.

The Immediate Impact on American Workers

Many economists grudgingly agree that there will be two effects of moving work overseas: displacement of U.S. workers and a change in the makeup of the U.S. workforce. The first effect is clearly negative, but many economists argue that the U.S. track record for the reemployment of workers is spectacular. They argue that workers will quickly find new jobs at the same or better wages. All it takes is some quick retraining.

The fact of the matter is that retraining programs, whether provided as part of the welfare system or as trade adjustment assistance, have never really proved their effectiveness in the United States. Instead, our policy has been to allow the unemployed coal miner or steel worker to somehow find his own way to a job, with few prospects that the replacement job will provide anywhere near the same wage.

There are many other reasons to doubt this particular leap of faith. In recent years, the U.S. economy has destroyed more jobs than it has created, so the rosy scenario that economists have portrayed has not happened. It is not clear when new jobs will begin to be created, but most economists have faith that history will repeat itself and the United States will start creating jobs again.

Others claim that displaced U.S. workers are now "freed" from tedious work and can engage in more interesting things such as "project management," which will stay onshore. They say colleges should focus on that training. But this thinking is flawed, for two reasons. First, the assumption that project management will remain onshore because it should be close to the customer is faulty when there is also the need to locate project management activities offshore, close to where the work is being done. Second, freshly minted graduates may not be able to leap right into managing a project without ever having experience working on projects. Just as a production plant supervisor must understand all the work being done on

the factory floor, technology managers are nurtured through a natural maturation process that includes getting their hands dirty as a technologist. Looking to the future, U.S. science and engineering graduates, for example, are unlikely to get that critical project experience, which will no longer be available in the United States.

Furthermore, while those Americans are out of work, they are no longer paying income taxes and are potentially drawing unemployment insurance and using other social services that help displaced workers. Once again, the offshoring advocates do not include in their calculations the costs of lost tax revenue and of greater demand for social programs. Moreover, it is simply ridiculous to think that we can have a national economy of 130 million managers.

Downward Wage Pressure

The impact of offshore outsourcing on a particular company's jobs should depend on the company's situation. For example, if a company is growing, U.S. workers may be redeployed within the company to assume new tasks, but if it's not growing, then those workers will likely be laid off. Gartner, a research firm, predicts that only 40 percent of the half-million IT workers displaced by offshoring will be redeployed within the same company.[1] But even if economists are right and the American economy will ultimately create new jobs, they do not consider the downward wage pressure that cheap labor from overseas will put on those new jobs (will the new jobs really be at the same wages as the old ones were?) and in what occupations the new jobs will be available.

Harris Miller, president of the Information Technology Association of America and the technology industry's leading lobbyist, put it very bluntly: "Americans must face the 'hard truth' that offshore companies not only offer information technology services for a fraction of the cost, [but they can] compete for increasingly more sophisticated and complex IT work. . . . The silver lining of this wage pressure is that a more competitive payroll picture may undercut [U.S. employers'] need to move jobs offshore."[2] In other words, some offshoring advocates actually argue that downward wage pressure is a good thing! The question is, good for whom? While we don't know what the long-term effects of this downward wage pressure will be, we do

know that the overall deterioration in wages is real and could be substantial.

An article in *BusinessWeek* relates the story of Jon Carson, an entrepreneur who needed to find some senior programmers for a new venture. He knew that programmers with that kind of experience commanded $80,000 salaries in the Boston area. He was offered the opportunity to get the work done in India at a net cost of $40,000 per programmer when all of the additional costs of coordination and brokering were included. Carson was willing to pay a slight premium to have the work done close by. To test the waters, he decided to place a job ad in the *Boston Globe* for the programmers with a salary offer of $45,000. The response to the ad shocked him. He was flooded with résumés from high-quality American programmers, all willing to work for $45,000—less than the average starting salary of a fresh bachelor's degree computer science graduate![3] This story is replicated thousands of times over as skilled high-tech workers find themselves accepting ridiculously low salaries because they now compete in a flooded labor market. Such anecdotes are supported by a study from an IT workforce research company, Foote Partners LLC, which determined that offshoring had eroded IT salaries by 8–23 percent for various specialties.[4]

The "Wal-Mart effect" describes the creation of big-box stores that push out smaller, more labor-intensive retailers and insist on lower wages and benefits for workers, as they push out possibilities for unionization. The Wal-Mart effect is currently putting America's working class in jeopardy in the retail sector, and seems to be ready to spread throughout the U.S. services economy. Surely American consumers are willing to pay a few extra pennies for each product to ensure that they and their neighbors can have decent working conditions, steady employment, and a manageable standard of living.

Companies also continue to cut benefits in a race to the bottom, which they claim is driven by global competition. Even the pension system in America is at a point of bankruptcy, as very few new companies are willing to offer pensions anymore and some major older companies are threatening to stop paying into their pension plans. If the economy has become so much more efficient, why are so many workers anxious about their futures?

American workers now have to deal with additional risk of layoffs throughout their careers, a factor that should increase their compensation,

often called a risk "premium." That is, the higher the risk you are willing to take, the higher the reward will be, which supports basic economic logic. However, in the current climate, workers are being asked to take on additional risk, while there is no noticeable jump in compensation; in fact, the opposite is happening. Can workers even think of employment as a career anymore? And if not, is this necessarily good for the economy? There is enormous overhead added to the system when people are constantly losing their jobs. *Flexible labor markets*, the euphemism that economists like to use, come at a very high cost.

It doesn't take an economics degree to realize that workers are also consumers, and that companies depend on consumers to buy their products and services. Without stable, high-wage employment, consumers will no longer be able to spend or borrow, thus returning the favor to those companies that are now consciously undermining our standard of living.

The Long-Run Impact on American Workers

The discussion about offshore outsourcing is overly focused on the macroeconomic picture and misses what really happens when a company destroys someone's livelihood. Even if the worker finds a new job, the broad view says nothing about how long it will take, how he makes up for the lost wages while looking, and the quality of the new job. But data on displaced workers are collected every other year by the Bureau of Labor Statistics (BLS). The bureau takes a snapshot of the employment status of workers who are displaced because their plants are closed, moved, or their position was eliminated. The data show that the results haven't been good in the early part of the twenty-first century, corresponding to the accelerating pace of offshore outsourcing.

From the beginning of 2001 to the end of 2003, more than 5.3 million workers who had held their jobs for at least three years were displaced (for all reasons, not just outsourcing). In January 2004, only 65 percent had found full- or part-time work, 20 percent were unemployed, and 15 percent had dropped out of the labor force altogether. Of those who were lucky enough to find full-time work, more than half—57 percent—earned less than their prior job; and of those, a third said that their pay was cut by at least 20 percent.[5] High-level white-collar workers—categorized as manage-

ment, professional, and related—fared only slightly better, with 67 percent being reemployed; and lower-level white-collar workers—categorized as office and administrative support occupations—fared worse, with 60 percent being reemployed.[6]

In fact, the evidence for displaced manufacturing workers over longer periods of time, 1979 to 1999, is similar. Approximately 65 percent of manufacturing workers who were displaced were reemployed at the time the BLS conducted its survey. That means that more than one in three were not! For those lucky enough to find positions, 60 percent experienced salary drops of 15 percent or more. And services workers who were reemployed had larger earnings losses than the workers with manufacturing jobs. Moreover, retraining doesn't seem to have much positive effect for displaced workers.[7] No matter how one spins it, the record for reemployment is abysmal: 35 percent were not reemployed, and another 40 percent earned significantly lower salaries.

The Impact on Individuals

No one can put numbers on the amount of personal suffering and anxiety that offshore outsourcing causes U.S. workers, either through job loss or the threat of job loss. As one worker put it succinctly, "I'm not a statistic." Or as Jeraldean Evans, a fifty-eight-year-old veteran programmer from Oakland, California, says about having to train her foreign replacement: "My value as a human being was taken away from me."[8] Even those who have not been displaced are terrified. One worker described offshore outsourcing as a threatening monster and told us that many engineers in Minnesota are "frightened of this thing [outsourcing] which seems to have only one outcome: All engineering jobs will go overseas or salaries will take a significant dip."

Economists could attempt to estimate the lost wages and benefits from unemployment and reemployment at lower salaries, but there is no way that they can calculate the costs extracted from individuals, their families, and their social networks. We have personally heard from hundreds of workers who have been pummeled by the outsourcing wave. Many of them have become embittered, despondent, and desperate as they cope with the prospect of losing their livelihood and, in some cases, their homes and marriages.

As you read the stories in this section, think about how someone you know has been hurt by a layoff. It is critical to put a human face on the story of offshore outsourcing because it is, in the end, a human story. Many of those who are suffering try to take personal action. They have their own Web sites, chat rooms, and e-mail lists that discuss the issue and plan ways to get policymakers to act. However, countless others are afraid to discuss their situation publicly, for fear of being blackballed by employers—a particularly treacherous position to be put in, especially during a soft labor market.

They Train Their Replacements

Many companies have forced their employees into the painful position of training their own replacements. Some of these situations have been well publicized, but most people are too reluctant to speak out, for fear of retribution from the companies. Bonny Berger, a twenty-one-year veteran AT&T computer programmer, had her job outsourced to IBM in 1999. Shortly thereafter, as a new employee of IBM, she was asked to train her replacement when the work was transferred to Canada. She was lucky enough to find other tasks within the company, but even that work was soon outsourced offshore, and she was asked to train her Indian replacement. By March 2002, after another round of finding work in the company and training another Canadian replacement, IBM laid her off.[9]

Mike Emmons and Pat Fluno worked as computer programmers for Siemens ICN, a major German multinational, in Orlando, Florida. They and twenty of their coworkers were told that their jobs were going to be outsourced to Tata Consultancy Services, an IT company in India. Emmons and his colleagues were going to be let go. In order to get their severance package, however, they would have to train their foreign replacements, who were here on L-1 visas and were being paid one-third the salaries Emmons, Fluno, and their colleagues earned. Emmons has two children, including one who requires special medical attention, and he has experienced firsthand the consequences from the loss of his job. He has since been reemployed with the State of Florida at a 60 percent cut in salary, but he is fortunate enough to have health-care coverage for himself and his children.[10]

The issue made Emmons mad as hell, and he began a grassroots campaign against this kind of behavior. He launched a short-lived campaign for Congress against U.S. Representative John Mica (Republican, from Florida), who he felt had betrayed him and the other Siemens employees.[11] Emmons operates a Web site, www.outsourcecongress.org. Former coworker Pat Fluno, a single mother, testified before Congress, describing how humiliating it was to train her replacement at Siemens.

In a story reminiscent of workers training their replacements, companies are even being forced to train their overseas competitors. After one of our appearances on a talk-radio show in Hartford, Connecticut, a software programmer told about her company's work with an insurance industry client. The client liked the work that her company was doing but wanted to cut costs, and so he asked her firm to outsource some of the work to an Indian firm as one of the conditions of the contract. After they agreed to the contractual terms and successfully delivered the product, the Indian firm learned enough to take over all future work, and her company was cut out of the arrangement.

Displaced Workers Struggle to Carry On

Time magazine reported the story of Vince Kosmac, from Orlando, Florida, who has twice experienced the deleterious effects of offshore outsourcing. He was hit by it the first time back in the early 1980s, when he was a trucker delivering steel to plants. At that time, he got training in computer science, which served him well until 2002, when his job was outsourced to a company overseas. Now forty-seven, he has not been able to find good work. He is disturbed that people so nonchalantly recommend that he retrain yet again, while supporting his family, which includes a child with cerebral palsy.[12]

Vince's story also highlights the practical problems that arise when individuals are out of work for an extended period of time. Fast-moving technology passes them by, and without support for retraining, they are likely to be forced to pursue other, low-paying professions. And when both spouses are working in fields that are susceptible to offshore outsourcing, families are particularly vulnerable. Forty-seven-year-old Lisa Pineau, of Plano, Texas, lost her job as a computer programmer in November 2002 to

nearshoring in Canada, and she is fearful that her husband, manager of an IT department in a bank, may be next—his company is outsourcing some of its technical work offshore.[13] Since being laid off as a programmer, Pineau has worked part-time doing administrative work for $10 an hour and, more recently, compiling credit reports for $15 per hour.[14]

Offshore outsourcing's effects on individuals are often indirect, exacerbating a depressed job market, which is leading an ever greater number of formerly middle-class white-collar workers into bankruptcy. Jeff Hester, a fifty-nine-year-old college-educated computer systems operator from Mountain View, California, recently filed for bankruptcy after losing his job. He now sells jewelry in a shopping mall.[15] While his job loss may not be directly attributable to outsourcing, his story points out how dependent so many people are on their regular paychecks. They can't afford to be out of work for an extended period of time. Unfortunately, for many educated workers, the only job opportunities are in retail shops at relatively low pay.

For older workers, displacement can be especially difficult, since prospective employers often shy away from them in spite of the age-discrimination laws. With increasing frequency, job losses force older workers, even former executives, into early retirement.[16] For fifty-seven- year-old senior credit administrator Arwilda Allen, the announcement came as a shock that her job and ten of her colleagues' jobs would be offshored to the Philippines. She expected that when Thomson, her employer of seventeen years, subcontracted the work to Accenture, her job would stay in Indiana and she would continue doing the same work. Instead, Accenture shipped her job overseas. The single mother of two is now contemplating early retirement. To earn extra income, she'll be renting out part of her house.[17]

The *Contra Costa Times* reported the saddest story of them all, the story of Kevin Flanagan. Flanagan was so distraught that the Bank of America laid him off after forcing him to train his foreign replacements, he committed suicide. By all accounts, the triggering event for Flanagan was his layoff. His grieving father, Tom, put it this way: "Kevin losing his job with Bank of America was the defining event in his decision to end his life. Certainly there were other issues, demons, with which he was unable to cope."[18]

It's Just the Tip of the Iceberg

These stories of individuals are examples of so many others who have been impacted by offshoring. They are a microcosm of a possible avalanche of effects that could come, and that will have a major impact on our communities. It does not take much imagination to multiply these individual circumstances by the thousands of people who have lost their jobs, with limited possibilities of finding other jobs, and also face family hardships. These are people who lost positions not through idleness or lack of effort but, rather, through specific decisions made by their employers, as well as decisions by U.S. policymakers to look the other way.

The companies are well aware of what they are doing to people. In Tampa, Capital One called in extra security and police cars before they announced they were exporting 1,100 jobs overseas.[19] This explains why the companies have tried to silence news and discourage debate about the issue—with great success so far, as discussed in Chapter 3. People are angry, and they have every right to be. They have been abandoned by the very people who are supposed to represent their interests—the politicians and companies that have profited from Americans' investment in research and development and in education.

But some individuals are beginning to fight back:

● Natasha Humphries, a former senior software engineer at Palm and a Stanford University graduate, provided dramatic testimony to the House Small Business Committee on October 20, 2003. She detailed the insidious process by which Palm slowly but surely had her unwittingly train her replacements in India, all the while assuring her that her job was not in jeopardy. She also testified that she was "discouraged [by her company] to enhance my professional skill set, either through poor direction or denied approval of coursework."[20] She is now active in a group (www.techunites.org) that aims to unionize information technology workers.

● Scott Kirwin, who lives in Wilmington, Delaware, has lost his job twice to offshore outsourcing and is under constant pressure to keep his family afloat. He became so incensed by how companies were treating their IT employees that he started the Information Technology Professional

Association of America (www.itpaa.org) to represent the interests of U.S. IT workers.

● John Pardon decided to leave his job at NCR before being displaced. Disgusted by how employers are treating IT workers, Pardon has left the IT field altogether and has turned into an activist, joining a group (RescueAmericanJobs.org) as a policy analyst. Pardon describes himself as a moderate conservative who has been alienated from the Republican Party because of the Bush Administration's favorable stance on offshore outsourcing.[21]

The Impact on Communities

The present wave of offshore outsourcing has important precedents. When the manufacturing exodus occurred in the 1980s, communities with lots of heavy industry were hurt disproportionately—cities like Pittsburgh (synonymous with steel), Cleveland, Buffalo, and Detroit. They were ignominiously dubbed the "Rust Belt," a sign of their reduced stature. For the current wave of offshore outsourcing, the impact may, in fact, be less concentrated geographically because many white-collar service jobs are distributed throughout the country.

Ironically, many of the Rust Belt communities have tried to reinvent themselves by attracting white-collar service jobs. Pittsburgh has a thriving financial services sector, and Buffalo recently outbid other cities to attract a Geico insurance office that will create up to 2,500 white-collar jobs in customer service and sales—just the kinds of jobs that offshore outsourcing advocates think are expendable. The price tag for the city and state was an astounding $100 million in tax breaks.[22] That turns out to be a whopping $40,000 per job. So, we have hundreds of thousands of jobs being offshored at the same time as cities are spending tens of millions of dollars to gain those same kinds of jobs.

Will we have something akin to a Rust Belt but for cities, such as Charlotte, North Carolina, with many financial services jobs? These cities have specialized in the types of services that are most vulnerable to offshoring. Economic development officials in San Antonio, Texas, are concerned about the implications of offshoring because of the high proportion of call centers in their city. More than 50,000 workers are employed by call

centers in San Antonio, and as a result they are trying to attract occupations and industries that are less likely to be outsourced.[23] And even communities that are able to bring in white-collar work have no guarantees that it will stay there. In 1996, Tampa, Florida, lured Capital One to bring jobs to that town with $4 million in tax subsidies, but the company found cheaper foreign labor too appealing and eliminated 1,100 Tampa jobs.[24]

Far-Reaching Consequences

Offshore outsourcing has serious social, economic, and financial ramifications for communities well beyond the loss of jobs. This type of outsourcing means the loss of a middle-class base with its tax, revenue, and employment source for many communities. The economic consequences go beyond the jobs that are offshored, also affecting local businesses from restaurants to retailers and the host of trades and other services that had supported the workers. As the tax base dwindles, local governments are less able to sustain the public services and infrastructures that their citizens expect. The entire community's quality of life begins to slide. This impact especially can be quite dramatic in smaller communities that lose primary employers.

For example, Clintwood, a small town in Virginia, lost 250 call-center jobs when Travelocity decided to offshore-outsource those tasks. It was a devastating blow to the town because the call center was the largest employer, and the town had already been experiencing double-digit unemployment (11 percent, raised to 15 percent after the loss of Travelocity). Local economic development officials were rushing to fill the vacant space by offering incentives to potential employers.[25]

In the late 1990s, Reading, a city in northeastern Pennsylvania, invested many public resources in attracting an Agere telecommunications equipment plant. But the city has lost the plant and more than 3,000 good-paying jobs, leaving empty facilities and creating a $500,000 shortfall in property taxes for Muhlenberg Township. Average annual salaries in the township have dropped from $42,000 to $31,000.[26]

Mainstream economists talking in the abstract assume that the economy will simply create new jobs. For communities and employees who depend on these jobs, the truth is much starker. These communities begin

THE HUMAN FACE OF OUTSOURCING

to compete fiercely with each other for jobs, lowering their taxes and social services to attract companies. More important, as more offshore outsourcing takes place, what industries or companies can replace the key employers in these communities? Economists have yet to answer this question. Just look at some of the towns in the Rust Belt, where manufacturing jobs were lost in the 1980s, to understand the consequences of yet another wave of unaddressed job losses.

Washington seems to have no answers for where new jobs can come from for those communities such as Allentown, Pennsylvania, which has lost the latest edge of service jobs, on the heels of a generation of lost manufacturing jobs. Local community leaders understand how difficult it is to attract and create good-paying jobs, and the officials are left holding the bag when businesses move offshore. Not only do the communities lose tax revenues but they also have to provide services to laid-off workers and their families.

What the Future Holds

As already discussed, the new wave of offshoring will affect particular white-collar occupations. Since this is an emerging phenomenon, we can only speculate what changes might occur. State and local government industrial recruiting efforts will be challenged. As companies now have more options, state and local governments are facing foreign competition for those jobs as well. The likely response will be to provide even greater tax incentives, resulting in a loss of revenue and a shift of greater tax burden onto individuals and existing businesses. Yet even when states do provide incentives, companies are lured by a combination of low labor costs and tax incentives in overseas locales.

Some indications of what might happen can be seen by examining the IT sector. Communities that are information technology–intensive, such as California's Silicon Valley and Austin, Texas, have been most affected. The topic of offshore outsourcing has been a regular feature in Silicon Valley's newspaper, the *San Jose Mercury News*. Persistently high unemployment rates have troubled that region. In 2000, San Jose, in the heart of the Silicon Valley, ranked best in employment among large metropolitan areas (>1 million in population), with an unemployment rate of just 2 percent. Just two years later, San Jose went from best to worst, with unemployment

at 8.5 percent, and the city retained that dubious distinction in 2003, with a slightly better rate of 8.2 percent.[27]

Of course, not all of that unemployment is due to offshore outsourcing, but when that factor is overlayed on an already weak job market, anxiety runs high in the Valley. A July 2004 survey showed that Bay Area workers are the most pessimistic in the nation, with 27 percent worried about losing their jobs, compared to a nationwide average of 18 percent.[28] And according to the Kroll & Deo Bardhan study, the Bay Area is the region most vulnerable to outsourcing, with one in six jobs at risk.[29]

When we made an outsourcing presentation in August 2004 to about 350 electronics engineers at a semiconductor conference, there were many who expressed concern that the Valley had lost its edge and would no longer be the center of the "next big thing." They worried about their children, who had grown up thinking that they would work in technology, and were now wondering whether anything would be left. A few expressed confidence that they would just move on to a higher level of work and that the electronics jobs that were being outsourced offshore would be merely complementary, pointing out that the Valley had made employment transitions in the past. And corporate leaders seem to support the idea that the transition may be different for this region. Craig Barrett, CEO of Intel, said, "Companies can still form in Silicon Valley and be competitive around the world. . . . It's just that they are not going to create jobs [there]."[30]

Table 7-1 suggests which states will be most impacted by offshoring in the field of IT, reflected as states with the highest concentration of technology jobs. While Virginia is vulnerable, its situation is buffered in part because of its proximity to Washington, D.C., and many contracts from the federal government. Those jobs are less likely to be offshored. Connecticut and Colorado, both states with a high proportion of technology jobs, have been hotbeds of grassroots activism. We would expect workers in other states listed in the table to follow suit.

Local and state politicians, unencumbered by the national political implications of offshore outsourcing and focused on jobs in their communities, are sponsoring studies of the effects of such outsourcing on their states. We recently spoke at a conference of state government officials, including many state legislators, and they expressed strong concerns about

Table 7-1. States with disproportionately large numbers of high-tech jobs.

(Median is 3.5%.)

State	Hi-Tech Jobs Concentration	Hi-Tech Jobs
District of Columbia	7.0%	41,490
Virginia	6.4%	217,460
Colorado	6.1%	128,960
Washington	6.0%	153,020
Maryland	5.9%	143,360
Massachusetts	5.6%	178,860
Connecticut	5.0%	81,850
California	4.9%	708,060
Michigan	4.9%	211,610
Minnesota	4.6%	120,540
New Jersey	4.5%	174,730
New Mexico	4.4%	32,430
Arizona	4.4%	99,250
Utah	4.3%	45,350
Texas	4.3%	397,420
Oregon	4.2%	64,740
Kansas	4.1%	53,320
New Hampshire	4.1%	24,600
Vermont	4.0%	11,700
Georgia	4.0%	151,130
Idaho	3.9%	22,250
Rhode Island	3.8%	18,210
Illinois	3.7%	216,180
Ohio	3.6%	193,430
Alabama	3.6%	65,090
Nebraska	3.6%	31,300
Delaware	3.6%	14,320

Source: Ron Hira analysis based on Bureau of Labor Statistics (August 15, 2004).

the employment bases in their regions. One official expressed particular concern that a defense contractor was offshoring the jobs in his district.

The threat of outsourcing is making people rethink their approach to economic development. Regions that are heavily dependent on the industries of information technology are turning instead toward biotechnology and nanotechnology to pull them out of a slump, a solution that we discuss with some skepticism in the final chapter.

The Indian-American Community: A Special Case

India has been the prime destination for white-collar offshore outsourcing, facilitated by the large Indian diaspora in the United States. This makes Indian-Americans a special case in terms of community impact. In fact, the Indian community in America has a keen interest in the debate about outsourcing, about the business and personal opportunities that are created for them, about how they are viewed by other Americans, about the negative impact that offshoring has had on American jobs (in many cases their own, since many work in IT), and about the positive impact offshoring has had on the Indian economy and on the relatives and friends they have there.

The U.S.-based newspapers, such as *India Abroad* and *India Tribune*, that cater to the Indian-American community have created regular "outsourcing" sections akin to a Sports or Business section. As Indian Americans, our discussions with friends and family have been insightful, and at times heated. They generally support the notion that people hear what they wish to hear and filter out the facts that conflict with their hopes and beliefs. Thus, most Indian Americans overly discount the downside of offshore outsourcing.

Despite the conflicted feelings within the Indian-American community about offshoring, there is a common feeling of pride in the progress being made by India. The December 8, 2003, cover of *BusinessWeek* magazine headlined "The Rise of India," and articles highlighted the country's brainpower, evoking a great sense of pride in the community. On the other hand, the Indian American Leadership Incubator, an organization that tries to get Indian Americans more politically active, hosted a discussion panel whose title was, "Your Cousin, Ramesh, in India Is Getting a Good Job, But You're Still Unemployed: Is Outsourcing Good?" In spite of its title, the

meeting ended up being less about the problems created for Indian-American workers by offshore outsourcing and more about how to fight the backlash against this outsourcing in the United States.

The Indian-American Center for Political Awareness, another lobbying group, has been more balanced in its outlook and more open to discussion of offshore outsourcing, including the downside. They realize that, in order to be a credible lobbying organization, they have to acknowledge valid claims made by the other side. The focus on India has also provided greater political voice for the Indian-American community, which is one of the wealthiest and best-educated ethnic groups in the United States. Both Republicans and Democrats are wooing the Indian-American vote and receiving campaign contributions.[31]

We have given numerous talks to Indian-American groups, and there is almost always an attendee who says that the outsourcing backlash is due to racism. The comment is usually framed something like, "If these jobs were going to Ireland or Australia, no one in the United States would be making a stink of this." The racism fears reached a crescendo when the largest Indian newspapers reported the "mysterious" death of an Indian software programmer in the United States. One newspaper implied that there was a cover-up and that the death came "in the wake of reports of xenophobic American professionals targeting Indians."[32] It turned out that there was no foul play involved and the story had no merit.

While there are elements of racism in a small number of grassroots worker organizations that oppose offshore outsourcing, we think that the Indian-American community is missing the primary reason for opposition: the destruction of U.S. jobs. The overwhelming majority of people in the grassroots organizations are concerned about the future they and their children will have, and could not care less where the jobs are going, only that they are disappearing.

Many Indian-American entrepreneurs are also benefiting greatly from the offshore outsourcing trend, leveraging their ties to the United States and Indian business communities. Some are high-profile, like Vinod Dham, the "father of the Pentium," who has started the offshore venture-capital firm NewPath Ventures; Sunil Wadhwani, CEO of Pittsburgh-based IT offshoring powerhouse iGate; and Atul Vashistha, who runs the offshoring advisory consulting firm NeoIT. There are countless smaller start-up com-

panies, like String Information Services, run by Prashant Kothari, and even more Indian Americans who are acting as the global supply coordinators for Fortune 500 firms.

Offshore outsourcing is also changing the migration dynamics for Indians and Indian Americans. For a very long time, the migration was unidirectional, with Indians coming to the United States for a better life. Many of these Indians, including our parents, were highly educated professionals who brought intellectual capital to the United States—this phenomenon has been dubbed pejoratively the "brain drain." Now, many Indians who came to the United States to study or work are returning to India, some even after staying in the United States for many years. Some observers refer to this as the "reverse brain drain" or "brain circulation" or even "brain gain" for India. The job opportunities in Bangalore and other Indian cities are better now, and returnees can afford to live a good lifestyle because of the low costs of living in India.

Indeed, an estimated 35,000 Indians have returned to Bangalore, and many, like Infosys executive Subhash Dhar, feel they have a better quality life there.[33] Upper-middle-class Indians are able to afford things that their counterparts in America couldn't dream of, like full-time servants, and are able to have their children grow up close to family and friends. And in some rare cases, even non-Indians are moving to India to work for lower wages. Joshua Bornstein, a twenty-three-year-old American who grew up in Chicago, went to work for Infosys in corporate planning in 2003, when he saw better prospects in India. He has thrived at Infosys and continues to rise in the company.[34]

It is likely that the focus on India will continue for the near future, since it is the most visible and leading destination for offshoring. As more countries become viable destinations for U.S. jobs, though, the spotlight on Indian Americans will likely begin to be diffused to other communities. These wider impacts will surely affect Indian Americans in the United States as much as other communities in the future, which, it is hoped, will lead to more sober assessments of the impact of offshore outsourcing.

Conclusion

In the last two chapters, we have discussed the real and potentially devastating impacts of offshore outsourcing on Americans—on the personal,

community, and national levels. We have shown that outsourcing is not some abstract or minute subject of economic discussion, but a phenomenon that is making a palpable impact on our standard of living. Offshore outsourcing represents one sign of a decline in the standard of living enjoyed by Americans, a superior standard that has been at the heart of the American identity. America is a unique country in the world, constructed on the premise that those who work hard enough can find a way to succeed. It was this identity that has allowed America to create the American Dream, attracting the best and brightest from around the world.

But offshore outsourcing signals that even hardworking, well-educated, and highly skilled American workers may no longer be able to achieve that dream. Despite the efforts of many young and middle-aged people to make a new life by retraining, there can be no retraining for positions that do not exist.

When large numbers of jobs are lost, the effects are felt not just by a few families whom economists assume will find their way. Whole communities may be the lifeblood of their neighborhoods and social fabrics, namely the opportunities for gainful employment. With the loss of key jobs, public services and tax bases are affected. There is much more than economic efficiency at stake here. For example, how are the benefits of lower prices from outsourcing going to be reaped, if no one has a job to pay for these goods and services? But perhaps the most devastating impact is felt by the next generation, who will enter the job market with few clear prospects for gainful employment. What motivation can our next generation of the best and brightest find, if the most high-paying and technically skilled jobs are following the wave of manufacturing jobs lost earlier? These impacts will reverberate on the national level, with equally important long-term consequences unless corrective actions are taken. We as a nation will begin to lose our capabilities in national security, in the ready supply of technical and engineering talent, and in the ability to maintain our economic competitiveness.

So, what types of actions should be taken to preserve the American way of life? We begin to examine some possible choices in the next chapter by examining how developing countries are attracting these high-wage jobs. When we peel away the surface, we see that this situation is not abstract economics or "market forces" at work. Rather, it is specific, proactive poli-

cies of Indian and Chinese companies working hand-in-hand with their governments that have led to their gains and our losses.

Notes

1. Sanford Nowlin and Travis E. Poling, "U.S. Jobs: Next Stop, India?" *San Antonio Express* (September 21, 2003).

2. Marilyn Geewax, "Pay Cuts May Reverse Tech Job Loss, Expert Says," *Atlanta Journal Constitution* (October 21, 2003).

3. David E. Gumpert, "U.S. Programmers at Overseas Salaries," *BusinessWeek Online* (December 4, 2003).

4. Lisa Vaas, "Offshoring Eats Away at IT Pay, Study Shows," *EWeek* (January 13, 2004).

5. "Back to Work for Less: Survey: 57% Who Lost Full-time Jobs 2001–2003 and Found Full-time Work Again Are Earning Less," *CNN/Money* (July 30, 2004).

6. Bureau of Labor Statistics, Displaced Worker Survey 2001–03, Table 5 (July 30, 2004).

7. Lori G. Kletzer, *Trade-related Job Loss and Wage Insurance: A Synthetic Review*, unpublished manuscript (June 2003).

8. Katherine Yung, "Job Security Hopes Fading," *Dallas Morning News* (June 26, 2004).

9. William M. Bulkeley, "New IBM Jobs Can Mean Fewer Jobs Elsewhere," *Wall Street Journal* (March 8, 2004).

10. Leign De Armas, "Mike Emmons Is Mad as Hell," *Orlando Weekly* (July 22, 2004).

11. Ben Worthen, "The Radicalization of Mike Emmons," *CIO Magazine* (September 1, 2003).

12. Jyoti Thottam, Karen Tumulty, and Sara Rajan, "Is Your Job Going Abroad?" *Time* (March 1, 2004).

13. Steve Lohr and Matt Richtel, "Lingering Job Insecurity of Silicon Valley," *New York Times* (March 9, 2004).

14. Katherine Yung, "Job Security Hopes Fading," *Dallas Morning News* (June 26, 2004).

15. Suein Hwang, "New Group Swells Bankruptcy Court: The Middle-aged Job Losses, Illnesses Can Push White Collar over the Edge," *Wall Street Journal* (August 6, 2004).

16. Rebecca Blumenstein, "Older Executives Find Job Losses Often Mean Having to Retire Early," *Wall Street Journal* (July 20, 2004).

17. Ted Evanoff, "Offshoring Trend Costs Thomson Jobs: 11 at Carmel Headquarters Seeing Work Sent to Philippines," *Indianapolis Star* (August 30, 2004).

18. Stephanie Armour, "Workers Asked to Train Foreign Replacements," *USA Today* (April 6, 2004).

19. Jeff Harrington, "Call Center Ends 1,100 Tampa Jobs," *St. Petersburg Times* (July 22, 2004).

20. See http://www.house.gov/smbiz/hearings/108th/2003/031020/humphries.html.

21. John Pardon, "Lost Your Job Yet?" *ComputerWorld* (April 12, 2004).

22. Sharon Linstedt, "Anatomy of the Geico Deal," *Buffalo News* (January 4, 2004).

23. Sanford Nowlin, "San Antonio: Call Center Friendly?" *San Antonio Express* (July 10, 2004).

24. Harrington, "Call Center."

25. Gail Russell Chaddock, "Outsourcing Resonates in Virginia Race: The Issue of Jobs Moving Overseas Remains Hot for 'NASCAR Dads' and Software Engineers in Many States," *Christian Science Monitor* (July 21, 2004).

26. Kathy Kiely, "As Jobs Go Overseas, a City Struggles to Reinvent Itself," *USA Today* (March 22, 2004).

27. Bureau of Labor Statistics, Local Area Unemployment Statistics, retrieved August 29, 2004.

28. "Silicon Valley's Slump Eroding Optimism," Associated Press (August 8, 2004).

29. Carrie Kirby and John Shinal, "Offshoring's Giant Target: The Bay Area," *San Francisco Chronicle* (March 7, 2004).

30. Rick Merritt, "Political Winds Hit Offshoring," *Electronic Engineering Times* (March 24, 2004).

31. Nishad H. Majmudar, "In the U.S., Indians Gain Campaign Clout— Democrats and Republicans Alike Seek Contributions from Highly Successful Group," *Wall Street Journal* (August 17, 2004).

32. "IITians Death: Is There More to It than Meets the Eye?" *Economic Times* (August 6, 2004).

33. Amy Waldman, "Indians Go Home, but Don't Leave U.S. Behind," *New York Times* (July 24, 2004).

34. Amy Waldman, "A Young American Outsources Himself to India," *New York Times* (July 17, 2004).

CHAPTER 8

How Developing Countries Attract American Jobs

This chapter examines the question of offshore outsourcing from the point of view of the developing country. First, outsourcing is not limited to a single-source country. While India has been the most mentioned site for outsourcing, there are many other countries that have successfully captured some market share in information technology (IT), including Ireland, Central and Eastern European countries (e.g., Russia, Bulgaria, Romania), Asian countries from China to Thailand, Latin American countries (Brazil, Chile, and Argentina), and even African countries (South Africa and Ghana).

Unlike the United States, these countries are implementing proactive strategies to attract jobs and industries. U.S. companies are encouraged to move work offshore because of the direct incentives these governments offer as part of their national industrial strategy. For example, Russia agreed to purchase Boeing planes only if it located some of its design engineering in that country. China ensures technology transfer in return for access to its domestic market. The history of "smoke-stack chasing" by various countries, offering incentives such as tax holidays, is several decades old, but the competition for the advanced technological industries is more recent.

Beginning in the early 1990s, Ireland was successful in wooing a number of U.S. companies during a serious wave of offshore outsourcing.

Ireland, whose emigrants for a century settled throughout the world, began for the first time to draw interest from its diaspora. The "Celtic Tiger" of the 1990s, with miraculously high growth rates and rising standard of living, demonstrated that the United States had no monopoly on information communications and technology.

At first, Ireland was seen as a strategic gateway to the European Union, being both located nearby and on the direct route of transatlantic airways. The Irish government offered a stable macroeconomic policy, tax breaks, and a lenient regulatory environment to attract the first outsourced telecommunication and call centers. The Irish government then developed a full-fledged strategy to begin attracting IT companies from the United States. The strategy included serious investments in technical education; a targeted marketing campaign for Ireland as an attractive place to do business; a complete revamping of its educational system, including setting up a national system of technological institutes and a few internationally competitive university departments; and development of a partnership among labor, government, and business for long-term job creation in new areas.[1]

The Irish miracle seems to be losing momentum now, but the example it provided of the ability to mobilize a national strategy and successfully move thousands of high-tech jobs in a short period has been reproduced in a number of other cases. In this chapter, we focus on explaining the policies guiding the most successful recent case—namely, India's software industry. By identifying the strategies India has so successfully used in attracting outsourcing contracts in IT, we can begin to understand our domestic weaknesses and recognize the policies that could keep jobs here. We also examine the differences in the approach taken by China as it moves to expand its own outsourcing options beyond the manufacturing sector.

Why Software Companies Move Overseas

Before explaining why offshore outsourcing in software has taken place, it is important to examine some basics about the industry. To begin, many textbooks identify three common types of software development models.[2]

1. In the "waterfall" model, the stages are: specification of user needs; design of software solutions; writing the actual code; test-

ing and integration into existing systems; and maintenance of the system.

2. In the "rapid prototype" model, the initial specifications are followed by a prototype; testing and integration of the prototype; evaluation, which leads to creating new specifications and a new prototype.

3. In the "spiral" model, the initial planning; prototype; evaluation; design; analysis of risks; and development of a new prototype are the logical steps.

Each model assumes that there will be distinct teams that work together with the business side to create the software. The software teams are involved with certain tasks: the systems analysis and interactions with the customer; the overall planning; system design, including the actual programming; the testing and integration; implementation; maintenance; quality assurance; documentation; and identifying reusable components for future projects. On the business side, companies are always concerned about the types of competition; what software becomes standard; which applications are linked to a type of software; time to market; how often updated versions need to be created; and what type of customer support is needed.

Software programming is often divided into parts, or "modules." Thus, many different programmers may be working on different aspects of the software simultaneously. The integration of these different codes is obviously a daunting task and must be considered in software design. The modularity of the software business, therefore, is key to understanding the expanded role of outsourcing. It is easy to guess which aspects of the business can easily be done elsewhere: the programming and testing. Furthermore, where the customer service requires answering simple questions about setting up or running a program, these tasks can be routed to an overseas telephone operator. Customer service can also be provided 24 hours a day by taking advantage of differences in time zones, though in many cases operators in developing countries work night shifts. The ability to work on software 24 hours a day in global offices operating in modular fashion obviously reduces the time to market of the product development.

Considering the wage differentials we pointed out in Chapter 5, it is no surprise that important aspects of the software industry have moved

overseas. Yet, looking only at this side of the industry misses some important questions: Why did software start to move overseas just in the last few
years? And, why wouldn't these software jobs go to countries with lower
wages and/or high concentrations of engineers, such as China and Russia?
In the next section, we outline the proactive strategy that India has followed
to capture the lion's share of these jobs.

Outsourcing to India

It is ironic and a sign of the times that Ross Perot, the famous two-time
presidential candidate who warned of the "giant sucking sound" of jobs
moving to Mexico because of NAFTA, has now moved some of his own
jobs overseas. Perot Systems has an Indian subsidiary with more than 3,500
employees.[3] Indeed, the companies operating in India include some of the
biggest names in American business: IBM, ORACLE, Sun, EDS, and
Microsoft. Tables 8-1 and 8-2 give some illustrative numbers.

However, these numbers don't tell the whole story. U.S. companies
have plans to hire thousands more foreign workers, and to move research
and development overseas. IBM has plans to add 4,000 employees in India
and China, and Accenture 5,000 people in India in the next year. Intel
plans to increase staff to 2,000 by 2006.

It's not just American companies that are setting up shop in India.
The earnings of Indian-owned companies have grown phenomenally, in
good part based on outsourced business, so these represent jobs that also
would otherwise have been located in the United States. The Indian big
three—Infosys, Tata, and Wipro—are starting to compete head-on with U.S.
firms for contracts. Surprise spread through the industry when the Indian
firm Infosys won a $25 million contract from DaimlerChysler—but why the
surprise? The offshore outsourcing trend just continues to grow.

There is evidence that U.S. operations in India are at a disadvantage
in terms of costs. They pay 20 percent higher wages than local counterparts, and have a higher turnover of employees in Bangalore. The savings in
labor costs for local companies has led to astounding increases in profits.
For instance, Wipro announced a 43 percent increase in its profits for
2004.[4] Infosys's revenue topped $1 billion for FY 2003–04, and profits
jumped 23 percent.[5] In response, some U.S. companies have begun to buy

Table 8-1. IT companies and employees in India.

Company	Number of Employees in India
IBM	6,000 (14 cities, 5,000 in Bangalore)
EDS	1,500 (7 cities)
Intel	900 (Bangalore)
Cognizant	13,000
GE	2,500 (Bangalore)
Texas Instruments	1,000
SAP (German)	2,000
Siemens	1,000 (Bangalore)
Oracle	6,000
Hewlett-Packard	10,000
Cisco	600 (Bangalore)
Sun Microsystems	500 (Bangalore)
Infosys (Indian)	22,000

Sources: These are numbers as reported in the press and cannot be verified. For IBM & EDS, Andrew Wahl, "Bangalore or Bust," *Canadian Business* 77, no. 4 (February 16–29, 2004), p. 17. For Infosys, Manjeet Kripalanai and Steve Hamm, "Scrambling to Stem India's Onslaught; Now Big Western Service Outfits Have to Fight Back on Both the High and Low Ends," *BusinessWeek* January 26, 2004, p. 81. For Intel, Don Clark, "Another Lure of Outsourcing: Job Expertise," *Wall Street Journal,* April 12, 2004, p. B1. For Cognizant, Thomas Claburn, "What's Next for India? Interest in Offshore IT Operations Keeps Growing, But Increased Competition for Talent May Dull Some Cost Benefits," *InformationWeek,* January 5, 2004, pp.45–46. For TI, IBM (Bangalore #s), and GE, Raju Chandrasekar, "Bangalore: India's Garden City Is Blossoming with More than Silicon," *Global Finance,* April 2001, p. 80. For Siemens, Shirin Madon, "Information-Based Global Economy and Socioeconomic Development: The Case of Bangalore," *The Information Society* 13 (1997), pp. 227–243. For SAP and Oracle, "The New Geography of the IT Industry—Information Technology," *The Economist,* July 19, 2003, p. 53. For Sun and Cisco, Manjeet Kripliani, "Calling Bangalore: Multinationals Are Making It a Hub for High-Tech Research," *BusinessWeek,* November 25, 2002, p. 52. For Hewlett-Packard, Kerry A. Dolan and Robyn Meredith, "A Tale of Two Cities," *Forbes* 173, no. 7 (April 12, 2004), pp. 94–101.

Table 8-2. Estimated number of outsourcing employees and companies by city.

City	Number of Employees	Prominent Companies
Bangalore	109,500	Intel, IBM, SAP, SAS, Dell, Cisco, TI, Motorola, HP, Oracle, Yahoo, AOL, E&Y, Accenture, Wipro, Infosys, Msource, Microsoft, 3M
Delhi	73,000	GE, American Express, STMicroelectronics, Wipro, Daksh
Mumbai	62,050	Morgan Stanley, Citigroup
Chennai (Madras)	51,100	World Bank, Standard Chartered, Cognizant, Polaris, EDS, Pentamedia Graphics
Hyderabad	36,500	HSBC, Microsoft, Satyam
Kolkata (Calcutta)	7,300	PwC, IBM, ITC Infotech, TCS
Pune	7,300	Msource, C-Dac, Persistent Systems, Zensar

Source: Justin Fox, "Where Your Job Is Going," *Fortune* (November 24, 2003), p. 91.

Indian firms. IBM, for example, recently purchased Daksh, with its 6,000 employees, for more than $160 million.[6]

Meanwhile, Indian companies are looking to move into other areas of application, including legal services, banking, and accounting. Prominent U.S. law firms have already begun to outsource work offshore, following the call centers that moved overseas long ago. Indian pharmaceutical companies have also begun to attract significant interest and outsourcing. And Indian IT firms have hired Americans to help them increase the amount of their outsourcing work. Indian firms have also begun to set up marketing sites in the United States, Mexico, and Canada to service local clients. Indian outsourcing business has also moved to Europe, leading to massive layoffs there in both IT and financial services, as we discussed in Chapter 4.

The Rise of Indian Software

The Indian economy is often cited by economists as one of the spectacular failures in history and a prime example of how planning, red tape, and over-protection can kill entrepreneurship and economic growth. Indeed, for most of its fifty years of independence, India has had an economy that has lagged in growth behind most of its neighbors to the East. As Indian scholar Basu states, "Nehru [India's postindependence leader and key shaper of its economic trajectory] did participate in the economic planning process; but his interest was not so much in the plans as in the prose of the plans. Not surprisingly, while Korea produced some of the most effective policy plans, India produced some of the most well-written policy plans."[7]

The liberalization of the Indian economy took place in a well-documented sequence of events that occurred because of a financial crisis in the late 1980s. Without getting into all of the details, the Indian government was unable to meet its debts and so suffered a severe foreign-exchange crisis. The appointment of Manmohan Singh as Finance Minister in 1991 (he is now Prime Minister) turned what was a short-term crisis into an opportunity for long-term change, from the socialist and relatively closed economic planning model to one that was more open to the world economy. Besides reforming fiscal, macroeconomic, and exchange policies, the government began to attack the jungle of regulatory red tape that continues to stifle economic activity—what is referred to locally as the "license raj."

Since liberalization of the economy, economic growth has significantly increased. However, that growth has been accompanied, as in many other developing countries, with increases in regional and individual inequalities. Moreover, India's exports did not, at least initially, show any signs of being able to compete with world-class leaders in the higher-value-added products that are so important to economic growth, such as automobiles, electronics, and high technology. So, it seems almost miraculous to see India as a world-class leader in any industry, especially a high-technology one.

Consequently, the growth of the Indian software industry has been nothing short of phenomenal. The increasing volume of software exports is illustrated in Table 8-3. These numbers are astounding when one considers that total Indian exports (of all products) in 2003 were less than $50 billion! The software industry currently employs 500,000 people, and this

number continues to grow.[8] The overall size of the IT sector in India rose from $2 billion in 1994–95 to $12.2 billion in 2000, so that approximately half of all of the industry is geared to exports. And the software industry is about four times the size of the hardware industry.[9] Yet these estimates undoubtedly underestimate the importance of the new exports, as there are many (out-)outsourced (subcontracted) processes and linked industries within India itself that feed off overseas exports.

It is tempting to explain India's explosive growth as the sole result of a freeing up of the market and the new entrepreneurship that resulted from the 1990s macroeconomic reforms. This would be a superficial view of the situation. However, an in-depth study of the development of the Indian IT industry, from state-dominated lackluster to emerging giant, notes the following:

> [D]id fewer regulations lead to growth? The analysis in this chapter indicates otherwise. A review of software policy clearly suggests that the level of state intervention in the industry did not decline substantially until the reforms of 1991; and that the Department of Electronics's policies played an important role in facilitating the growth of the industry. Keeping the state out of the industry would not have worked. While private telecommunication companies could have provided the infrastructural facilities, private firms are unlikely to have organized trade missions. The state's helping hand was essential. A close examination of the policy changes, especially during the late 1980s and early 1990s, indicates that the policies were not so much liberalized as fine-tuned.[10]

Hence, the key to India's rise as a software giant is the combination of activities by its long-achieving diaspora and local government encouragement of the industry.

The Indian Diaspora Brought High-Tech Home

The Indian software miracle in the late 1990s would not have happened without active efforts on the part of the Indian diaspora in the United States. Indeed, part of the major advantage India has had in software out-

Table 8-3. Growth of Indian software exports.

(U.S. $ billions, unless otherwise noted.)

1985	1998–99	1999–2000	2000–01	2001–02	2008 (est.)
$24 million	$2.7	$4	$6.2	> $8	> $50

Sources: Kaushik Basu, "The Indian Economy," pp. 3–31 in Kaushik Basu, ed., *India's Emerging Economy: Performance and Prospects in the 1990s and Beyond* (Cambridge, MA: MIT Press, 2004), p. 19. For 1985, N. R. Narayana Murthy, "The Impact of Economic Reforms on Industry in India: A Case Study of the Software Industry," in Kaushik Basu, ed., *India's Emerging Economy: Performance and Prospects in the 1990s and Beyond* (Cambridge, MA: MIT Press, 2004), p. 217.

sourcing over its potential competitors is this human link between the two countries. In the mid-1980s, with a shortage of technical talent, Silicon Valley firms began using large numbers of Chinese and Indian engineers— a classic case of "brain drain" benefiting the United States.

These foreign-born engineers began to branch out and form their own start-ups later in the decade. By 1998, Chinese and Indian immigrants made up 29 percent of all Silicon Valley high-tech start-ups, and of these, Indians were heading 778 firms.[11] As labor and rental costs rose in the Valley by the mid-1990s, some Indians began to look back home for a competitive edge. The Indian government, by all accounts, was hardly welcoming in those early years. But the Indian diaspora in the Silicon Valley began to organize itself to pool knowledge and venture capital. Several informal network organizations were formed, including the TiE (IndUS Entrepreneurs) and the SIPA (Silicon Valley Indian Professionals Association), which also served to acclimate new immigrants to U.S. ways of life.

Anna Lee Saxenian has completed the most exhaustive work on the Indian and Chinese diaspora in the Valley, including extensive surveys in the late 1990s and again in 2000.[12] Saxenian claims that the IC (Indian Chinese) factor was vital to understanding the success of the Valley as opposed to other areas, such as Route 128 in Massachusetts. She found that most of the diaspora were young, first-generation (newly arrived) immigrants. She discovered that many of the diaspora who later set up businesses in their home countries did so while continuing to maintain a presence in the United States. Therefore, she states that, with the exception of

Taiwan in the early 1990s, the movement was more one of "brain circulation" than of "brain drain reversal."

While it is not within the scope of our purpose to try to answer the
question of why the Indian diaspora—and not the Chinese one—was successful in activating home-country production, there are several possible
reasons. (It should be noted, nonetheless, that the Chinese diaspora has
been instrumental in helping Chinese and Taiwanese industry to move
toward high technology, and both countries have successfully moved into
hardware elements of the international IT market, where Indians have fall-
en short. They have not, however, had the same success yet with software[13]
or the customer service field.) The principal reason could be as simple as a
lack of language capability, since Indians speak English. Moreover, the
Chinese government seems much more intent on protecting and developing
its domestic market than does the Indian government. The strongly coordinated Chinese state vs. the disorganized Indian democracy may ironically
have worked in India's favor in this case, in the sense of providing space for
an unanticipated development.

Why Bangalore? The Development of the Indian Software Cluster

It should be evident by now that industry doesn't go to the lowest-cost wage
areas, otherwise Silicon Valley would have been out of business a long time
ago. Instead, industries often seem to develop in regional clusters, as has
the fashion industry in Milan and publishing in New York City. This seems
to be the same dynamic in Bangalore, which has some similarities to Silicon
Valley.[14] Lying at a high altitude in southern India, it boasts a moderate climate and is known as "the Garden City." Bangalore has a relatively modest
population of some 5 million, and so it has none of the problems of the
megalopolises of India. Bangalore was a most livable place, therefore, well
before the tech boom.

More important, Bangalore is home to an Indian Institute of
Technology (IIT), which provides a ready supply of world-class engineers,
thus serving as the educational anchor for the process—much as MIT and
Stanford have in Massachusetts and California, respectively.[15] Originally,
IIT-trained engineers were exclusively employed in an Indian-government-

sponsored aerospace research and development laboratory, so that there was the seed of a basic cluster present—as Nehru defined Bangalore as India's "city of the future."

Once Texas Instruments (TI) opened a research lab in 1985 in Bangalore, the way was set for other companies to follow. TI was also instrumental in helping the local and national governments to develop the infrastructure and strategies for attracting further businesses. Upon noting these possibilities, the state government of Andhra Pradesh stepped in to increase the momentum. Among other things, Andhra Pradesh set up HiTEC city, a campus-like facility of over 55,000 square feet that was donated by the state government.[16] This set up a wave of reinforcing actions by the federal government to encourage the IT cluster, including other IT parks, as described below. Complaints about pollution, traffic, infrastructure, and especially electricity, skilled labor shortages, and high turnover rates have increased in recent years, but no other Indian city seems to have been able to catch any of Bangalore's luster.

The Indian Government's High-Tech Policies

India has clearly been the most successful country in attracting outsourced jobs in high technology, so it bears examination in some detail. While for many years India has invested heavily in advanced technical education, spearheaded by the world-famous Indian Institute of Technology, only in the last decade or so has there been a strong local demand for these world-class engineers. Indeed, the Indian government kicked IBM out of the country in 1977 when it refused to dilute ownership of its subsidiaries. This created much greater possibilities for the national development of the industry, including an interesting twist of fate.

After IBM left, Indian programmers continued to use the Unix system throughout the 1980s, while companies abroad developed proprietary systems. In the 1990s, Unix made a comeback, thus India had an abundance of a scarce commodity.[17] In addition, Texas Instruments pioneered the offshore outsourcing phenomenon by setting up a research and development center in Bangalore in 1985.[18] However, the great wave of outsourcing came a decade later. The timing is explained in a general sense by the liberalization of the Indian economy, beginning in the early 1990s, and the dot-com

boom later in that decade in the United States, which created a spillover effect through the diaspora, as described above.

By the late 1990s, governments at all levels in India recognized the country's tremendous export growth and began to construct clearly proactive policies to encourage that growth even more. Bureaucratic control was decentralized, and more pro-industry export policies were adopted. Companies now rely on local Software Technology Parks of India (STP or STPI) offices for regulatory feedback, thus removing the need to deal directly with the federal government. The STPI have been the key government actors in the growth of software, for example.

One of the most crucial steps was setting up a satellite-based communications infrastructure, which increased bandwidth availability and reduced costs by more than 40 percent! It is crucial to note that the satellite effort is one that could have been accomplished only with government cooperation. Within the STPs, there are no restrictions on equity; there is duty-free import on all inputs, including capital goods (with some exceptions); and there are exemptions from payment of corporate taxes for a block of five out of the first eight years of operation. In return, participating companies are obliged to export 150 percent of the cif (cost, insurance, and freight) value of the imported hardware plus wages. Companies can sell up to 25 percent of their production to the domestic market after the export obligation is met.[19]

Financial Considerations for Indian Companies

Indian IT companies also have significant tax rate advantages over U.S. firms. As shown in Table 8-4, the tax rate for Indian majors is less than half that of U.S. majors. These advantages show up in the bottom line for the companies' investors and enable the Indian firms to underbid their competitors to gain market share.

The 1990s reforms improved access to finance for local companies. For the first time, they were able to set their own prices for their initial public offerings (IPOs), which is quite important for new software companies with limited tangible assets for collateral. In 1998, employee stock option plans were permitted, including ones denominated in a foreign currency. And from 1993, Indian companies were allowed to list on foreign stock

Table 8-4. Tax rate advantages for Indian IT companies.

Company	Country	Effective Tax Rate 5-Year Average (%)
Wipro Limited	India	13.42
Infosys Technologies Limited	India	14.01
Satyam Computer	India	14.02
Computer Sciences Corporation	US	30.55
Cognizant Technology Solutions	US	31.23
Electronic Data Systems	US	35.87
Affiliated Computer Services	US	38.64
Perot Systems Corp.	US	54.37

Source: Reuters.com (August 29, 2004).

exchanges, leading to Infosys becoming the first India-registered company on an American stock exchange, the NASDAQ.

The Royal Bank of India also eased foreign currency access, which made it easier to deal with foreign companies and consultants, and eventually, foreign offices. There are an estimated 750 overseas offices for Indian IT today, up from 167 in 1995. More recently, multinational companies were allowed to maintain 100 percent ownership of their subsidiaries. As a result, IBM, ORACLE, SAP, Microsoft, and Sun all set up shop, with important spillover effects on local companies, infrastructure, and training.[20]

India has set up free-trade zones; software parks, where infrastructure and tax holidays are guaranteed; and tax and regulatory breaks for the system generally. Tariffs for imported inputs and duty procedures were vastly simplified from the 1990s reforms. There is no duty on imported software. These tax holidays are so important for the fledgling BPO market that NASSCOM, the Indian software industry trade association, reacted strong-

ly against the possibility that the government might begin taxing multinational corporations' offshoring arrangements.

India has also been promoting the industry abroad. The recognition of
success in the industry led to the development, from October 1999, of a
new Ministry of Information Technology to handle strategic national planning in coordination with NASSCOM (National Association of Software
and Services Companies), the private-sector business association.

Vulnerabilities in the Indian Software Industry

Anthony D'Costa points out that the U.S. offshore outsourcing phenomenon has important limitations in terms of benefits for India.[21] This outsourcing so far has not led to a virtuous circle of development, in which
linked industries, finance, and government investments in infrastructure follow suit. Likewise, offshore outsourcing has not really developed a domestic market, in either industry or consumers, or moved the "core" operations
of multinational companies to India. By its nature, the movement of software business to India is susceptible to movement elsewhere, as discussed
in the next section. Moreover, the Indian software industry is intimately
tied to U.S. partners and industries, though there are signs of growing independence.

The ongoing volatility of macroeconomic conditions and questions
about political stability, as well as the possibility of new regulations on the
industry, could also limit business's confidence in long-term growth and
investment in India. There is always the possibility for supply bottlenecks
in certain personnel areas; infrastructure, including electricity, remains
poor; and so far, at least, there seems to be great turnover among workers
in the industry.

Up to this point, Indian software work seems to have been concentrated in the more labor-intensive programming and testing areas, on the
one hand, and the cheap labor aspects of customer service, on the other.
For example, work on the Y2K problem accounted for a tremendous 46 percent of total software exports from 1996 to 1999! There is little indication
that Indian companies will be able to sell in the market niches of packaged
software or customized solutions on a level with American competitors,
and the efforts to create a viable international hardware industry have not

succeeded.[22] Furthermore, there is strong concentration in Indian software, with a few companies dominating most revenues and exports. Industry concentration seems particularly pronounced in custom design, with more than 70 percent of revenue accruing to just four companies.[23]

An Overview of China's Proactive IT Policy

By way of contrast, let's now turn to how China has approached its IT development and its growing interest in attracting offshore outsourcing of IT work. Thus far, China's miraculous growth over the last decade has been concentrated in manufacturing. China has not yet made significant inroads into the U.S. service market. Perhaps the language barrier is one problem, as well as the strategic restrictions the Chinese government uses to guide foreign investment. But perhaps it is simply that China has other priorities at the moment. China's accelerated development reflects a unified military-civilian government dedication to developing self-sufficiency, a primary motive ever since China's embarrassment at Western bullying a century ago.

Unlike India, China's growth has been fueled in good part by a more balanced and consumer-led demand. Therefore, foreign investors are drawn to China to tap into the rapidly growing middle class, rather than to use it as an export platform. Moreover, the Chinese government has had a long-standing, carefully considered industrial policy. China has used its state-owned enterprises and limited foreign investment to develop internationally competitive but nationally controlled industries at the "commanding heights" of the economy, such as steel, electronics, pharmaceuticals, chemicals, and automobiles. The Chinese government's 863 Project lists for key areas of development include integrated computer manufacturing systems and robotics; biotechnology; energy; IT; lasers; new materials related to technology; and space technology.[24]

The Chinese government, going back to the opening of the export processing zones (EPZs) in southern China, has sought to limit the influence of foreign investors and to force foreign investors to produce for export markets. Via the EPZs, the Chinese economy seems to be developing concentrated clusters of industries. This has allowed for the development of regionally targeted sectoral policies and reduced interregional competition for foreign investment in certain areas (also unlike India).

In addition, China is implicitly showing favoritism to foreign companies that bring in more product development and research centers. For example, China instituted a policy change in the auto sector, offering tax breaks for companies willing to add research jobs. While the labor costs in China are attractive (recent Ph.D. graduates command salaries of $12,000 per year[25]), the primary concern for U.S. companies is the weak intellectual property protection.

Nevertheless, China's nascent efforts show great promise. For instance, the share of industrial high-technology exports increased from just 7.9 percent in 1995 to 22.5 percent in 2001.[26]

China's Science and Technology Policy

According to Turpin and Liu, China's science and technology policy has been dominated by three types of institutions. The first is the Chinese Academy of Science Institutes; the second are institutions attached to universities; and the third is units within the industrial sector.[27] Complementary efforts, coordination, and subsidization are being made at the regional and local levels. The Chinese government has emphasized pushing research into applied "downstream" production settings, including allowing business spin-offs from public research institutions. These spin-offs are called New Technology Enterprises (NTEs) and receive favorable treatment and subsidization from the government. In addition to "product" and "manufacturing technology" institutes, the new initiatives are designed to bring Chinese science and technology efforts much closer to actual production and consumer demand.[28]

The Chinese government, unlike India's, has been pouring more and more effort into creating quality technical institutions, including offering incentives to its engineers and researchers abroad to come home. The latter include support of business, technical, and educational exchanges, as well as actual recruitment by government officials of Silicon Valley Chinese workers of all levels. And recent reports cite measurable success in doing so.[29] Nor has China shied away from research in leading-edge industries. China's efforts are present in biotechnology, space transport, and nanotechnology, among others.

Looking to Compete

China's entry into the World Trade Organization (WTO) is not necessarily going to lead to major inroads by foreign companies, according to many analysts. Rather, joining the WTO was designed to ensure China access to external markets, as its industries begin to compete through exports. As the Korean government has helped manufacturers such as Samsung, China's government has encouraged joint ventures with foreign multinationals, so its businesses can learn the game with a long-run view to independent production and marketing. China has already made significant inroads into emerging technology markets, including semiconductor and hard-drive design and production, cell phones, and DVDs.[30]

While China's software industry remains far behind that of India's, it has ambitions to match its prowess in hardware. China's 9th Five-Year Plan from the late 1990s targeted the software industry for growth and usage expansion, under the leadership of the Ministry of the Electronics Industry. At present the Chinese software industry seems to be focused on converting software to Chinese applications, but this is viewed as a stepping stone for future exports. In 1985, the government set up an Institute of Software under the Chinese Academy of Sciences, as well as a National Research Center for an Intelligent Computing System. Hence, the government has started several joint ventures with foreign companies under the guise of these two institutions. The government also has developed software parks in Shanghai and Zhuhai, with plans for several more.[31]

In 2003, the Semiconductor Industry of America and consulting firm Dewey, Ballentine released a report stating that China's industrial policy was succeeding in challenging U.S. companies in the industry.[32] The report underscores the commonly held view of the strategic importance of semiconductor chips, which led to the SEMATECH government-industry consortium that saved the industry from an onslaught by Japanese and other manufacturers in the 1990s.

The Impact of the Chinese Diaspora

Perhaps the most significant reason China has been able to leapfrog technologically in both manufacturing and services capability is the influence of the Chinese diaspora, including partnerships with overseas Chinese

located in Taiwan, Hong Kong, Singapore, and the United States. The overseas Chinese have provided both ready capital and technological and business know-how to lay a solid foundation for the miracle. Overseas Chinese have prospered in Southeast Asia and elsewhere for hundreds of years, and so they provide an important link between China and outside markets.

It is clear that the overseas Chinese operate in a fashion quite different from that of Western corporations. Not only is there the factor of the extended family but also the informal decision making that make studying them so difficult. A strong level of trust (*guanxi*) means that long-term capital investments can be made by such networks without a clear paper trail or formal loan documentation. Therefore, the importance of the Chinese diaspora for technology transfer and investment is probably underestimated.

While it is hard to trace the growing impact of the overseas Chinese, there is no doubt of its significance. For example, Anna Lee Saxenian, as part of her studies of Silicon Valley noted earlier, points to the importance of the overseas Chinese there who went home to set up hardware plants in Taiwan, taking advantage of Taiwanese government policies, infrastructure, and incentives. According to Saxenian, this parallels with the movement of mainland Chinese entrepreneurs who are now returning home.[33]

The Implications for Other Developing Countries

Undoubtedly, from the perspective of the developing countries that are gaining these outsourced jobs, there are many positive impacts. Many of the countries have identified this as the best path to growth as they try to replicate India's success. By having an export orientation, these developing countries are building up hard-currency reserves and strengthening their macroeconomic position vis-à-vis other developed countries.

Their comparative advantage is lower labor costs. They are not only gaining technological knowledge but, more important, learning the business practices of the leading corporations in the world. They are also moving up the ladder of innovation, where there are many macroeconomic advantages, particularly with respect to current accounts. Most important, these countries have finally found a way to begin to utilize a hitherto idle labor force. A number of developing countries have strategies to move beyond call centers and program-

ming, and they are targeting research, development, and design jobs.

Still, it is important to distinguish India's software- and export-dependent strategy from China's more broadly based one in regard to IT. China seems to be focused on servicing its domestic market and in producing hardware and peripherals, not just software. This is probably a more sound strategy for the long run, considering that IT tends to cluster not just in regions but also in product chains. Part of the reason for India's success is the very nature of the software work, which has become more mobile. Therefore, India could lose the software industry if its advantages in labor costs and expertise are overcome. Hardware industries, which rely on investments of equipment and continual upgrades in processing, are less mobile, and so provide a more steady base for a country's IT sector.

Moreover, the recent election reversal of the BJP (Bharatiya Janata Party) on the federal level, and at the state level in Andhra Pradesh, indicate that there is disquiet in India with regard to the lack of linkages and employment creation in the software industry so far. The software boom in India has naturally been soaking up the excess capacity of the highly skilled and educated workers in India. Now, the political implications of unmet expectations regarding the sharing of the wealth generated by the software sector has led to serious discussion by the Indian government to levy some taxes on the industry. It remains to be seen what form those taxes will take, and if they will negatively affect obtaining further outsourced work.[34]

There are also some questions about whether the best and brightest in these developing countries are being lured to solve problems and meet the needs of the United States instead of their own countries. For example, the best scientists may be working on new pharmaceuticals that address problems for people in developed countries, like male pattern baldness or obesity instead of malaria or tropical diseases.

Then there are the issues of whether developing countries will lose some of their sovereignty to the multinational corporations, who can extract concessions like tax breaks and other subsidies. More important, since these companies have figured out how to move these jobs from America to one developing country, it is likely to be easy for them to move again. Right now, jobs in Mexican manufacturing *maquiladoras* are moving to China, and this may be a trend that is replicated in services, as more developing countries target these jobs and industries. In fact, in some ways

it might be even easier to move services jobs, potentially leading to an ongoing cascade of job movement around the world.

Unlike the free-market ideologues who dominate the conversation in the United States (as our country backslides), other countries use active industrial policies to pick winners. The next time you hear some long diatribe about the glory of free markets, think about all the defense contracts going to Boeing, the European help to Airbus, or the South Korean government's help to Samsung and Hyundai. The Chinese miracle is not due to free-market forces alone, by any stretch of the imagination.

What's Down the Road?

It is likely that an even lower-cost competitor, particularly China, could eventually undercut India's positioning in the software industry, as costs are estimated to be lowest there and in Russia.[35] Part of the reason for the slowdown in Ireland was that the country limited its strategy to IT and financial services, and did not link to manufactures and hardware, which made it vulnerable to undercutting by lower-labor-cost countries.

The contrast between India and China shows that, for the same reason, as well as because of a more unified government strategy, China may end up winning the competition in the long run. There are some reports of increases in wages and office space in India owing to the IT boom; however, the Indian educational system already is responding to the boom by increasing the number of graduates.[36] Nevertheless, there are already some reports of Indian outsourcing to China.[37]

It may take a while for the wage-rate differentials and growing Chinese government support to overcome India's advantages, including the English language and established ties between Indians in the United States and those at home. However, the foremost factor is the proactive and focused efforts of the government to promote industry and the well-established educational infrastructure through the IITs. Whether and how soon China could overcome these advantages remains to be seen, but the Chinese government seems to recognize the importance of the sector and has taken major steps in that direction. In the meanwhile, Indian companies continue to grow in their knowledge of how to sell in the U.S. market on their own, and so continue to increase the space between them and erstwhile competitors in the developing world.

The backbone of any technology industry is a large pool of employed engineers. Table 8-5 illustrates that, though the quality may temporarily be higher in the United States, in terms of sheer numbers the developing countries have a fast-growing pool of available graduates. The difference today from even five years ago is that these engineers actually have employment opportunities in their home countries, which may encourage higher-quality students to pursue these degrees.

Just as India has created both timing and other built-in advantages through its government policies, China and other developing countries can do the same. Indeed, cost differentials are not the only factors determining where software factories are located. Studies of software teams point out that the camaraderie and regular interactions of a consistent team located in the same area can lead to better results. Moreover, teams who are familiar with the American market can more easily make intuitive and quick judgments on the basis of their local knowledge.

Conclusion

Here in the United States, we must wake up to the facts that offshore outsourcing is accelerating every day and that more and more countries are or

Table 8-5. Undergraduate degrees in engineering awarded annually.

Country	Number of Graduates
China	195,354
India	129,000
Japan	103,440
Russia	82,409
US	60,914
South Korea	45,145

Source: Don Clark, "Another Lure of Outsourcing: Job Expertise," Wall Street Journal, April 12, 2004, p. B1.

soon will be offering offshore alternatives to American companies. However, the companies themselves would be wise to wake up and look down the road, too. There's much more at stake than simply cutting costs.

American companies can ensure quality control and recruitment by keeping jobs at home. As a result of complaints regarding its outsourced customer service department, Dell recently moved corporate support back to the United States.[38] Companies such as Holiday Inn that rely on outside designers of software for their database systems may feel held hostage if major modifications need to be made. Thus, price obviously is not the only criterion for whether a product works or not—quality and long-term reliability have to be considered as equally important. Relative laissez-faire toward the IT industry may have worked initially—owing to the United States being the pioneer and the site of the by far largest market, and having the greatest concentration of employed engineers—but that policy is clearly not working anymore.

Nor should we be so naïve as to think that IT is the only industry under fire. India, China, and other countries are actively targeting other key and emerging sectors, such as pharmaceuticals, biotechnology, and nanotechnology. For example, in response to the offshore outsourcing of its own jobs, Singapore has started a massive project, called Biopolis, as a cornerstone for its plans to develop an internationally competitive biotech industry. The Biopolis will employ 2,000 researchers, and has attracted international talent, including researchers from MIT. The project has already attracted investment plans from U.S. biotech firm Chiron and from Novartis, a Swiss pharmaceutical company.[39]

There are parallel efforts being made in other countries. India has created the Genome Valley to develop the biotech industry, again around Hyderbad. There are already signs that these efforts are succeeding—many companies commonly run clinical trials abroad now. And as in IT, salaries for biotech workers abroad are a fraction of those of their U.S. counterparts.[40]

The day is coming when the United States may no longer be the dominant source for innovation in the world economy, and offshore outsourcing—set within the current policies—is narrowing the gap between the leader and the followers. In order to compete with countries such as India, the time is now for the U.S. government to develop a direct and proactive

strategy to maintain and build upon its lead in key industries. In the final chapter, we recommend policy responses that will help to ensure that lead.

Notes

1. See Part II, "Ireland: The Enterprise Isle," pp. 59–108, in Jeff Saperstein and Dr. Daniel Rouach, eds., *Creating Regional Wealth in the Innovation Economy* (Toronto: Financial Times and Prentice-Hall, 2002).

2. Examples of introductory texts with good overviews are Ronald J. Leach, *Introduction to Software Engineering* (New York: CRC Press, 2000), and Dick Hamlet and Joe Maybee, *The Engineering of Software: Technical Foundations for the Individual* (New York: Addison Wesley, 2001).

3. Stephen Gandel, "Where's Perot?" *Money* (May 2004), p. 108.

4. "Wipro Ltd.: India-Based Software Maker Posts 43% Surge in Net Profit," *Wall Street Journal* (April 19, 2004), p. 1.

5. Joanna Slater, "Infosys' Revenue Surges 41% on Outsourcing Boom," *Wall Street Journal* (April 14, 2004), p. B8.

6. See Brad Stone, "Should I Stay or Should I Go?" *Newsweek* (April 19, 2004), pp. 52–54.

7. Kaushik Basu, "The Indian Economy," pp. 3–31, in Kaushik Basu, ed., *India's Emerging Economy: Performance and Prospects in the 1990s and Beyond* (Cambridge, MA: The MIT Press, 2004).

8. Basu, "The Indian Economy," p. 24.

9. Nirvikar Singh, "Information Technology and India's Economic Development," pp. 223–261, in Kaushik Basu, ed., *India's Emerging Economy: Performance and Prospects in the 1990s and Beyond* (Cambridge, MA: The MIT Press, 2004).

10. Vibha Pinglé, *Rethinking the Developmental State: India's Industry in Comparative Perspective* (New York: St. Martin's Press, 1999), p. 154.

11. The numbers are 20% Chinese and 9% Indian. See Joel McCormick, "Asia's Best and Brightest Flock to Silicon Valley," *Electronic Business* (August 1999), p. 40.

12. Anna Lee Saxenian, *Local and Global Networks of Immigrant Professionals in Silicon Valley* (San Francisco: Public Policy Institute of California, 2002), and "Transnational Communities and the Evolution of Production Networks: The Cases of Taiwan, China, and India," *Industry and Innovation* (December 2002), pp. 183–202.

13. Anna Lee Saxenian, "Government and Guanxi: The Chinese Software Industry in Transition," conference paper for Global Software from Emerging Markets: An Engine for Growth? London Business School (March 12, 2003).

14. According to historical accounts, Silicon Valley got its start in the 1950s through defense contracts. Fairchild and HP were two of the pioneering firms. The clustering was cemented as chip manufacturers began to settle there in the 1960s. As in the case of India, it appears that a few entrepreneurs really pushed the effort to expand into a cluster.

15. Technically, the IIT in Bangalore is called the Indian Institute of Science. There are six other IITs in different cities across India.

16. Radha Roy Biswas, "Making a Technopolis in Hyderbad, India: The Role of Government IT Policy," *Technological Forecasting and Social Change*, forthcoming.

17. Anna Lee Saxenian, "Bangalore: The Silicon Valley of Asia?" pp. 169-210, in Anne O. Krueger, ed., *Economic Policy Reforms and the Indian Economy* (Chicago: University of Chicago Press, 2002).

18. Justin Fox, "Where Your Job Is Going," *Fortune* (November 24, 2003), pp. 84-91.

19. Jitendra Kohli, ed., *The Business Guide: India* (Singapore: Butterworth-Heinemann Asia, 1996), pp. 308-309.

20. N. R. Narayana Murthy, "The Impact of Economic Reforms on Industry in India: A Case Study of the Software Industry," in Kaushik Basu, ed., *India's Emerging Economy: Performance and Prospects in the 1990s and Beyond* (Cambridge, MA: MIT Press, 2004) p. 219.

21. Anthony D'Costa, "Software Outsourcing and Development Policy Implications: An Indian Perspective," *International Journal of Technology Management* 24, nos. 7/8 (2002), pp. 705-723.

22. Singh, "Information Technology," pp. 229, 242; and Naushad Forbes and David Wield, *From Followers to Leaders: Managing Technology and Innovation in Newly Industrializing Countries* (New York: Routledge, 2002), p. 33.

23. Changdana Chakraborty and Dilip Dutta, "Indian Software Industry: Growth Patterns, Constraints and Government Initiatives, pp. 317-333, in Raghbendra Jha, *Indian Economic Reforms* (New York: Palgrave Macmillan, 2003), p. 321.

24. Evan Feigenbaum, China's *Techno-Warriors: National Security and Strategic Competition from the Nuclear to the Information Age* (Stanford: Stanford University Press, 2003), p. 178.

25. Robyn Meredith, "China Wants Brains, not Just Brawn," www.Forbes.com, June 30, 2004.

26. Saxenian, "Government and *Guanxi.*"

27. Tim Turpin and Xielin Liu, "Balanced Development: The Challenge for Science, Technology and Innovation Policy," pp. 191–211, in Charles Harvie, ed., *Contemporary Developments and Issues in China's Economic Transition* (New York: St. Martin's Press, 1999).

28. Shulin Gu, *China's Industrial Technology: Market Reform and Organizational Change* (New York: Routledge, 1999).

29. Anna Lee Saxenian, "Transnational Communities and the Evolution of Global Production Networks: The Cases of Taiwan, China, and India," *Industry and Innovation* 9, no. 3 (December 2002), pp. 183–202.

30. Jonathan R. Woetzel, *Capitalist China: Strategies for a Revolutionized Economy* (Rexdale, Ontario: John Wiley and Sons, 2003).

31. Michael Pecht, Chung-Shing Lee, Zong Xiang Fu, Jiang Jun Lu, and Wang Yong Wen, *The Chinese Electronics Industry* (New York: CRC Press, 1999), pp. 135–142.

32. See www.semichips.org for the SIA report.

33. Saxenian, *Local and Global*; "Transnational Communities"; "Government and *Guanxi.*"

34. Anthony Mitchell, "Outsourcing Could be Affected by Indian Taxes," *E-Commerce Times* (August 4, 2004), found at www.ecommercetimes.com.

35. Forbes and Wield, *From Followers*, p. 34. China is the cheapest, lower than Russia. See also David E. Gumpert, "A New Tide in Offshore Outsourcing," *BusinessWeek Online* (January 14, 2004), for a story on a company that moved to Colombia for programming after experiencing problems in India.

36. Thomas Claburn, "What's Next for India? Interest in Offshore IT Operations Keeps Growing, but Increased Competition for Talent May Dull Some Cost Benefits," *Information Week* (January 5, 2004), pp. 45–46.

37. Jen Lin-Liu and Seema Singh, "Indian IT Firms Connect with Chinese Counterparts," *IEEE Spectrum* 41, no. 1 (January 2004), p. 26.

38. Justin Fox, "Hang-ups in India," *Fortune* (December 22, 2003), p. 44; and Maryfran Johnson, "Colliding with Customers," *Computerworld* (December 15, 2003), p. 50.

39. See David Tong, "Singapore's Reply to Offshoring—Build Biopolis," *San Francisco Chronicle* (April 18, 2004), found at www.sfgate.com; and David Swinbanks and Richard Nathan, "Singapore Attracts Foreign Talent," *Nature* 394, no. 6693 (August 6, 1998), p. 604.

40. Bernadette Tansey, "Are Biotech Jobs Next to Go?" *San Francisco Chronicle* (April 18, 2004), found at www.sfgate.com.

CHAPTER 9

Ten Policy Recommendations

In Chapter 3, we pointed out how legitimate studies have been seized and distorted by advocates, pundits, and news organizations to show that not only is offshore outsourcing a win-win situation for both countries but it is also good in the long run for the American workers who are displaced. Unfortunately, rather than moving the discussion forward, these advocates and pundits have impeded progress in solving the real problems created by offshore outsourcing. They have allowed many people to maintain the absurd position that there are no problems with offshore outsourcing. Indeed, most politicians either agree with the "don't worry, be happy" approach—all but ignoring that a problem exists—or come up with tepid proposals that are marginal at best. Few seem to grasp the major implications of offshore outsourcing and the long-term consequences for the American economy.

In this book, we have not denied the positive effects of this brand of outsourcing. We recognize the enormous potential of offshoring to enhance people's lives, here and abroad. For instance, offshore outsourcing lowers costs for U.S. consumers and makes companies more efficient, and it offers opportunities to many heretofore underutilized workers in developing countries. The opportunity to improve the lot of developing countries is important. However, the advocates are only partially correct when they say that offshore outsourcing is not a zero-sum game. The correct way to think about it is that

outsourcing does not have to be a zero-sum game if we install the right poli-cies. The costs and benefits are maldistributed, with some parties, like cor-porate executives, reaping large benefits at almost no cost, and others, like displaced U.S. workers, bearing most of the costs with meager benefits as consumers. At present there are no policies in place to correct the inequity.

As we said back in Chapter 1, the problem isn't so much that offshore outsourcing is happening as it is *how* it is happening. The proper distribution of costs and benefits from offshore outsourcing should be an explicit policy objective, not an afterthought, as so many advocates treat it. To move to a more constructive, positive type of outsourcing, we first need to go beyond the simplistic and dogmatic framing that has characterized the argument thus far.

For example, potential policy responses are often grouped in the vague, artificial categories of either "free trade" or "protectionism." The political culture construes protectionism negatively, and as a result, many potential policy responses have been slowed or stopped because they have been tagged as protectionist. Indeed, industry groups with an interest in accelerating the movement of work offshore have targeted any policy proposal they do not like as protectionist. Some of these ideas include pragmatic and internationally common government procurement policies and better enforcement of guest-worker visas regulations. Remember that many of these same industry groups favored the "protectionist" relief in the 1980s when their companies were under assault—industries that include steel, autos, and semiconductors. Voluntary quotas and major subsidies were created to help these industries out, such as the bailout of Chrysler and the formation of the Sematech semi-conductor government-industry consortium. In short, there are no silver bul-lets, and we don't advocate shutting down offshore outsourcing. Instead, we can and should be taking practical steps for improving the ways in which this outsourcing impacts all Americans. Our intention in this chapter is to sketch out the broad areas of policy actions that can be taken rather than to provide specifics, which can come only with further study and discussion of particu-lar industries and groups of workers.

What makes finding these policy solutions so difficult is that most of our established policy mechanisms have historically been company-centric—that is, they were designed to help companies become more productive and competitive. This approach served us well as more productive companies translated into more jobs and greater prosperity for all. Unfortunately, now

that the bond between U.S. companies and U.S. workers has been severed, we have to search for new policy mechanisms that benefit America as a whole, not just companies that are headquartered here.

Instead of U.S. companies competing with overseas companies, as we had in the 1980s, it is now U.S. workers who are competing head-to-head with foreign workers. And it is often in the short-term interests of large U.S. companies to increase the competition that U.S. workers face so that they can drive down their costs. That's why we call for a long-term national strategy that is worker-centric, that focuses on how to make American workers significantly more productive and protect their interests. This is no small task, and will require a paradigm shift in the ways in which we currently devise economic policies. Let's begin with the initial steps that need to be taken.

1. Acknowledge that a Problem Exists

Remarkably enough, many influential people continue to argue that offshore outsourcing creates no or only negligible negative effects; this includes key politicians from both parties. Indeed, a Computer Systems Policy Project report, Choose to Compete, which is typical of many recent suggestions, has sensible recommendations such as improving K-12 education, making permanent the R&D tax credit, increasing natural science research spending, and improving the technology infrastructure.[1] However, almost none of the recommendations, save for a very small reference to worker retraining, addresses how to solve the problems that offshore outsourcing create for American technology workers.

So, our first recommendation is for the government to formally recognize that offshore outsourcing creates problems. This should be done formally through legislation and informally by the opinions and proposals that policymakers articulate in speeches. Congressman Donald Manzullo (Republican from Illinois) has done both. He held the only two Congressional hearings on outsourcing in 2003 long before it became a household word. And he continues to raise outsourcing in speeches to a broad set of audiences.

In May 2004, Senator Joe Lieberman (Democrat from Connecticut) introduced legislation that would establish a bipartisan blue ribbon commission to examine the pluses and minuses of offshore outsourcing. The idea is modeled after the Young Commission, named after John Young, then CEO of

HP, that was established in the 1980s to address the problems of manufacturing and high-tech competitiveness for U.S. companies. Senator Lieberman's commission would have representatives from industry, academia, and worker groups. We think that this is a very good idea and hope that it gets bipartisan support and is enacted. The legislation does not presuppose a particular policy recommendation or the scale and scope of the problem. It just acknowledges that there are real problems created by offshore outsourcing and that something should be done about them. By having an independent commission, Lieberman hopes to take the politics and rhetoric out of the process.

Our only concern is that industry has mounted such a concerted campaign to present the rosy side of this outsourcing that it may be difficult to find industry leaders willing to participate. This is where political leaders have to step up and inform corporate leaders that they not only have a responsibility to participate but that it's in their best interest to do so.

2. Gather the Right Data to Study the Problem

There is a near consensus that we don't have sufficient data on how much outsourcing is going overseas and what its impacts, positive and negative, are. This is a major failing of government policy. It is absurd that we spend $130 billion on research and development every year, and yet the government can't find a few million dollars to collect better data on outsourcing and study its effects. Think about the amount of time and effort that has been wasted, including our own, in speculation and irrational discussion of outsourcing rather than formulating actions based on clear information and informed analysis.

We place the blame for this squarely on leaders who have been unwilling to direct or redirect a small amount of the enormous resources at their disposal toward understanding this issue. For political reasons they have decided that no information is better than some information. An important driver for this decision is the overwhelming number of industry-funded studies that find few problems created by offshore outsourcing, and those that are can be easily solved. Industry lobbyists obviously prefer controlling the message, because an independent government study offers the chance of derailing their well-honed public relations message.

The federal government (Departments of Labor and Commerce) must begin regularly tracking the volume and nature of the jobs that are moving

offshore. The lack of objective data creates too many opportunities for dueling studies. With objective data, we can make some progress in trying to solve the problems instead of debating whether it is a problem or not. To date the effort to collect data has been minimal. There has been $335,000 allocated to the Department of Commerce to study the numbers, which is not nearly enough to do anything particularly useful.

Some have said that it is too difficult to measure this phenomenon, but they are wrong. There are many practical methods to estimate the number of jobs moving offshore, including charting the employment trends of multinational corporations and tracking the increases in employment of major foreign offshore outsourcers. The impact on U.S. workers can be tracked by counting the number of workers displaced and how long they are displaced, as well as tracing their reemployment, including the quality, wage level, and nature of the new jobs they get.

What Kinds of Data?

Following are our specific recommendations on the kinds of data that should be collected. These are not meant to be exhaustive. They are purposely written to answer key policy questions rather than interesting economic questions. All too often data are collected and not used, so by focusing on the policy questions that need to be answered, rather than specifying how or what specific data is collected, we hope that it will be more pertinent to policy decisions. Data should be collected from existing sources and new surveys, and it should then be disseminated widely. We need, at minimum, the data on:

- The numbers and types (by occupation, skill level, and wages) of jobs that are moving offshore
- The reemployment prospects and success (level of new wages and type of new job) for American workers displaced by outsourcing
- The numbers and types of jobs being created overseas by U.S.-owned companies for the purpose of exporting to U.S. markets compared to those created to serve foreign markets
- The numbers and types of jobs being created in the United States by foreign-owned companies for the purpose of selling in the U.S. market compared to those created to produce exports for overseas markets

- Companies' near-term and long-range plans for relocating facilities and transferring jobs to overseas locations
- The impact of offshore outsourcing on academic and career choices made by American students
- The role of the H-1B and L-1 temporary visa programs in offshore outsourcing operations by U.S. and foreign-owned companies

Who Would Conduct the Study?

Because of the size and complexity of the data-collection effort, and the very real limits on the ability of government agencies to conduct surveys and collect new data, it is unlikely that any single organization or group of individuals will be able to plan and implement the proposed study. The overall effort could be managed by a private-sector organization with a national reputation for objectivity, as well as extensive capabilities and experience in the conduct of policy-oriented survey research. Subcontracts should be awarded on an as-needed basis. Information and opinion should also be collected from stakeholders in business, education, and government, as well as from labor unions, professional societies, and other worker organizations.

Offshore outsourcing will be a growing influence on our economy for the foreseeable future, and it is important that the government begin to regularly track outsourcing-related data. Accordingly, the study should launch a process that brings policymakers, experts, and industry representatives together on a long-term basis with government statistical agencies to identify the data required and to make recommendations for regular and consistent data collection, as well as policy discussions and recommendations.

Congressman Frank Wolf (Republican from Virginia) has assumed a leadership role in addressing the dearth of data. He sponsored the Department of Commerce study of outsourcing, which was completed in 2004, and also authored legislation for a follow-up $2 million study to be conducted by the well-respected nonpartisan National Academy of Public Administration. This legislation passed in December 2004.

3. Reform U.S. Visa Policies that Encourage Offshore Outsourcing

Let us preface this section by saying that we believe that the H-1B and L-1

visas have been important policy tools that have improved America's technological prowess. Since we have worked most of our careers in research labs
and universities, we can personally attest to this. These visas should not be
eliminated, but they should be reformed to meet the American public interest. Unfortunately, they are being used to take away one of the most important comparative advantages that American workers have—physical presence
in the United States. They are, in fact, encouraging companies to outsource
to foreigners.

In an increasing number of cases, the visas are being used to bring in
cheap foreign workers who replace Americans. The visas should be used as a
last resort, not a first choice for cheap labor. With unemployment rates for IT
personnel and engineers at record levels, it was unbelievable that industry
used up its quota of H-1Bs for 2004 and 2005.[2] The exploitation of lax visa
regulations has actually accelerated the process of offshore outsourcing.

Our own research has shown that a number of offshore outsourcing
companies have stretched the guest-worker visa regulations (H-1B and L-1) to
gain competitive advantage in the U.S. market.. Many of the offshore outsourcing business models rely heavily on H-1Bs and L-1s. So, it is long over-
due for Congress to align the law and the program's implementation to its
intent. The current H-1B and L-1 system is tantamount to dumping, defined
by the U.S. International Trade Commission as "the sale or likely sale of
goods at less than fair value." In this case, these companies are bringing in
labor from abroad and selling it at below fair value. There is no way that competitors could hire equivalent U.S. workers at that cost. For example, in 2001,
EDS requested 452 H-1B's at a median salary of $71,251; while Wipro
requested 3,120 positions at salaries of $50,648; and Tata, 11,982 positions at
salaries of $36,502. The latter two are able to bring in large numbers of cheap
foreign workers to underbid their rivals like EDS. More remarkably, many of
these H-1B dependent companies are winning federal and state government
procurement with these guest workers.

Congress should strengthen H-1B and L-1 workforce protections and
their enforcement to ensure that the programs serve their respective purposes
without adversely affecting employment opportunities for U.S. high-tech
workers. There were at least five bills introduced in Congress in 2004 that
would reform the L-1 and H-1B visa rules. Of the legislation introduced, the
one cosponsored by Senator Christopher Dodd (Democrat from

Connecticut) and Representative Nancy Johnson (Republican from Connecticut) seems to be the most sensible because it adds safeguards for U.S. workers without reducing the benefits the programs provide to America's technological competitiveness.

4. Adopt More Pragmatic Approaches to Government Procurement

Government procurement has been one of the primary areas of outsourcing policy debate, since about forty states have legislation either pending or passed that restricts offshore outsourcing to some degree. Tennessee was the first state to pass this kind of legislation, but it is likely to pass in many more states. An outright ban does not make sense, but instead we should take a pragmatic approach to what should and should not be outsourced overseas. A simple one-size-fits-all approach just does not work.

American taxpayers have a right to know that government expenditures at any level are being used appropriately to boost innovation and help U.S. workers. The public sector—federal, state, and local government—is 19 percent of the economy and is an important mechanism that should be used by policymakers. There is a long, strong, and positive link between government procurement and technological innovation. The federal government funded not only most of the early research in computers and the Internet but also was a major customer for those technological revolutions. Also, our billions in defense expenditures have helped to fund technological innovations, such as the Internet, that have commercial applications.

It is no coincidence that many of our major technology companies had the federal government as an early customer. Whether it is in the hardware area, where Texas Instruments sold the first-ever integrated circuit to NASA, or Ross Perot's building Electronic Data Systems on a Social Security Administration contract, or Microsoft originally being located in Albuquerque to support Department of Energy laboratories located there, we should recognize the enormous value of keeping certain types of government procurement onshore, especially in a time when we are far from full employment. When those jobs go offshore and none are created in their place, the United States is a net loser. In terms of high technology, creating strong preferences for American workers not only is in the national interest but is in the interests of national security.

As globalization narrows U.S. technology leadership, the Department of Defense and other government security agencies will need to enhance their ability to acquire and assimilate foreign technologies. The same will be true for American companies as they are passed by foreign competitors in certain market segments. This will require significant shifts in operating procedures and organizational change.

5. Overhaul Assistance Programs for Displaced Workers

There is no disagreement from objective observers that people are being displaced by offshore outsourcing, but their reemployment at substantially their prior wages is critical to calculations that show the U.S. benefit from trade. Yet all of the data show that the likelihood of reemployment is poor. And even worse, outside of the bromide that the higher a person's education level, the better chance for a good job, we know very little about what works and what does not in terms of moving to a new job or career. This situation needs to radically improve if we are serious about addressing the negative effects of offshore outsourcing.

We need to overhaul the systems that identify and help displaced workers, and we need to track their outcomes. That means that we need to spend significant resources on programs whose singular focus is to get people back to work. In effect, the sooner we can get folks back to work, the better we can put their skills and knowledge to productive use, benefiting both them and our nation. Unfortunately, the existing employment assistance programs are underfunded, understaffed, and not helpful for a large number of white-collar workers. This is not a negative reflection on the dedicated staff at these employment offices, but the reality is that they are more experienced helping people who need English-as-a-second-language training than helping displaced IT workers figure out whether they should stay in the profession or train to do something else, what that something else might be, and how to move into that job.

Improving Retraining Efforts

Congress should create special new U.S. workforce assistance programs to help displaced high-tech workers become productive again. We are in a new

era of work and lifelong learning, and new and more flexible methods are needed to provide meaningful assistance. This recommendation will require extensive experimentation and resources—something that will be very difficult to pass with the current budget deficit.

To their credit, some people in industry have begun this discussion. Most (like Andrew Grove, former CEO of Intel, and Alan Greenspan, Chairman of the Federal Reserve) have zeroed in on the idea of improving education and retraining efforts. While attractive, this is a problematic answer, because none of the proposals so far have offered details, let alone where the resources will come from. As we discussed earlier, there are serious questions about the effectiveness of retraining programs:

- What exactly will we retrain people to do?
- Will it be skills that don't quickly diffuse overseas?
- Who will come up with the resources to do this?

For example, Sam Palmisano, CEO of IBM, is the Cochair of the Council on Competitiveness's National Initiative on Innovation (NII), an initiative that is making policy recommendations on how America can improve its competitiveness. At the kickoff of the NII, Mr. Palmisano announced that IBM was setting aside $200 million to retrain 100,000 of its workers. This sounds like a lot of money until you do the math and figure out that it is $2,000 per trainee—about the cost of one college course. In other words, the proponents of education and retraining are vastly underestimating the cost and, more important, the difficulty in retraining.

Also, it is often difficult to directly identify workers who have been displaced because of trade; given the secrecy of company plans, sometimes even workers do not know why they have been let go. Companies are increasingly reluctant to reveal their plans for fear of the bad publicity that will result. And many workers are too intimidated to publicly identify themselves. They fear losing their severance package or being blacklisted if they speak out. Even if we could identify those who have been adversely affected by trade, it is not clear how we should compensate them. Should we offer subsidized retraining in some other profession? Is it realistic to expect an electrical engineer with twenty years of experience to spend four years studying to become a nurse—one of the few occupations that is predicted to grow?

Because it is so difficult to identify which workers are displaced by off-shore outsourcing versus some other cause, such as technology or just plain bad business decisions, we propose that training funds be available for anyone who is out of work. It just makes economic sense to make people more productive, get them back to work rapidly, and give them a set of skills that will keep them employed for a long period of time.

Matching Workers to Job Openings

There is more to getting people back to work than training. If it were that simple, then there would not be so many underemployed college graduates in the United States. So we need to devise a better matching system between job openings and available employees. We have heard from many employers who say that they cannot find the right workers. Some of this is being said for political reasons. For example, Harris Miller of ITAA sponsored a terribly flawed survey that inflated the number of openings in order to bolster the importation of cheap foreign labor through the guest-worker visa programs. But there are cases when employers genuinely cannot find the right people. At the same time, we have heard from thousands of highly qualified workers who cannot find a job.

We could begin to improve the rehiring process by building on the existing private headhunters and Internet job boards. For example, one could provide incentives to those private-sector service providers to improve the quality and speed of the matching. It is in everyone's interest that unfilled jobs get filled by the right people and get filled quickly.

We also have very poor information on the nature and scale of job openings in the United States. The Bureau of Labor Statistics has initiated a new survey, called the Job Openings and Labor Turnover Survey. In time, this should provide some high-level information for policymakers, labor economists, and policy wonks. But what we really need is real-time intelligence that is useful for the unemployed or soon-to-be unemployed workers. And it has to be presented in a form that a layperson can readily assimilate. Let's leverage the information technologies that we have all spent so many tax dollars creating to develop a truly world-class matching system.

6. Establish Better Protections for Workers

As we've said throughout this book, individual American workers are the big
losers from offshore outsourcing. They are at the mercy of a system that
offers few protections in the face of the potentially devastating loss of their
jobs, benefits and, in fact, their careers. There are some ways we can set up
better protections for American workers—if not to actually prevent their jobs
from being outsourced overseas, then at least to make the situation somewhat
less demoralizing.

First off, workers should not be forced to train their replacements as a
condition of severance or eligibility for unemployment insurance. Quite simply, this indignity should be made illegal.

Giving Adequate Notice

Too many workers have been blindsided by their layoffs and provided little or
no notice. The reason for the short notice is not that companies execute their
decisions on offshore outsourcing in a matter of weeks. On the contrary,
most companies plan this outsourcing over a fairly long period of time.
Instead, the reason is that companies are afraid that if they give too much
notice, workers will leave, and company morale will quickly decline.

Any worker who is displaced because of offshore outsourcing should
have adequate notice—at least ninety days—so that he or she can plan for the
transition. Tom Daschle (Democrat from South Dakota), the former minority leader in the U.S. Senate, introduced legislation to this effect in 2004, but
no action was taken on it.

The current system is destructive in a number of ways, but most importantly, it makes no economic sense for the United States or for the workers.
Workers need to find new employment, and the more time they have to plan
their finances and transition, the less time they will be unemployed and the
higher the likelihood they will find better jobs. While companies have fought
this idea, for them it may actually take some of the stigma out of outsourcing.

Providing Reasonable Relief for Displaced Workers

We know from our discussions with displaced workers that many of them
are unemployed for extended periods. The Trade Adjustment Assistance

(TAA) program was put in place in the 1960s to help workers with monetary and counseling assistance if they have been displaced by trade. A number of government and private studies have shown that the program has had limited success, but one obvious problem is that it never extended its reach beyond manufacturing workers. It is silly that the current law doesn't help services workers, who make up the vast majority of our workforce and are the ones who are increasingly at risk because of offshore outsourcing.

Remarkably, the legislation introduced by Senator Baucus (Democrat from Montana) to extend the TAA program to services workers was shot down in 2004. The reason cited was a lack of funds. Furthermore, many manufacturing workers who are eligible for benefits do not receive them because the current program is underfunded. The result is that they have exhausted their savings, sometimes losing everything and being forced to declare bankruptcy. And as offshore outsourcing continues to rise, the story will become even more common. We can deal with this by looking the other way, which is to maintain the status quo, or we can provide reasonable relief.

For those who are lucky enough to be reemployed, many times their success is muted because they are forced to take a significant pay cut. Some have argued that a new form of insurance could be available to make up for lost wages when the new job pays less than the last one. In such a program, sometimes referred to as *wage insurance*, if a displaced worker finds new employment, but it pays less than his original position, the insurance program would supply some of the difference. Proponents argue that this would create a further incentive for workers to take a job more quickly rather than holding out for better pay.

Uncoupling Health Care and Pensions from Employment

One of the greatest fears for all workers, but especially those with families, is to lose their health-care benefits. Many workers hang on to jobs that they actually dislike primarily because they fear losing that health care. At the same time, companies cite rising health-care costs as a major disincentive to hiring new full-time employees. They prefer temporary workers. We also know that one of the incentives to nearshore work in Canada is their national health-care system, which means that employers don't pay those benefits.

So, the U.S. health-care system creates a disincentive for workers to take risks and find better employment opportunities, and it makes U.S. workers artificially more expensive than their overseas counterparts. We need to detach the employment decisions, by companies and workers, from health care. Jobs should be matched to workers for productivity reasons, not health care. To say that the program is broken is an understatement.

By the same token, the pension systems in this country are distorting corporate and employee decision making. Shorter vesting times and greater portability are necessities in this new, more flexible labor market.

7. Train the Next Generation of Workers to Have Lifelong Marketable Skills

Employers repeatedly say that they are looking for workers who can "hit the ground running." They say that they have neither the time nor the resources to hire people who are unable to contribute from day one. At first glance, it might seem that this desire should lead colleges to concentrate more on specific skills and less on learning how to learn. Actually, we advocate just the opposite in the face of offshore outsourcing. If, indeed, our young people are facing a future in which they will have five careers rather than five jobs within one career, then adaptability is the desirable attribute for students.

This points to a primary emphasis on learning how to learn and a secondary emphasis on specific skills. Such a reform could leave gaps between what employers want and the skills of workers, and those gaps will need to be filled by specialized course offerings and maybe with a lowering of expectations by employers as to what they actually need. We also need a systematic method of collecting information on the skills needed now and in the future. Too often, when they are asked about what skills their companies need, business leaders are guessing at the answer rather than having objective data. More important, as we discuss below, part of the employers' gripe about inadequate skills points to a larger problem: the breakdown of trust between workers and employers. That trust normally comes from a long-term partnership.

Our current education system is designed around intensive and expensive degree programs. We are all aware of the expense of obtaining an undergraduate liberal arts degree, and our B.A./B.S. system is not appropriate for many labor market needs. There are lower-cost alternatives for providing

skills training, and they should be subsidized by the government, just as we subsidize higher education. We need a much greater array of courses delivered more cheaply and in ways that are convenient for students. For lifelong learning to be effective, agility and responsiveness to market needs are at a premium, but unfortunately colleges are almost by necessity characterized by inertia. That would point to a different kind of institution as the leader in providing these courses.

How can we encourage employers to invest in their employees? With the disintegration of employer-employee loyalty, it should be no surprise that employers are less generous in supporting continuing education for their employees. From the point of view of the employer, the educational investment made in an employee may never pay for itself if that employee leaves to work somewhere else.

Some have proposed a human-capital tax investment credit—essentially a way to subsidize employers who invest money to improve their employees' skills. We think that the idea is on the right track, but it is a mistake to offer the tax credit to the employer. It should go directly to the workers. For instance, the workers' future interests may not be tied to their current employers, and they may choose different courses from those that interest their employers. In other cases, employers may not see the need in having workers train even if the tax credit is available, thereby depriving the workers of training. And in corporations that do not pay any taxes, the tax-credit incentive wouldn't work.

Revamping our education and training system to ensure lifelong learning is one of the investments that the offshore outsourcing trend is making obvious—a goal we need to maintain long-term national competitiveness in a global economy.

How do we pay for all of these programs? Many companies are getting significant windfalls from trade, and it is reasonable enough to ask them to pay a small portion for maintaining our long-term national interests. The money could be put into a special fund that goes specifically for retraining assistance and lifelong learning. Putting a small toll on the services trade will hardly distort our economic system in comparison with the billions of dollars spent by communities in tax breaks to recruit companies. In the latter strategy, taxpayers are bearing the entire burden. In the former, company executives, shareholders, and consumers are taking on some of the burden.

This is not as radical an idea as it might seem. For instance, the pro-out-sourcing advocacy group McKinsey Global Institute recommended something similar to in their offshore outsourcing study. Polls of high-level IT managers also show that they think this is a sensible approach for addressing the problems of offshore outsourcing. The nature of this problem demands government coordination and leadership—no company alone can propose or take on such tasks.

8. New Institutions Are Needed to Represent the Interests of Workers

All of these labor-market issues point to the major need for some institution that represents the interests of U.S. workers. Corporate executives are able to influence politicians not only with their campaign contributions and other favors but also by funding a large public relations blitz, including policy "studies." In an attempt to make the studies appear unbiased and authoritative, the corporations fund academics and think tanks that they know will come up with conclusions favorable to them.

For any group to get policies enacted beneficial to them, it takes diligence as well as resources. Policymaking includes myriad meetings and committees, and unless a group has a physical presence at these meetings, its interests are likely to be ignored. Right now, U.S. workers are not represented at many of these forums. We have seen this lack of representation firsthand. Even sophisticated workers such as engineers are only marginally represented in the policymaking process. For instance, no engineers' groups, outside of the unions, are even participating in the committees advising the U.S. Trade Representative about trade negotiations.

The reason for this situation is simple. The government relations offices that represent workers just don't have adequate resources. Whereas corporate coffers support the executives and shareholders' interests, there is no equivalent mechanism to fund workers' interests. Is increased union membership the right answer? Even with their small numbers, the positives that unions have achieved for their members have spread far wider to touch most of us. Their efforts should be acknowledged and boosted. However, it is unlikely that union membership will increase significantly anytime soon. So, there have to be new types of organizations and institutions established to represent workers' interests.

Many of the grassroots organizations that represent displaced IT workers were formed on shoestring budgets and do not have experience organizing people or influencing public debate. We need stronger organizations, perhaps initially funded by foundations and other philanthropists, that are eventually recognized, if not directly supported by the government.

Also, there are some scholars who do important work on labor issues, but we need many more of them. Universities increasingly operate like businesses, and if there is money available to do research in a particular area, it will entice faculty to work in that area. But having more academics is not enough. We also need advocacy organizations to represent workers. These organizations would play a number of roles, such as synthesizing research and translating it into information that can be used by policymakers, doing original research on offshore outsourcing, publicizing facts about this outsourcing, and ensuring that workers have a seat at the table when the United States makes domestic policy and considers trade agreements.

9. Maintain Our Technological Leadership

We can all agree that U.S. technological leadership is an objective that we should strive to achieve. But this leadership no longer means having the most advanced companies headquartered in the United States, since many of these companies are essentially global entities. Instead, it means having the most advanced work performed in the United States by U.S. workers, and a large and healthy science engineering labor market to provide those workers. By healthy, we mean that the pay is good enough and the work interesting enough to attract the best and brightest Americans to these professions. A healthy labor market is also one in which unemployment levels are low and wages are rising.

The "Holy Grail" Solution: Increase Software Productivity

In his speech at the Business Software Alliance in October 2003, Andy Grove, former CEO of Intel, suggested that we try to double software productivity by investing in research and development and in new technology. The concept is to eliminate the labor-cost advantages of developing countries by making American software engineers more productive. While this is an attractive goal, many of the same problems apply.

First, can it be done? Software makers have been searching for ways to automate the process for years because it is still essentially a labor-intensive craft industry whose major input cost is labor. In fact, higher productivity is the "holy grail" of software development. The federal government's Defense Advanced Research Projects Agency has been pumping money into Computer-Aided Software Engineering tools for years, and while there has been some progress in automating the processes and making software production more reliable, it has been mostly incremental in nature. Grove used a figure of about $1 billion in his talk, but Microsoft alone spends about $8 billion per year on R&D.

Second, if it could be done, there is still the question of how to prevent the better technology or know-how from diffusing quickly to the developing countries, especially since U.S. companies have shown a penchant for taking the latest tools and techniques to cheap foreign labor.

The Techno-Optimist Solution: Be Patient for the "Next Big Thing"

The other answer proposed from the point of view of technology is to just wait for the "next big thing." The United States will supposedly be able to move "up the ladder of innovation." The techno-optimists say that this new field will be biotechnology or bioinformatics or nanotechnology. In fact, our own National Science Foundation, a bastion of techno-optimism, has predicted that more than 2 million jobs will be created in nanotechnology. One can only speculate on the impact that nanotechnology will have on the economy and jobs, and hope that it will be significant as some predict—and considering the current employment situation, that it happens soon. However, we have already seen that a number of countries are able to leap up that ladder of innovation.

As a nation, we are not alone in our pursuit of the frontiers of nanotechnology. China is currently the second largest producer of technical papers in nanoscience and nanotechnology, even ahead of Japan. With great cost advantages in addition to this advanced technical knowledge, we should anticipate that China will compete strongly for new nanotechnology jobs and manufacturing opportunities. Of course, all of this is speculation that an unproven and unknown technology will somehow create thousands of new jobs.

But if nanotechnology is somewhat speculative, biotechnology is more mature. The U.S. government already spends about $28 billion every year on

health research through the National Institutes of Health. We are the clear leader in drug development, but as we discussed in Chapter 8, we are not the only country targeting biotechnology as a growth area. For instance, Singapore is actively pursuing biotechnology, and India wants to be the low-cost drug discovery location. Even if we become more successful in biotechnology breakthroughs, the industry is not a major employer, and it isn't clear that achieving those breakthroughs will create many jobs here.

Many of the policies that are being proposed by industry, such as increased government R&D and infrastructure spending, make good sense and should be adopted. However, they must be designed so that they focus on increasing the number and quality of American jobs.

10. Institute Trade Policies in the U.S. National Interest

We have also seen throughout this book how American companies and the pundits that support offshore outsourcing claim that this trend benefits the consumer and the bottom line, and is the result of "market forces." However, in Chapter 8 we discussed the ways that first Ireland, then India, and now China were able to capture thousands of American jobs. We showed that in each case, a government-business strategy was put in place to help entrepreneurs, including tax breaks, infrastructure provision (for example, actually creating software parks), and financing. We also showed how government and business had to work together with universities to create conditions that would keep the country's highly skilled workers at home instead of emigrating, as had earlier been the case. We saw how both an overseas diaspora and the cost-cutting goals of American companies were decisive in making this jump.

In light of the above, therefore, we would have to ignore the facts to claim that offshore outsourcing is simply the result of market forces. Deliberate actions and coordination were needed by both American companies and host governments and universities to support the offshore outsourcing. Nor are any of these governments slowing down their efforts. Indeed, we can predict that as offshore outsourcing continues, more countries and more incentives will be offered in the competition for leading sectors.

Manipulating the Markets

Free markets, as we demonstrated in Chapter 2, are a theoretical possibility
but not a reality. Markets everywhere are regulated and modified and imper-
fect. In a sense, markets are living entities that change shape constantly. For
example, tax structures change markets. Worker safety rules and immigration
rules change markets. Government education policies and support for education change markets. For years, the United States was able to dominate
world markets and set the rules of trade. However, the situation has changed.
Now the trade game is like what the U.S. Olympic basketball team faced—
some teams in the world have figured out how to take advantage of existing
rules to make points in their favor.

The basic principles of international trade after World War II have
moved toward increasing trade liberalization, using nondiscriminatory means
(attempting to extend the same agreement to all nations who sign it) based
on reciprocity, but allowing for safeguards and contingent trade measures.[3]
What this has meant in practice varies considerably from country to country
and from time to time. However, clearly there is no simple thing as free trade.
Countries such as Japan have created protections for their local rice and beef
producers that are perfectly legal within current trade regulations. Similarly,
the United States has been accused of abusing its power to impose counter-
vailing and antidumping duties in order to protect some of its industries, such
as steel.

There are a whole host of ways that countries attempt to skew trade
results in their favor, from undervaluing their currency, as China has been
accused of doing, to using defense spending to subsidize research and development that helps the private sector, as is the case with the United States. So,
while international trade agreements have been quite successful in reducing
tariffs—that is, the customs duties countries place on imports and exports—
they have been nowhere near successful in creating free trade.

Adjusting Policy to Deal with New Problems

The United States has yet to deal with the economic impact of trade on labor
and the environment, a situation that has earlier parallels. For example, at the
turn of the twentieth century, there were heated battles over the wildly fluc-
tuating economy that lasted through the Great Depression, until President

Franklin D. Roosevelt put into place some of the safeguards that would help smooth out the economy. These safeguards are aspects of our life in the United States that we take for granted, and the value of which few economists would dispute—safeguards such as a Federal Deposit Insurance Corporation that guarantees bank accounts up to $100,000 and Social Security and unemployment benefits.

In our opinion, we are at a similar historical crossroads in regard to international trade and its unanticipated effects on our livelihood. Unfortunately, there has scarcely been the recognition, let alone the leadership, to begin to adjust our domestic and international policies to deal with the problems of our new global situation.

Our principal negotiating body, the United States Trade Representative (USTR), basically has carte blanche to develop the national trade and investment negotiations strategy. USTR has meetings with different sectoral groups; however, it is notable that different industries are treated separately, and labor consultation groups are usually treated separately from business groups. This allows the USTR to use a "divide and conquer" strategy. The USTR can pick and choose which industries it wants to prosper and isolate the others. That would be the case for textile industries, for instance. It can avoid considering workers' interests, as reflected in the total lack of consideration of outsourcing and labor rights issues, which have not been included in any trade agreement. The exceptional U.S. free trade agreement with Jordan, which includes monitoring, enforcement, and educational efforts for the Jordanian government and workers, shows that labor standards can be included in free trade agreements.

Rather than looking past our responsibility to give our workers a fair chance, we should try to lift up the basic working standards of foreign workers. There is no logical argument for not including basic (safe) working conditions, environmental, and labor rights in agreements, and the enticement of access to the U.S. economy—the largest in the world—means that we have the leverage to make positive and true win-win agreements. Above all, even if the USTR consults, it has no need to heed particular suggestions. This is because most trade agreements have been signed as a take-it-or-leave-it package. The reasoning is that this gives the USTR, working for the president, greater simplicity in negotiating with foreign counterparts.

Seeking Accountability for Trade Policy

In the interests of easing the ability to create trade agreements, we have allowed the USTR to dictate the terms of trade agreements. In essence, the agreements the USTR makes have domestic impact—the USTR is making domestic policy, after all. Yet, there is no clear line of accountability between the USTR and the American people, or for that matter, to Congress. We need to take back our trade policy and make it work for the American people, not privileged corporations that work behind a veil of secrecy and personal relationships with trade negotiators, and who ultimately show no loyalty to our country as they funnel profits into overseas accounts and employment abroad.

The USTR and its advocates would likely argue that taking domestic policy stances on issues not directly linked to trade will make the negotiating process unduly complex. Yet, we cannot see why, for simplicity's sake, agreements that are not in our interest should be signed. While before NAFTA, the effects of trade were so indirect or widespread so not many paid notice, the effects of trade agreements are now quite palpable and significant. Public hearings should take place on trade negotiations before those negotiations actually take place. This way, when negotiators make deals that affect the lives of Americans, they can do so with genuine confidence that there is consensus on a long-term national strategy, including compensation or retraining for affected industries, rather than simply playing God to certain industries, regions, and workers.

To be sure, this approach will require much more work in actually educating and engaging the public about trade agreements and the trade-offs involved in different stances. But in the end, won't this lead to a more sustainable and nationally beneficial trade strategy, which is supposed to be the USTR's goal? At the moment, the USTR does not avoid special-interest lobbying; it simply embraces certain industries over others, based on unclear criteria. We are certain that this will lead to a backlash at some point, as has occurred not only in the United States but in other countries as well. This certainly has been the case with the highly controversial Chapter 11 section of NAFTA, with the falling apart of the Multilateral Agreement on Investment talks, and with the major crisis in Mexico over agricultural imports. As Winston Churchill once quipped, "It has been said that democracy is the worst form of government except all the others that have been tried."

It seems clear that simplicity is not always the best route to achieving sustainable trade agreements that are in the interests of the majority of Americans. Just as millions of the world's population would love to come to work in the United States, so the premise of the global economic system is based on access to the American market more than anything else. We should leverage access to our market to ensure that the global rules for trade and investment include considerations of the overall welfare of the world's workers. Nor does any other country want the engine of the world's economy derailed. We are, after all, not slaves to the world's market but shapers of it. Which type of world market do we want to choose?

Conclusion

We need a national strategy on offshore outsourcing and trade that explicitly considers quality employment. On a more fundamental level, we need to change the way we think about economics. For the last few years, we have seen "positive" economic indicators—a major tax cut, historically low interest rates, and other signs of consumer activity. Yet, Americans as a whole recognize something that economists don't figure into their simplistic models. We may be better off now than at the start of the twentieth century, but this is in good part because we often have two people working in the family. It is no wonder that despite our greater wealth, we are overly stressed out: We have traded time for money. More important, while women have more choices and chances, and there are more choices in terms of types of employment, the unity between employer and employee has gone out the window.

Most Americans now live in perpetual fear of two things: that they will lose their job and that they will lose their health care. You can spend your life as an aerospace engineer one day and be training your foreign-born replacement the next. The reaction that economists have trained us to give is that it is all market-driven. Yet, we have shown in this book that markets can and are shaped, so the main concerns of economists should not just be inflation and interest rates but also quality and stable employment.

For example, we have highlighted here the growing nexus of impacts between trade and immigration policy, yet both sets of policies lack clear coordination. The same is true in terms of not only our technology policy but also our labor and environmental policies. In the past, the U.S. government recognized that there are key sectors in the economy that are important to

our quality of life. That is why we bailed out Chrysler in the 1980s and the government stepped in to save the semiconductor industry in the 1990s. These ad hoc efforts need to be replaced by a long-term national strategy to recapture and maintain our lead in innovation and job creation.

We are facing a "new competitiveness debate." While *competitiveness* became a buzzword with the rapid rise of imports in the 1980s, the difference is that now it is the workers who are being adversely affected rather than the companies. That means that the present chaos of isolated and blind public-sector and company responses will not address the problem that offshore out-sourcing represents. We are not advocating blind protectionism; we recognize the importance of helping developing countries to prosper. However, no developing country can gain in the long run if the United States economy takes a downward spiral.

The United States needs a coordinated national strategy to sustain its technological leadership and promote job creation in response to the con-certed strategies used by other countries to attract U.S. industries and jobs. We need a partnership among different levels of government and across agen-cies to tackle this problem. As it stands now, we have localities and states competing with each other for plants and businesses, sometimes marketing themselves, replicating the efforts of our federal agencies. We have agencies of the federal government that lack clear coordination and planning around a national innovation system.

Perhaps most worrisome is that the gap between the workers and the owners of businesses has grown far too wide, as it was in earlier periods of American history, such as the Gilded Age of the "Robber Barons." In reac-tion to that period, the U.S. economy rebounded with reforms, including basic labor legislation and antitrust rules. Similarly, we have demonstrated that, in fact, there is no such thing as free trade—all trade is negotiated by governments and affected by regulatory and countless other policies. These earlier reforms of our economy are things we now take for granted—and we no longer see as a questioning of some abstract supremacy of "the market." We need to take similarly historic and comprehensive steps to create a gov-ernment-business-university-labor pact for America in the next century.

The government's roles would include helping to fund technological and human capital development and helping business and labor adjust to changes in the market. More important, we need to develop something that

has never really existed in U.S. history: a means to coordinate labor and business to maximize international competitiveness. For instance, workers should be willing to relocate, retrain, and accept lower salaries when the market dips in exchange for some basic job security.

There is an important concept in economics besides markets, called transactions costs. Transactions costs in this case would mean the costs of moving workers to other jobs. If we consider the costs to society, and to the worker him/herself of training as an engineer or computer programmer, as well as the potential for that person to contribute in that capacity, then we can recognize that workers are not just commodities but are long-term assets and partners in a country's wealth. To ask a computer programmer to become a food service manager overnight, in short, is not an efficient use of resources, looking purely at the economic side of things (the personal costs are obvious). Moreover, if the market for IT suddenly picks up, then we have to spend money again retraining new programmers. So, to allow highly trained workers to move with the whims of the market just does not make much sense to us.

The same would be true at the company level. If companies hire and fire according to the cycles of the market, they are going against the lessons taught to business students in Management 101, as well as continually retraining new employees. Study after study shows that employees need to "buy in" to a company's goals, and to be consulted in ways to maximize their productivity. This requires some sense of loyalty and sacrifice on both sides—something that is not likely to happen when businesses cut short-term costs by hiring foreign employees. As we noted, numerous reports on offshore outsourcing note that there is a great deal of "churning," or moving around, of foreign employees from one American company to another. Moreover, the foreign companies that have begun to undercut American ones are drawing away the best offshore workers. After all, why would Indian men or women want to work for an American company, with decisions made thousands of miles away, when they can run their own companies on their own terms and in their own country?

American businesses need to share both the costs and the benefits of company growth with their workers. After all, if American workers are unemployed, who will buy their products? American workers need to be flexible in their expectations, especially during downturns, and be open to reasonable

adjustments so that they are continually employed and upgrading their skills. The end result will be a longer-term strategy that leads to stable employment, which is good for everybody.

We do not believe that the American people see price as the only important indicator in economics. Americans are smart enough to make the connections between the treatment of workers, the environment, trade agreements, company and public responsibility, and the products they buy. They are smart enough to recognize when price alone may not be in their own long-term interests. A national strategy and a change in consciousness could bring forward a new kind of economics that offers long-term, sustainable, and stable middle-class prosperity, rather than short-term, volatile, and insecure economics based on disposable workers and the lowest-price good at any cost.

A final thought: We hope that even if you are not persuaded by our recommendations, that you are now aware that something should be done about offshore outsourcing. Our interactions with staff in Congress and in the state legislatures have been very positive, even if we are critical of their nonresponse to the problems created by outsourcing. They read letters from constituents and understand that many people have been adversely affected. We hope that you continue to write to your elected officials at the local, state, and federal levels. It has become as easy as writing an e-mail. We do live in a democracy, and politicians tend to respond to their constituents' wishes.

Notes

1. "Choose to Compete: How Innovation, Investment and Productivity Can Grow U.S. Jobs and Ensure American Competitiveness in the 21st Century," Computer Systems Policy Project (December 2003).

2. Ron Hira, "U.S. Immigration Regulations and India's Information Technology Industry," *Technological Forecasting and Social Change* 71, no. 8 (October 2004), pp. 837–854.

3. Theodore H. Cohn, *Global Political Economy: Theory and Practice*, 3rd ed. (New York: Pearson/Longman, 2005).

Defining Outsourcing

There are several different ways to characterize the outgoing and incoming job flows between the United States and other countries. The following terms have been used, sometimes erroneously, by the media in describing the processes. Here we try to explain what they mean and why they are important. We also provide some concrete examples for each term in Table A-1.

Outsourcing

Outsourcing happens when a company decides to purchase a product or service from a source outside of the company. It generally refers to products or services that were once done in-house, now purchased from a source external to the company. We do outsourcing in our everyday lives, such as dining out, whereby we purchase our prepared food from an external source—a restaurant—instead of making the meal ourselves. In business parlance, outsourcing is sometimes known as *vertical de-integration*.

Companies have been outsourcing an increasing array of processes and functions that they used to do in-house, such as accounting, payroll processing, and even engineering design. The strategy for many companies

Table A-1. Examples by types of outsourcing.

Type of Outsourcing	Example
Outsourcing	Procter & Gamble (P&G) decided to outsource its IT function to Hewlett-Packard (HP) in a contract worth about $3 billion over 10 years. Nearly 2,000 P&G workers were transferred to HP in the deal.[1]
Offshore Outsourcing	Companies such as Cognizant, IBM, EDS, Infosys, and Igate provide IT services to US clients from India and other overseas locations.
Offshoring	IBM plans to move nearly 5,000 of its programming positions to India and China.[2] Microsoft is building a large development center in India.
On-Site Offshore Outsourcing	Companies such as Tata, Cognizant, Wipro, Infosys, and Satyam service US clients on location in the US by using foreign workers. Tata Consultancy Services (TCS) proposed to bring approximately 65 guest-worker programmers to service a $15 million contract with the State of Indiana, which was subsequently canceled. According to TCS, those workers would be paid approximately $36,000 per year, which is significantly below the starting salary of a graduating computer science major, which is about $50,000.[3]
On-Site Offshoring	Companies bring in workers from overseas operations on intra-company transfer visas to learn from their US colleagues. This is often referred to as "knowledge transfer."
Insourcing (incorrect usage by media and politicians)	BMW built an assembly plant in Spartanburg, SC, in 1994, where they produce 500 vehicles every day and employ 4,700 workers.[4]
Insourcing (correct usage)	America Online's (AOL) purchase of Time Warner (TW). The Internet provider, AOL, merged with up-stream media content provider TW.
Near-Shore	Stream International is moving between 100 and 200 technical support call-center jobs from Beaverton, Oregon, to Chilliwack, British Columbia. The work supports its contract with Hewlett-Packard. Lower health care costs are one reason.[5]

Sources:
1. Sandeep Junnarkar and Ed Frauenheim, "HP Lines Up Outsourcing Deals," www.CNET News.com, April 11, 2003.
2. William Bulkeley, "IBM to Export Highly Paid Jobs to India, China," *The Wall Street Journal,* December 15, 2003.
3. Kevin Corcoran, "State Job Agency Hires India Firm," *Indianapolis Star,* September 29, 2003.
4. http://www.bmwusfactory.com/, retrieved August 18, 2004.
5. Jeff Kosseff, "Beaverton Jobs Bound for B.C., Stream International Looks North and not to Asia for Cost Savings for as Many as 200 Lower-Level Technology Service Jobs," *The Oregonian,* April 7, 2004.

is to focus only on what is deemed its core competency and outsource the rest. This has had a profound effect of shaping the current movement of work overseas.

Offshore Outsourcing

When a company purchases a product or service from a supplier that operates overseas, the term offshore outsourcing is used. It doesn't matter where the supplier is headquartered—in the United States or overseas—just that the work is performed overseas. As we highlight throughout the book, the geographic location of a company's headquarters is becoming less and less relevant.

Offshoring or Offshore Sourcing

When a multinational company moves or expands some of its operations and jobs to overseas locations, this is referred to as offshoring or offshore sourcing. In some cases, work is currently done in the United States but is being shifted to an offshore location. In other cases, expansion that normally would have happened in the United States instead happens in offshore locations. Major companies are rapidly expanding their facilities and workforces in countries like China and India.

On-Site Offshore Outsourcing

When companies bring in lower-cost foreign labor, via guest-worker visas such as the H-1B or L-1, to complete work on-site in the United States, the term used is on-site offshore outsourcing. Not all work is easily offshored. On-site offshore outsourcing typically involves work that requires a physical presence with the customer, from software architecture to sales to pizza delivery, so companies are now increasingly bringing in foreign workers for that part of the service delivery.

A new business model, employed by the Indian IT firms, emerged in the mid-1990s. The model is designed around using low-cost foreign labor on guest-worker visas in the United States to service U.S. customers. Because of their significant labor-cost advantages, these companies are able to underbid their competitors using U.S. workers. The work is being done

by imported labor, so it is a form of offshore outsourcing, but it is distinct because the work is done in the United States.

Insourcing

The term *insourcing* has been used erroneously by the media and some politicians.[1] They are trying to describe foreign multinationals that set up or expand operations in the United States. However, offshoring advocates generally do not distinguish whether the operations are set up to make products for sale in the United States or for export outside of the United States—an important distinction. In some cases, foreign multinationals establish operations in the United States to be close to their U.S. customers for logistical reasons—if, for example, it is more cost-effective. In other cases, operations are established in the United States to "localize" the product—that is, to customize it to meet U.S. customer preferences. In still other cases, foreign multinationals set up plants in the United States because the U.S. government has explicitly or implicitly insisted that they have a production presence in order to sell in the U.S. market.

It is no accident that Japanese automakers Honda and Toyota have automobile assembly plants in Marysville, Ohio, and Georgetown, Kentucky, respectively. They were a direct result of U.S. policies for meeting parts content rules and a voluntary quota in the 1980s. In fact, Toyota regularly runs ads in major magazines touting the number of jobs it creates in the United States, with pictures prominently featuring their non-Japanese workers. While insourcing does occur and does benefit many U.S. workers, its impact has been somewhat distorted by offshoring advocates. For example, they point to the 6.4 million Americans who work for foreign-owned companies, but they never distinguish what share of those operations are to serve the U.S. market or go for export, and which ones were the result of U.S. government policy, let alone how many U.S. jobs are created and at what wage level.

Insourcing (correct usage) happens when a company decides to bring work that was previously purchased from an external supplier in-house. They may do this by purchasing the supplier—known as *growth by acquisition*—or by expanding their internal capabilities and workforce, known as *organic growth*. Insourcing is often referred to as *vertical integration* in business and economics literature.

Global Sourcing

This happens when a company uses sources that span multiple countries to produce a product or deliver a service. The sources could be in-house or external suppliers. A form of global sourcing is called *blended sourcing*, whereby a company delivers some of the services using U.S. operations and some with offshore operations. In the IT sector, companies are now offering so-called blended rates, which are prices that average on-site and off-shore labor rates.

Best-Shore, Near-Shore, All-Shore, Etc.

Many permutations of the *-shore* and *-sourcing* terms have been invented by consultants who are hawking the procedures. *Best-shore* refers to using the best, based on the customer's criteria, set of suppliers regardless of where they are located. *Near-shore* refers to using suppliers in Canada, Mexico, or sometimes Central and South America. Dell Computer's president described his sourcing as *all-shoring*, meaning to him that they will both source from and sell to all shores.

In addition to the terms listed above, there are a few other important outsourcing-related terms here. Business process outsourcing (BPO), which is also known as IT-enabled services (ITES) in India, is the outsourcing of business processes, such as insurance claims processing or accounting. It is the fastest-growing sector in Indian offshore outsourcing.

Companies are also using two euphemisms to describe the destruction of U.S. jobs. Corporate executives will often refer to the process of destroying U.S. jobs and creating overseas jobs as *rebalancing the workforce*. This has replaced the layoff euphemism of the early 1990s, *right-sizing*. The other euphemism is *knowledge transfer*, whereby a company forces a U.S. worker to train his or her foreign replacement before being laid off.

Note

1. See, for example, the Web site for the trade group Organization for International Investment, "The Facts About Insourcing," www.ofii.org/facts_figures. Among others, they quote Senate Majority Leader Bill Frist (Republican from Tennessee) talking positively about

Nissan's automobile plant in Smyrna, Tennessee, and House Majority Leader Tom DeLay (Republican from Texas) referencing a Toyota plant in San Antonio, Texas. There is some irony to these quotes, since these leaders have supported outsourcing and are against "protectionism." The plants referred to are a result of U.S. government policy intervention that forced Japanese automakers to establish a presence and workforce in the United States, and could certainly be called a form of protectionism.

Analysis of Key Outsourcing Studies

There have been numerous pro-outsourcing studies issued by corporate lobbying groups. Most of these studies cite the same recycled findings—which are only positive—in slightly different ways. Here is a more detailed look at the three key pro-outsourcing studies we referenced in Chapter 3, along with our critical analysis of each one.

ITAA Study

In March 2004, the Information Technology Association of America (ITAA), a wealthy, influential lobbying group, was concerned about Congress's growing doubts about offshore outsourcing. They paid Global Insight, a Massachusetts-based economics consulting firm that was founded by a Nobel Prize-winning economist, to conduct a study of outsourcing.[1]

Global Insight forecast that more than twice as many jobs will be created than will be destroyed as a result of offshore outsourcing. They did acknowledge that this outsourcing will destroy more U.S. IT jobs than are created, but said that the rest of the economy will create many jobs in other sectors. They also found that offshore outsourcing will create many other economic benefits, such as lower inflation and higher GDP.

This sort of result is unsurprising since it is based on standard eco-

nomic models and simply puts speculative numbers on the standard theory. Forecasts such as these are almost always wrong. The standard economic models cannot account for some of the most important real-world variables that affect the economy, such as technological innovation and wars—and of course it cannot measure losses or gains in U.S. national security. But for a body like ITAA, having a number when your opposition doesn't makes you appear more authoritative, especially since it is accompanied with the unabashed title for the report, "The Comprehensive Impact of Offshore IT Software and Services."

The more interesting story about the study was the unusual way it was released and how its public distribution was limited. ITAA, a lobbying organization that is well versed in how news is picked up, pulled out every stop to control the message. ITAA took the unusual step of embargoing the executive summary of the study, sharing it only with reporters if they agreed to not share the information with anyone outside of their organization. So, in essence, reporters were asked to write stories without getting a critical review from anyone with the technical expertise to interpret the findings and limitations, something that reporters would normally do.

ITAA was successful in ensuring that most of the initial articles were favorable and held a successful press conference at the National Press Club in Washington, D.C., to highlight their findings. Of course, no other viewpoints were shared at the conference. To further control the message, ITAA released only the executive summary of the study and sold the full study for $350, a price so high that it dissuaded critical examination by independent academics or other organizations. The purpose of this study was not to invite an open and honest dialogue about offshore outsourcing's impacts, but instead to market only the upsides of it.

Mann Report

Dr. Catherine Mann wrote perhaps the most important study on offshore outsourcing so far, because of both its timing and the way it supported the outsourcing advocacy coalition.[2] Mann is a fellow with the prestigious think tank Institute for International Economics (IIE) in Washington. Her study was released in December 2003, just before the public debate about outsourcing reached a peak.

Because of its timeliness, Mann's report became a ready and credible resource for proponents of offshore outsourcing, and her findings were quoted uncritically in major publications such as *The Economist* and *Time* magazine. Ambassador Carla Hills, former U.S. Trade Representative, was almost falling over herself quoting from Mann's report on ABC's "This Week with George Stephanopoulos" during a panel discussion about outsourcing just after Mankiw's remarks. Shortly thereafter, IIE held a luncheon for reporters to highlight Dr. Mann's findings, without inviting anyone with an alternative viewpoint to speak at the meeting. This led to media stories that once again highlighted the virtues of offshore outsourcing with little discussion of its downsides.

Contrary to the ITAA study, Dr. Mann's major finding is that IT services outsourcing will actually create many more U.S. IT jobs than it destroys. Her thesis is that offshore outsourcing will result in lower IT services costs, which will make it cheaper for businesses to buy IT equipment and services. The lower prices will result in greater purchases—more people will buy a $500 software package than a $1,000 one—which will result in more IT labor demand.

How does she get to this result? She argues that the U.S. IT boom in the 1990s is a good predictor of what will happen in this decade—that is, the 1990s is analogous to the current decade. Her report notes that in the early 1990s, computer hardware manufacturers began to move their production offshore, to places such as Taiwan. The result was lower hardware costs in the United States, leading to higher demand for these products.

With more affordable hardware, companies expanded their purchase of related products, such as software, peripherals, and consulting. The latter were produced in the United States, so that U.S. companies and their employees actually enjoyed the benefits of hardware outsourcing as the cycle made its way through the U.S. economy. Mann thus argues that the current wave of offshore outsourcing will cause software prices to decline and that there will be greater adoption of software in U.S. industries.

On the one hand, it is possible that lower software prices might be good for consumers and for businesses adopting IT. But Mann does not explain how American IT workers will benefit this time, since there is no related industry in the United States involved, as was the case with hardware (with software benefiting). Even if there is a demand for services com-

plementary to software, such as consulting or maintenance, there is no indication that these aspects will not also be outsourced overseas.

Mann's initial premises raise several issues. While hardware prices did decline in the early 1990s and software and related products demand did rise, offshore outsourcing was only a small reason. She attributes all of the increases in labor demand to this outsourcing, which is simply not the case. For example, the explosion in the use of the Internet led naturally to greater demand for software and IT services, something totally unrelated to the offshore outsourcing of hardware. A number of other factors also led to increases in labor demand, including the introduction of new types of software for businesses, such as enterprise resource planning software; the stock market and dot-com bubbles; the movement away from mainframe computers to client-server systems; the demand resulting from Y2K fears; and the shift from functional programming languages to object-oriented ones.

There were also business strategy reasons for massive IT spending by companies. This is what economists call *consumer* or *demand preference changes*, and in fact some, like *Harvard Business Review's* Nicholas Carr, have argued that IT spending no longer provides a strategic advantage. It is unlikely that any of these conditions will apply in the current decade (we cannot expect another technology revolution like the Internet to transform things), so it is a major hope or assumption by Mann—one that has not been borne out by the facts in 2004, during which offshore outsourcing boomed but the U.S. IT job market remained dismal.

Even if we assume that Mann's speculation is right, and IT demand in the 2000s skyrockets, then what stops the demand from being filled by cheaper overseas labor? She claims that what will be left in the United States are high-skill jobs that require customer interaction. In fact, the clear evidence shows that high-level work has begun to move offshore and that the overseas countries are targeting it. Mann also never addresses the fact that many IT companies are filling the jobs that require customer interaction in the United States with foreign guestworkers on H-1B & L-1 visas— what is essentially on-site offshore outsourcing. What stops companies from bringing in cheaper foreign workers to fill those new jobs that need to be filled in the United States? The number of H-1B and L-1 holders in the United States is estimated to be close to 1 million, with more than half in

IT—certainly enough to make a substantial impact on the labor markets here.

In sum, Mann's study should be viewed as an unreasonably optimistic forecast based on faulty logic and a poor understanding of technology and strategy. More troubling, it offers false hope to American IT workers and bad practical advice to them. According to her thesis, if you have been laid off from your IT job, you should just wait out the current downturn because offshore outsourcing is going to unleash a tremendous boom in hiring very soon.

McKinsey Report

The other study that has had the most impact on the debate over offshore outsourcing was completed by McKinsey Global Institute, an arm of the influential international management consulting firm McKinsey & Co.[3] Like the Global Insight study, McKinsey relies on numbers to bolster the appearance that the study is definitive. McKinsey had two reinforcing objectives for their report. First, they wanted to market their outsourcing services to potential clients by convincing companies that outsourcing overseas would result in tremendous savings. Second, they wanted to convince policymakers and the public that offshore outsourcing is a win-win situation. The latter goal would control any criticism of this outsourcing, thus allowing them to freely expand their consulting business.

One can debate whether companies will actually save the estimated 70 percent or more by the overseas outsourcing that McKinsey claims, but let's focus on the national impacts. They conclude that India would gain 33 cents for each dollar offshored to it, and the United States would gain a net of 14 cents. So, if you believe that their study is sound, the U.S. economy gets a 14 percent boost for every dollar that goes offshore—a good but certainly not tremendous gain. But buried within the numbers is the fact that for every dollar going offshore, U.S. workers lose tremendously. Before outsourcing, American workers got 72 cents of that dollar, but afterwards only 45 cents. Why? Because a large portion—at least 31 percent—never get jobs after being laid off, and many of those who were reemployed experience substantial wage loss.

So, even if McKinsey's rosy assumptions are correct, they conclude

that the U.S. workforce is a clear and absolute loser. Offshore outsourcing will shred the purchasing power of U.S. workers. McKinsey coolly says that this inequity can be easily solved by creating an insurance fund for workers. Nowhere in the report do they estimate the actual costs of doing so, however.

There are many other weaknesses in this study. Most of the data were gathered from case studies done by McKinsey consultants—the data were not available for others to review. Moreover, the McKinsey authors have unrealistically accurate estimates—to the penny on the dollar—in their forecasts. Also, there are no models provided in the study, so there is no way to even discuss whether the assumptions and models are realistic and/or to complete a sensitivity analysis on the models—something that any good analyst would do.

The study assumes that many U.S. workers displaced by offshore outsourcing will be reemployed soon, at substantially the same wages. They base this on an economy that is creating 3.5 million jobs every year—something that is completely unrealistic. As we showed in Chapter 6, the United States actually had fewer jobs in 2004 than it had in 2000. So their rosy reemployment scenario is not even close to the reality of 2000–2004. But the study's most critical weakness is that it's devoid of any discussion of potential impacts (costs and benefits) on U.S. innovation and security (also covered in Chapter 6). In sum, this study should be viewed as a self-interested lobbying document that presents an unrealistically optimistic estimate of the impact of offshore outsourcing and an undeveloped and politically unviable solution to the problems they identify.

Notes

1. Global Insight (USA), Inc., "The Comprehensive Impact of Offshore IT Software and Services Outsourcing on the U.S. Economy and the IT Industry," March 2004.
2. Catherine Mann, "Globalization of IT Services and White Collar Jobs: The Next Wave of Productivity Growth," Institute for International Economics, PB03-11, December 2003.
3. McKinsey Global Institute, "Offshoring: Is It a Win-Win Game?" San Francisco, August 2003.

A P P E N D I X   C

Legislation Introduced Related to Outsourcing

Federal Legislation

H-1B and L-1 Visa Reform and Expansion

HR 2849/ S 1457　　**USA Jobs Protection Act**
Rep. Nancy Johnson (R-CT)/ Sen. Chris Dodd (D-CT)
Introduced in House and Senate (July 2003)
*Strengthens H-1B attestation requirements, prohibits placement of Specialized Knowledge workers at worksites operated by unaffiliated employers.

HR 4166　　**American Workforce Improvement and Jobs Protection Act**
Rep. Lamar Smith (R-TX)
Introduced (April 2004)
Enacted (December 2004) – Public Law 108-447
*Restores H-1B dependent attestations and training fees, prohibits placement of L-1B workers at unaffiliated work sites, establishes a new H-1B and L fraud and abuse fee, and exempts 20,000 foreign nationals with M.S. and Ph.D. degrees from U.S. colleges and universities from the H-1B admissions cap.

S 1635　　**L-1 (Intra-Company Transferee) Visa Reform Act**
Sen. Saxby Chambliss (R-GA)
Introduced (September 2003)
Enacted (December 2004) – Public Law 108-447
*Prohibits placement of L-1B (Specialized Knowledge)

workers at sites operated by unaffiliated employers, mandates collection of statistics on L-1 visas.

HR 4415   **Save American Jobs Through L Visa Reform Act**
Rep. Henry Hyde (R-IL)
Introduced (May 2004)
*Caps annual L visa admissions at 35,000; eliminates specialized knowledge as a basis for obtaining an intra-company transfer visa.

S 2715   **International Student and Scholar Access Act**
Sen. Norman Coleman (R-MN)
Introduced (July 2004)
*Expedites visa processing and admissions procedures for temporary visitors, including foreign students and researchers.

Notification Requirements

S 1873/HR 3816   **Call Center Consumers Right to Know Act**
Sen. John Kerry (D-MA)/ Rep. Ted Strickland (D-OH)
Introduced (November 2003)
*Requires call center employees to disclose where they are located.

S 2090   **Jobs for America Act**
Sen. Tom Daschle (D-SD)
Introduced (February 2004)
*Amends Worker Adjustment and Retraining Notification Act to require that companies planning to move jobs overseas to provide affected workers, communities, and employment assistance agencies with 90 days, advance notice.

Government Procurement Regulations

HR 2989   Amendments to **FY 04 Transportation, Treasury and Independent Agency**
Approps Sens. Thomas (R-WY) and Voinovich (R-OH)
Enacted (January 2004) – Public Law 108-199
*Temporarily restricts the performance of certain federal government contracts at overseas locations.

S 2094/HR 3820   **United States Worker Protection Act**
See also S 1637
Sen. Chris Dodd (D-CT)/Rep. Rosa DeLauro (D-CT)
Introduced (February 2004)
*To prohibit the performance of certain federal and state government contracts outside the United States.

Data Collection Requirements

HR 2673

FY 2004 Consolidated Agency Appropriations Act
(includes Commerce Department Appropriations
Rep. Frank Wolf (R-VA)
Enacted (December 2003) – Public Law 108-199
*Earmarks $335,000 for the technology administration to study the extent and implications of workforce globalization on knowledge-based industries in the United States.

HR 4754

FY 2005 Commerce, Justice, State Appropriations
Rep. Frank Wolf (R-VA)
Passed House (July 2004)
Enacted (December 2004) – Public Law 108-447
*Earmarks $2 million for an independent assessment of the effects of offshore outsourcing on the economy and employment in the United States.

Tax and Trade Policy

S 1637

Jumpstart Our Business Strength (JOBS) Act
Sen. Charles Grassley (R-IA)
Passed Senate (July 2004)
Enacted (October 2004) – Public Law 108-357
*Amends the Internal Revenue Code to comply with World Trade Organization (WTO) rulings on U.S. tax treatment of foreign sales corporations and extraterritorial income. Establishes new business tax incentives and foreign income repatriation rules to help promote manufacturing and jobs creation in the United States.

Technological Competitiveness

HR 3598

Manufacturing Technology Competitiveness Act
Rep. Vernon Ehlers (R-MI)
Passed House (July 2004)
*Establishes an interagency committee to coordinate federally funded manufacturing research and development.

S 2747

Commission on the Future of the U.S. Economy Act
Sen. Joseph Lieberman (D-CT)
Introduced (July 2004)
*To establish a bipartisan commission to review competitiveness challenges facing the United States and recommend appropriate public policy responses.

State Legislation

Bills calling for restrictions on offshore outsourcing have been introduced in thirty-three states in 2003 and 2004. Most ban or restrict the use of foreign labor in state government contracts and propose one or more of the following:

- Bans on the performance of any work under state government contracts by persons who are not U.S. citizens or authorized by federal law to work in the United States
- Prohibitions on procurement contracts for work involving the personal information of state residents when any portion of the work is performed at overseas locations, directly or indirectly through subcontractors
- Requirements that call-center staff disclose their locations to callers

The thirty-three states include Alabama, Arizona, California, Colorado, Connecticut, Florida, Georgia, Hawaii, Idaho, Illinois, Indiana, Iowa, Kansas, Kentucky, Maryland, Michigan, Minnesota, Mississippi, Missouri, Nebraska, New Jersey, New Mexico, New York, North Carolina, Pennsylvania, South Carolina, South Dakota, Tennessee, Virginia, Washington, West Virginia, Wisconsin, and Vermont.

Bibliography

Expert Reports on Globalization, Trade, Development, and IT

Audley, John, Sandra Polaski, Demetrious Papademetriou, and Scott Vaughan. *Nafta's Promise And Reality: Lessons from Mexico for the Hemisphere.* Washington, DC: Carnegie Endowment for International Peace, 2003. A highly critical assessment of the outcomes of NAFTA.

Basu, Kaushik, ed. *India's Emerging Economy: Performance and Prospects in the 1990s and Beyond.* Cambridge, MA: The MIT Press, 2004.

Biswas, Radha Roy. "Making a Technopolis in Hyderbad, India: The Role of Government IT Policy." *Technological Forecasting and Social Change.* Vol. 71, no. 8, October 2004, pp. 823–836.

Carmel, Erran. *Global Software Teams: Collaborating Across Borders and Time Zones.* Upper Saddle River, NJ: Prentice-Hall, 1999.

Cohn, Theodore H. *Global Political Economy: Theory and Practice*, 3rd ed. New York: Pearson/Longman, 2005.

Feigenbaum, Evan A. *China's Techno-Warriors: National Security and Strategic Competition from the Nuclear to the Information Age.* Stanford: Stanford University Press, 2003.

Forbes, Naushad, and David Wield. *From Followers to Leaders: Managing Technology and Innovation in Newly Industrializing Countries.* New York: Routledge, 2002.

Fruin, W. Mark, ed. *Networks, Markets, and the Pacific Rim: Studies in Strategy.* New York: Oxford University Press, 1998.

Gu, Shulin. *China's Industrial Technology: Market Reform and Organizational Change.* New York: Routledge, 1999.

Hamlet, Dick, and Joe Maybee. *The Engineering of Software: Technical Foundations for the Individual.* New York: Addison Wesley, 2001.

Harvie, Charles, ed. *Contemporary Developments and Issues in China's Economic Transition.* New York: St. Martin's Press, 1999.

Hira, Anil. "The Brave New World of International Education." *The World Economy,* 26 (36), 2003, pp. 911–931.

_____. "The FTAA as a Three-Level Bargaining Game." *Problemas del Desarrollo,* no. 133, November 2003, UNAM-Mexico.

_____. "Implications of China's Rise for the Rest of the World Economy." Chapter in a submitted manuscript comparing Latin American and East Asian industrialization.

_____. "Regulatory Games States Play: Managing Globalization Through Sectoral Policy." Chapter in Marjorie Griffin Cohen and Stephen McBride, eds. *Global Turbulence: Social Activists' and State Responses to Globalization.* London: Ashgate, 2003, pp. 41–58.

Jha, Raghbendra. *Indian Economic Reforms.* New York: Palgrave Macmillan, 2003.

Kohli, Jitendra, ed. *The Business Guide: India.* Singapore: Butterworth-Heinemann Asia, 1996.

Leach, Ronald J. *Introduction to Software Engineering.* New York: CRC Press, 2000.

Lederman, Daniel, William F. Maloney, and Luis Servén. World Bank. *Lessons from NAFTA for Latin America and the Caribbean Countries: A Summary of Research Findings.* Washington, D.C.: World Bank, December 2003.

Maddison, Angus. *The World Economy: Historical Statistics.* Paris: OECD, 2001.

Mukherjee Reed, Ananya. *Corporate Capitalism in Contemporary South Asia: Conventional Wisdoms and South Asian Realities.* New York: Palgrave Macmillan, 2003.

Pecht, Michael, Chung-Shing Lee, Zong Xiang Fu, Jiang Jun Lu, and Wang Yong Wen. *The Chinese Electronics Industry.* New York: CRC Press, 1999.

Pinglé, Vibha. *Rethinking the Developmental State: India's Industry in Comparative Perspective.* New York: St. Martin's Press, 1999.

Qu, Zonghua, and Michael Brocklehurt. "What Will It Take for China to Become a Competitive Force in Offshore Outsourcing? An Analysis of the Role of Transaction Costs in Supplier Selection." *Journal of Information Technology* 18, 2003, pp. 53-67.

Saperstein, Jeff, and Dr. Daniel Rouach, eds. "Part II: Ireland: The Enterprise Isle." In *Creating Regional Wealth in the Innovation Economy,* pp. 59-108. Toronto: Financial Times and Prentice-Hall, 2002.

Woetzel, Jonathan R. *Capitalist China: Strategies for a Revolutionized Economy.* Rexdale, Ontario: John Wiley and Sons, 2003.

Sources of Statistics and Information Portals

- Bureau of Labor Statistics, www.bls.gov
- Lou Dobbs Tonight, http://www.cnn.com/CNN/Programs/lou.dobbs.tonight/
- Organization for International Investment, "The Facts About Insourcing" Web site, www.ofii.org/facts_figures
- World Bank, International Comparison Program: World Development Indicators, World Bank Group, Washington D.C., 2002.

Worker Web Sites

American Engineering Association: http://www.aea.org/

Displaced Techies: http://www.displacedtechies.com/

Hire American Citizens: http://www.hireamericancitizens.org/

IEEE-USA:
http://www.ieeeusa.org/forum/issues/Offshoring/index.html

Information Technology Professionals Association of America: http://www.itpaa.org/

NoSlaves: http://www.noslaves.com/

Professor Norm Matloff's Writings:

http://heather.cs.ucdavis.edu/itaa.others.html

Rescue American Jobs: http://www.rescueamericanjobs.org/

Organization for the Rights of American Workers:
http://www.toraw.org/

TechsUnite: www.techsunite.org

WashTech: www.washtech.org

Zazona: http://www.zazona.com/

Expert Reports on Outsourcing

Alarcón, Rafael. "Recruitment Processes Among Foreign-born Scientists and Engineers in Silicon Valley." *American Behavioral Scientist* 42, no. 9, June/July 1999, p. 1381.

Atkinson, Robert D. "Understanding the Offshore Challenge." Policy report, Progressive Policy Institute, May 24, 2004.

D'Costa, Anthony. "Software Outsourcing and Development Policy Implications: An Indian Perspective." *International Journal of Technology Management* 24, nos. 7/8, 2002, pp. 705–723.

Deo Bardhan, Ashok, and Cynthia Kroll. "The New Wave of Outsourcing." Fisher Center for Real Estate & Urban Economics, Fisher Center Research Reports: Report #1103, November 2, 2003.

Dobbs, Lou. *Exporting America: Why Corporate Greed Is Shipping American Jobs Overseas.* New York: Warner Business Books, 2004.

Drezner, Daniel W. "The Outsourcing Bogeyman." *Foreign Affairs*, vol. 83, no. 3, May/June 2004.

Global Insight (USA), Inc. "The Comprehensive Impact of Offshore IT Software and Services Outsourcing on the U.S. Economy and the IT Industry," March 2004.

Hira, Ron. "U.S. Immigration Regulations and India's Information Technology Industry." *Technological Forecasting and Social Change*, vol. 71, no. 8, 2004, pp. 837–854.

Lin, Anthony. "Law Firms Offered Outsourced Support Staffs." *New York Lawyer,* June 7, 2004, www.nylawyer.com.

Lin-Liu, Jen, and Seema Singh. "Indian IT Firms Connect with Chinese Counterparts." *IEEE Spectrum* 41, no. 1, January 2004, p. 26.

Mann, Catherine L. "Globalization of IT Services and White Collar Jobs: The Next Wave of Productivity Growth." Policy Brief 03-11, International Economics Policy Briefs, Institute for International Economics, December 2003.

Mattoo, Aaditya, and Sacha Wunsch. "Pre-empting Protectionism in Services: The GATS and Outsourcing." *Essential Reading from the Institute,* Institute for International Economics, January 2004.

Saxenian, Anna Lee. "Government and *Guanxi:* The Chinese Software Industry in Transition." Conference paper for Global Software from Emerging Markets: An Engine for Growth? London Business School, March 12, 2003.

_____. "Transnational Communities and the Evolution of Global Production Networks: The Cases of Taiwan, China, and India." *Industry and Innovation* 9, no. 3, December 2002, pp. 183–202.

_____. *Local and Global Networks of Immigrant Professionals in Silicon Valley.* San Francisco: Public Policy Institute of California, 2002.

_____. "Bangalore: The Silicon Valley of Asia?" In *Economic Policy Reforms and the Indian Economy,* Anne O. Krueger, ed. Chicago: University of Chicago Press, 2002, pp. 169–210.

(Some) News Reports on Outsourcing

Armour, Stephanie. "Workers Asked to Train Foreign Replacements." *USA Today,* April 6, 2004.

Babcock, Pamela. "America's Newest Export: White Collar Jobs." *HR Magazine* 49, no. 4, April 2004.

Bajkowski, Julian. "PM at Odds with Ministers Over Offshoring Government IT Jobs." *Computerworld,* Australia Edition, August 17, 2004.

Bhagwati, Jagdish. "Why Your Job Isn't Moving to Bangalore." *New York Times,* February 15, 2004.

Biers, Dan, and Sadanand Dhume. "In India, A Bit of California." *Far Eastern Economic Review* 163, no. 44, November 2, 2000, p. 38.

"Big Mac Index: Food for Thought." *The Economist,* May 27, 2004.

Bjerklie, David. "The Whole Outsourcing Thing Is Getting Tricky." *Time,* April 19, 2004, p. 100.

Blumenstein, Rebecca. "Older Executives Find Job Losses Often Mean Having to Retire Early." *Wall Street Journal,* July 20, 2004.

Blustein, Paul. "Implored To 'Offshore' More: U.S. Firms Are Too Reluctant to Outsource Jobs, Report Says." *Washington Post,* July 2, 2004, p. E1.

Bulkeley, William. "IBM to Export Highly Paid Jobs to India, China." *Wall Street Journal,* December 15, 2003.

Bulkeley, William M. "IBM Documents Give Rare Look at Sensitive Plans on 'Offshoring': When Shifting Jobs Abroad, It's $12.50 Vs. $56 In Pay, and 'Sanitize' the Memos." *Wall Street Journal,* January 19, 2004.

_____. "New IBM Jobs Can Mean Fewer Jobs Elsewhere." *Wall Street Journal,* March 8, 2004.

Chaddock, Gail Russell. "Outsourcing Resonates in Virginia Race: The Issue of Jobs Moving Overseas Remains Hot for 'NASCAR Dads' and Software Engineers In Many States." *Christian Science Monitor,* July 21, 2004.

Chand, Fakir. "World Bank to Take Up Visa Curbs Issue at WTO." www.Rediff.com, May 23, 2003.

Chandrasekar, Raju. "Bangalore: India's Garden City Is Blossoming with More than Silicon." *Global Finance* 15, no. 4, April 2001, p. 80.

Chanen, Jill Schachner. "Moving To Mumbai." *ABA Journal* 90, April 2004, p. 28.

Chittum, Ryan. "Call Centers Phone Home: Small-Town Economics Lure More Companies to Outsource in Remote Corners of the US." *Wall Street Journal,* June 9, 2004, p. B1.

Chorghade, Mukund S. "Collaboration Time: Indian Firms Can Provide Advantageous Partnerships." *Chemical Week* 166, no. 7, February 25, 2004, p. 1.

Claburn, Thomas. "What's Next for India? Interest in Offshore IT Operations Keeps Growing, but Increased Competition for Talent May Dull Some Cost Benefits." *Informationweek,* January 5, 2004, pp. 45–46.

Clark, Don. "Another Lure of Outsourcing: Job Expertise." *Wall Street Journal,* April 12, 2004, p. B1.

Corcoran, Kevin. "State Job Agency Hires India Firm." *Indianapolis Star,* September 29, 2003.

Cox, W. Michael, Richard Alm, and Nigel Holmes. "Where the Jobs Are." *New York Times,* May 13, 2004.

Crow, David. "More Consider Passage to India." *Australian Financial Review,* July 14, 2004.

"Daimler, Workers Strike Wage Deal." Associated Press, July 23, 2004.

Datz, Todd. "Outsourcing World Tour." *CIO Magazine,* July 15, 2004.

De Armas, Leigh. "Mike Emmons Is Mad as Hell." *Orlando Weekly,* July 22, 2004.

De Ramos, Abe. "The China Syndrome: U.S. Companies Are Beginning to Outsource Technology Research and Development to India and China. Will a Meltdown in Tech Jobs Follow?" *CFO Magazine,* October 15, 2003.

Dolan, Kerry A., and Robyn Meredith. "A Tale of Two Cities." *Forbes,* April 12, 2004, pp. 94-101.

Durfee, Don, and Kate O'Sullivan. "Offshoring by the Numbers: Results of Our Survey of 275 Finance Executives at a Broad Range of Companies." *CFO Magazine,* June 1, 2004.

Dvorak, John C. "Scams, Lies, Deceit, And Offshoring." *PC Magazine,* April 28, 2004.

Dyer, Geoff. "How India Hopes to Reshape the Drug World." *New York Times,* August 17, 2004.

Earnshaw, Aliza. "Intel Holds Job Fairs for 'Redeployed' Employees, While Hiring Overseas." *Portland Business Journal,* August 26, 2002.

"EDS Plans to Expand BPO Ops to Chennai, Gurgaon." *Economic Times of India,* June 17, 2003.

Evanoff, Ted. "Offshoring Trend Costs Thomson Jobs: 11 at Carmel Headquarters Seeing Work Sent to Philippines." *Indianapolis Star,* August 30, 2004.

"500,000 US IT Jobs Projected to Move Overseas by Year-End 2004; IEEE-USA Sees Continued Loss in U.S. Economic Competitiveness, National Security." IEEE-USA press release, July 21, 2003.

Fox, Justin. "Hang-Ups in India." *Fortune,* December 22, 2003, p. 44.

_____. "Where Your Job Is Going." *Fortune,* November 24, 2003.

Fraunheim, Ed. "Q&A: The Facts on Offshoring." www.CNETnews.com, August 11, 2004.

"Fresh BPO Investments May Dry Up, Alerts Nasscom." *Business Line,* India, January 22, 2004.

Friedman, Thomas. "Secret of Our Sauce." *New York Times,* March 7, 2004.

_____. "Small and Smaller," *New York Times,* March 4, 2004.

_____. "Software of Democracy." *New York Times,* March 21, 2004.

Gandel, Stephen. "Where's Perot?" *Money,* May 2004, p. 108.

Gilbertson, Dawn. "ON Semiconductor Stays a Step Ahead in China: Phoenix Chipmaker Blazed a Trail Inland Toward Cheaper Labor." *Arizona Republic,* August 2, 2004.

Goodman, Peter S. "White-Collar Work a Booming U.S. Export." *Washington Post,* April 2, 2003, p. E1.

"Great Hollowing Out Myth." *The Economist,* February 19, 2004.

Griffin, Greg. "Offshore Money Machine." *Denver Post,* May 4, 2004.

Grimes, Brad. "IBM to Build Navy Supercomputer." *Washington Technology,* July 27, 2004.

Gumpert, David E. "A New Tide in Offshore Outsourcing." *Businessweek Online,* January 14, 2004.

Harrington, Jeff. "Call Center Ends 1,100 Tampa Jobs." *St. Petersburg Times,* July 22, 2004.

Hayes, Simon, and James Riley, "Vaile Greenlights Offshoring." *Australian IT,* August 17, 2004.

Hilsenrath, Jon E. "Behind Outsourcing Debate: Surprisingly Few Hard Numbers." *Wall Street Journal,* April 12, 2004.

Hopkins, Stella M. "Bofa Expands into India Outsourcing: Up to 1,500 People May Be Hired at New Facility." *Charlotte Observer,* May 9, 2004.

_____., and Ted Mellnik. "Outsourcing Draining Jobs Nationwide." Knight Ridder Newspapers, July 6, 2004.

Horvit, Mark. "Delphi Among Firms Sending Engineering, Research Work Out of US." *Fort Worth Star-Telegram,* June 22, 2004.

_____. "Exporting Jobs: Offshoring Transforms The Global Workplace." *Fort Worth Star Telegram,* June 19, 2004.

Hwang, Suein. "New Group Swells Bankruptcy Court: The Middle-Aged Job Losses, Illnesses Can Push White Collar Over the Edge." *Wall Street Journal,* August 6, 2004.

"IBM Prefers South Africa as Back Up for Outsourcing." *ComputerWeekly,* August 4, 2004.

"Iitians Death: Is There More to It than Meets the Eye?" *Economic Times,* August 6, 2004.

"India's Software Giant Starts Taking Orders Ahead of IPO." Associated Press, July 29, 2004.

"Intel Looks to Russia to Build R&D." *Financial Times,* May 24, 2004.

Johnson, Maryfran. "Colliding with Customers." *Computerworld,* December 15, 2003, p. 50.

Junnarkar, Sandeep, and Ed Frauenheim. "HP Lines Up Outsourcing Deals." www.CNETnews.com, April 11, 2003.

Keenan, Robert. "Brecis Trims Engineering Staff, Turns to Offshore Development." *Commsdesign,* February 3, 2004.

Kiely, Kathy. "As Jobs Go Overseas, a City Struggles to Reinvent Itself." *USA Today,* March 22, 2004.

Kirby, Carrie. "Group Says U.S. Overreacting to Offshoring: Tech Association Urges Congress to Delay Protectionist Measures." *San Francisco Chronicle,* March 24, 2004.

_____. and John Shinal. "Offshoring's Giant Target: The Bay Area, Silicon Valley Could Face Export of 1 In 6 Jobs—Worst in the Nation." *San Francisco Chronicle,* March 7, 2004.

Koenig, David. "EDS Says It Will Cut 2,700 Jobs, Sell Some Assets." Associated Press State & Local Wire, June 18, 2003.

Konrad, Rachel. "Donohue Endorses Outsourcing of Jobs." Associated Press, June 30, 2004.

Kosseff, Jeff. "Beaverton Jobs Bound for B.C., Stream International Looks North and not to Asia for Cost Savings for as Many as 200 Lower-Level Technology Service Jobs." *The Oregonian,* April 7, 2004.

_____. "Not All That's Outsourced Gone Abroad: Some Analysts Fear that Domestic Outsourcing Poses as Big a Threat to U.S. Jobs as Offshoring, A View Reflected in Unemployment Data." *The Oregonian*, June 15, 2004.

Kripliani, Manjeet. "Calling Bangalore: Multinationals Are Making It a Hub for High-Tech Research." *Businessweek*, November 25, 2002, p. 52.

_____. and Ira Sager. "India's Next Outsourcing Coup: Drugs." *Businessweek*, January 19, 2004.

_____. and Steve Hamm. "Scrambling to Stem India's Onslaught; Now Big Western Service Outfits Have to Fight Back on Both the High and Low Ends." *Businessweek* January 26, 2004, p. 81.

Larson, Jane. "Competing Is Key, Says Intel CEO." *Arizona Republic*, June 5, 2004.

Lazarus, David. "A Tough Lesson on Medical Privacy: Pakistani Transcriber Threatens UCSF Over Back Pay." *San Francisco Chronicle*, October 22, 2003, p. A-1.

Levine, Greg. "Gates: Microsoft to Boost China R&D." www.Forbes.com, July 1, 2004.

Linstedt, Sharon. "Anatomy of the Geico Deal." *Buffalo News*, January 4, 2004.

"Lloyds Faces Legal Challenge to Outsourcing."www.Reuters.com, August 18, 2004.

Lochhead, Carolyn. "Economists Back Tech Industry's Overseas Hiring; Workers Deny U.S. Lacks Qualified Staff." *San Francisco Chronicle*, January 9, 2004.

_____. "Incentive Plan for Firms that Train Workers: Tax Credits Could Help Compensate for Jobs Lost Abroad." *San Francisco Chronicle*, March 17, 2004.

Lohr, Steve. "An Elder Challenges Outsourcing's Orthodoxy." *New York Times*, September 9, 2004.

_____. "High-End Technology Work Not Immune to Outsourcing." *New York Times*, June 16, 2004.

_____. and Matt Richtel. "Lingering Job Insecurity of Silicon Valley." *New York Times*, March 9, 2004.

Madon, Shirin. "Information-Based Global Economy and Socioeconomic Development: The Case of Bangalore." *The Information Society* 13 (1997), pp. 227-243.

Majmudar, Nishad H. "In the U.S., Indians Gain Campaign Clout— Democrats and Republicans Alike Seek Contributions from Highly Successful Group." *Wall Street Journal,* August 17, 2004.

Marshall, Matt. "Executives in Valley, Workers Offshore: Newpath Ventures Pushes Strategy for Its Start-Ups." *San Jose Mercury News,* May 16, 2004.

_____. "VC's Offshoring Push Goes into Overdrive: Everett Prods Start-Ups to Turn to Labor Abroad as Cost-Strategy." *San Jose Mercury News,* May 16, 2004.

Matlack, Crol, et al., "Job Exports: Europe's Turn." *Businessweek,* April 19, 2004.

Mattera, Phillip. "Your Tax Dollars at Work . . . Offshore: How Foreign Outsourcing Firms Are Capturing State Government Contracts, Corporate Research Project of Good Jobs First." July 2004. Unpublished report.

Maykuth, Andrew. "India's Drug Firms Aim to Compete with Giants." *Philadelphia Inquirer,* May 4, 2004.

McCormick, Joel. "Asia's Best and Brightest Flock to Silicon Valley." *Electronic Business* 25, no. 8, August 1999, p. 40.

Melcer, Rachel. "It Firms Weigh Patriotism Vs. Cheaper Overseas Labor." *St. Louis Post-Dispatch,* May 25, 2003, p. E-1.

Meredith, Robyn. "China Wants Brains, Not Just Brawn." www.Forbes.com, June 30, 2004.

Merritt, Rick. "Political Winds Hit Offshoring." *Electronic Engineering Times,* March 24, 2004.

Mitchell, Anthony. "Outsourcing Could Be Affected by Indian Taxes." *E-Commerce Times,* August 4, 2004, found at www.ecommerce-times.com.

"Mr. Mankiw Is Right." *Washington Post,* February 13, 2004.

Nachtigal, Jeff. "Microsoft's India Workforce Doubles: Internal Documents Detail Contract Employee Work Agreements." *Washtech News,* July 28, 2004.

"Nasscom Fears More Visa Restrictions Against IT Pros." *Press Trust of India*, May 24, 2003.

"New Dell CEO Vows to Increase Jobs Worldwide." *AFP*, July 27, 2004.

"New Geography of the IT Industry—Information Technology." *The Economist* 368, no. 8333, July 19, 2003, p. 53.

Nowlin, Sanford. "San Antonio: Call Center Friendly?" *San Antonio Express*, July 10, 2004.

_____. and Travis E. Poling. "U.S. Jobs: Next Stop, India." *San Antonio Express*, September 21, 2003.

"Pakistani Threatened UCSF to Get Paid, She Says." *San Francisco Chronicle*, November 12, 2003, p. B-1.

Pardon, John. "Lost Your Job Yet?" *Computerworld*, April 12, 2004.

Pereira, Joseph. "IBM Declines to Comment on Reported Job Transfers." *Wall Street Journal*, July 23, 2003.

Plender, John. "How Companies Keep Tax Low Within the Law." *Financial Times*, July 20, 2004.

"Political Timing, Outsourced." *New York Times*, February 17, 2004.

"Poor Payers to a Degree." *The Economist*, June 10, 2004.

Porteus, Liza. "Outsourcing Targeted in 2004 Campaign." Fox News, March 31, 2004.

Rai, Saritha. "Financial Firms Hasten Their Move to Outsourcing." *New York Times*, August 18, 2004.

Raum, Tom. "Bush Economic Team Under Fire, Hands New Ammo to Democrats." Associated Press, February 19, 2004.

Rayner, Abigail. "IBM Deal Boosts Presence in India Despite U.S. Anger." *London Times*, April 9, 2004.

Reich, Robert B. "High-Tech Jobs Are Going Abroad! But That's Okay." *Washington Post*, November 2, 2003, p. B3.

"Reuters Offshore Experiment." *Businessweek Online*, March 4, 2004.

Shannon, Brad. "Workers Anxious as Jobs Head Overseas: Millions Spent by Washington's State Agencies on Work Done Offshore." *The Olympian*, August 1, 2004.

Sharma, Amol. "India Winning Higher-Status Jobs From Us." *Christian Science Monitor*, June 18, 2003.

"Siemens and Unions Strike Deal." *International Herald Tribune*, June 25, 2004.

"Silicon Valley's Slump Eroding Optimism." Associated Press, August 8, 2004.

"Simmons Cements Indian Dominance." *TheLawyer.com*. February 23, 2004, p. 10.

Singh, Shelley. "U.S. Visas are Not a TCS–Specific Issue." *Business World India*, June 30, 2003.

Slater, Joanna. "Infosys' Revenue Surges 41% on Outsourcing Boom." *Wall Street Journal*, April 14, 2004, p. B8.

Solomon, Jay. "A Global Journal Report: Outsourcing to India Sees a Twist." *Wall Street Journal*. April 1, 2004, p. A2.

Srinivasan, S. "Most Siemens Software Jobs Moving East." Associated Press, February, 16, 2004.

_____. "Sap to Add 1,900 Programmers in India: The Business Software Vendor Will Invest Another $24 Million and Add the Programmers by the End of 2006." *Informationweek,* August 3, 2004.

Stewart, Christopher S. "Outsourcing Joins The M.B.A. Curriculum." *New York Times*, March 28, 2004.

Stone, Brad. "Should I Stay or Should I Go?" *Newsweek*, April 19, 2004, pp.52-54.

Takahashi, Dean. "HP Results Solid In 4th Quarter: Revenue Growth Strong; 2,000 More Job Cuts." *San Jose Mercury News*, November 20, 2004.

Thibodeau, Patrick, and Sumner Lemon. "R&D Starts to Move Offshore." *Computerworld*, March 1, 2004, pp.1-3.

Thottam, Jyoti, Karen Tumulty, and Sara Rajan. "Is Your Job Going Abroad?" *Time*, March 1, 2004.

Treanor, Jill. "HSBC Cuts to the Core." *Guardian*, July 26, 2004.

Trigaux, Robert. "Capital One: The Political Drama." *St. Petersburg Times*, July 29, 2004.

"U.S. Tech Workers Training Their Replacements." Associated Press, August 11, 2003.

Wahl, Andrew. "Bangalore or Bust." *Canadian Business* 77, no. 4, February 16–29, 2004, p. 17.

Waldman, Amy. "A Young American Outsources Himself to India." *New York Times*, July 17, 2004.

_____. "Indians Go Home, but Don't Leave U.S. Behind." *New York Times*, July 24, 2004.

Warner, Melanie. "The Indians of Silicon Valley," *Fortune*, May 15, 2000, pp. 356–366.

Will, George. "The Economics of Progress." *Washington Post*, February 20, 2004.

Wintour, Patrick. "U.K. Can Benefit from Jobs Heading to India, Say Blair." *Guardian*, March 23, 2004.

"Wipro Ltd.: India-Based Software Maker Posts 43% Surge In Net Profit." *Wall Street Journal*, April 19, 2004, p. 1.

Witte, Griff. "Reuters to Move Editorial Jobs from U.S. and Europe to India." *Washington Post*, August 10, 2004.

Worthen, Ben. "The Radicalization of Mike Emmons." *CIO Magazine*, September 1, 2003.

Yung, Katherine. "Job Security Hopes Fading: Offshoring, Automation and More Are Leaving Workers Unsure How to Adapt." *Dallas Morning News*, June 26, 2004.

Zielenziger, David. "Reuters Summit-Tech Cos Focus on Asia to Expand Jobs." www.Reuters.com, February 27, 2004.

Index